To my daughter, Danielle:
When all seems dark, do not forget to follow your light.
It will never lead you astray.

Disclaimer

While best efforts have been used in preparing this book, neither the author nor the publisher shall be held liable or responsible to any person or entity with respect to any loss or damages caused, or alleged to have been caused, directly or indirectly, by the information contained herein. Every situation is different, and the advice and strategies contained in this book may not be suitable for you.

In the following pages you will find recommendations for the use of certain herbs and essential oils. If you are allergic to any of these items, please refrain from use. Do your own research before using an essential oil. Each body reacts differently to herbs, essential oils, and other items, so results may vary person to person. Essential oils are potent; use care when handling them. Always dilute essential oils before placing them on your skin, and make sure to do a patch test on your skin before use. Never ingest essential oils.

Always do your research before handling a crystal, especially if you have never worked with that specific crystal before. Before placing a crystal in water, make sure it is insoluble. Please keep in mind that all objects and tools used in this book, including elixirs, are not intended for human consumption. Some crystals are toxic, harmful, or poisonous if left on the skin; other crystals are toxic, harmful, or poisonous if ingested in any way. If you are allergic to any of the crystals suggested in this book, please refrain from use.

CONTENTS

EXERCISES

ACKNOWLEDGMENTS

I always loved reading as a child, and as a teenager, I wrote poetry, but I believed that being an author was something only a few people could accomplish. Ten years ago, I would have never believed that I would have my first book published by the very publisher whose books on energy, paganism, and witchcraft I had read for a very long time. But with the assistance of others, that dream has become a reality.

When you put your desires into the universe, they will come back to you. If you truly believe something will happen, then it will. Our world is unique in this way. Everything that you have ever wanted will become true if you put your heart and soul into it. That is how this book on water and energy came into my life and into existence. The law of conservation of energy states that energy cannot be created nor destroyed; it can only be transformed from one form into another. I have found this to be true in my own life.

I wanted to first thank Annwyn Avalon, because she introduced me to the magical life of water. You have been an amazing mentor. To my husband, for being supportive at home while I spent many hours writing. To both the universe for blessing my life and to the water for her inspiration that set my passion for this subject in motion. To the goddess, The Morrigan, for she gave me the courage and strength to continue when I had none. And finally, to Llewellyn Worldwide, for giving me this opportunity.

The Call of the Water

Will I ever be at peace,
Or will I be restless forever,
By tears that swell as I remember,
Dropping down to kiss my lips,
The deep longing,
Of complete and utter bliss,
I'm reminded of an eternal heart's desire,
A pounding sensation that I must acquire,
Frantic to hear the waves crashing at the shore,
    To awaken each morning, seeing ships of great galore,
The life I crave relentlessly,
Dragging me in,
I can't resist,
    The pull of the glimmering glass topped water against the shore,
The more I watch the closer I get,
    Walking past the twisted roots turning upon the sandy shore,
The watery caress fills me with longing for the sea,
The sirens' deep whispering melody,
A song that is only sung for me,
A sweet lullaby,
    This sensation is twisting at my core,
    And I cannot fight it anymore,
I'm mesmerized,
It is pulling me,
Into the depths,
So willingly,
Am I drowning,
No,
The Call of the Water,
Has taken me,
    Deep within the waters I plunge,
My unsaid plea,
Was granted,
To take away the deep misery,

Spinning,
Twisting,
Under the blue,
I struggle,
To catch my breath,
Transforming,
Evolving,
Becoming anew,
The water guides me,
As we become one,
Intertwined,
So intimately,
The Call of the Water,
Has taken me.

—Cat Robinette

FOREWORD

Water, the earth's most precious resource, our primordial mother, the life force of this planet, is in danger. It is in danger of being polluted, destroyed, and possessed by those who wish to profit from it. Much of the water on this planet has already been destroyed, poisoned, and polluted, but there is still time and still so much that can be done. Each person called to the aid of water has their part to play. It is going to take a collective of folks that specialize in many different things coming together with a sacred purpose to make the necessary change we need to heal and protect the waters of this planet.

Water is unique in that it seems to have an intelligence that can mimic or play back our thoughts, feelings, and words, and it can even mirror physical objects. The groundbreaking work of Veda Austin has shown us that water is more than what we know. It can communicate with us through pictograms and formations in ice. In my own experience, my ability to communicate with the spirit world is increased while I am in or near water. So much of my sacred water work has been born in a bathtub, shower, or body of water.

The bodies of water on this planet don't just include natural sites such as lakes, rivers, oceans, and springs. People are made of water—that makes us bodies of water. We are sacred vessels, each unique on our own, and each full of our own potential. Together we can make change through powerful acts such as research, activism, and energy work and healing modalities that restore the purity of water. When we work to heal the water, we are working to heal an intelligent being who is not only part of us, but who we are in a symbiotic relationship with. When we work to heal the water, we are working to heal ourselves.

It is not new that water has a consciousness and an intelligence. Stories of water speaking and having wisdom abound throughout time and across the planet. There are stories of water creatures and water sprites acting as the embodiment of water who aid humanity in various ways. There are also stories of water healing and transforming. There are even stories of wells speaking or having voices, such as the Celtic stories of the Horned Women and the Well Maidens.

Well maidens were beautiful women who resided within wells and were the voice of the water. They tended these sacred places and freely gave food and water to all who passed by. The well maidens welcomed visitors and served them using golden cups and bowls. They were oracles who were one with the water. One day when King Amangon and his men passed by a beautiful well maiden, they disregarded her hospitality. Their greed and lust overcame them, and they coveted the maidens, the golden bowls, and the abundance of ever-flowing waters. King Amangon kidnapped a well maiden so he could force her to serve him; his men assaulted other well maidens and took their golden bowls. Some well maidens saw this and quickly retreated back into the well. The water dried up and no longer flowed forth. The well maidens became silent, and the water no longer had a voice. Because of this, the land became desolate and fell into ruin.

The story does not end there, though. The well maidens went into hiding, and eventually King Arthur's knights found a lush forest grove where the beautiful well maidens and their children lived. The well maidens had sons who they taught to become knights and protect the women, the wells, and the sacred waters. We see that through surviving the acts of violence against them they were able to retreat, heal, and rise up once again to tend the precious landscape. This time they trained their sons (and perhaps daughters) to become their protectors, and they were fierce warriors who protected their water mothers with their lives. We are now in a time when this story is becoming a reality once again. We have seen what greedy corporations have done in their quest for their own golden bowls: their profits.

The waters of this planet extend far beyond just the beautiful bodies of natural water. They extend to our own bodies as well. We are, after all, made of water and therefore are sacred vessels of water that contain unlimited potential. We have the power to wield our vessels as forces of change by speaking up and getting involved in activism and shoreline cleanups. Most of all, we have the potential to heal and to be a sacred vessel or conduit for healing the waters of this world.

Some may find that healing takes the form of activism to bring about radical change, choosing to stand at the front of a protest using your powerful words to lead the way. Or you may find that you are more like the gentle well maidens, quietly pouring your gifts of healing into the sacred waters. Energy work also has the potential for powerful healing and change, but it will not remove the physical impurities of water. However, with proper filtering processes, the water will be pure once again. That is where energy work can come in. It can help to restructure the water, bringing it back to balance and harmony and raising its vibration, and over time it can heal.

In the following pages, Catharine Robinette weaves together a magical tome that not only shows her love for water but also helps raise awareness of how our precious bodies of water are being polluted, destroyed, and controlled by greedy corporations for profit. She provides beautiful rituals and energy work techniques to not only protect the water, but to heal and help restore the water of this planet. Catharine's dedication as a water priestess and water protector is evident throughout the pages of this book. She has written a beautiful guide that will help others begin their own practice of healing the water through energy work and ritual.

It is not enough that we raise energy, pray, or sing songs to the water. Just like it is not enough to simply clean and filter natural bodies of water of physical impurities. Though they may be cleaned from toxins and restored physically, that does not necessarily mean they are restored spiritually. It takes both. We need tools; we need rituals; we need boots on the ground; we need real change in the physical world, and in the spiritual and energetic as well. It doesn't matter if you are a sweet, singing well maiden or a water warrior—your magic is desperately needed. Together, we can heal the future of water.

—Annwyn Avalon
Author of *The Way of the Water Priestess*,
Water Witchcraft, and *Celtic Goddess Grimoire*

INTRODUCTION

The essence of life has been sacred since the beginning of time, and there are various cultures throughout the world that honor our sacred water with the ingrained wisdom of the ancient past. Their devotion to water is shown through the captivating ceremonies held within their beautiful and spiritual traditions. However, there are thousands of individuals and corporations who, unfortunately, have taken our life-giving water for granted. Instead of nourishing our once clear and pristine waters, humankind has instead polluted our water extensively, destroying it by changing its physical and vibrational structures.

The water that our ancestors had access to was pure, vibrant, and full of life. Today the physical and vibrational healing properties of our water are being transformed at an alarming rate by brackish poison that has been created by the human race and the human race alone. While we do need water to survive, we have manipulated water for purposes that do not pertain to human survival.

We never needed plastic, oil, or artificial chemicals—they could have been avoided entirely, but we made them in the name of convenience because it was easier than taking the time to find a more environmentally friendly solution. Our initial unawareness has caused worldwide water pollution within a relatively short amount of time. Our water and our planet have been bearing the desperately heavy weight of human decisions and suffering the consequences for far too long.

We are living in a time when circumstances and consequences do not have to be considered permanent anymore. We now have the energy, intention, and knowledge to manifest transformation, and as healers, we can rejuvenate and imbue nourishing life back into the sacred waters humanity has been taking from. Water has always had the capacity to be healed and we, as living vibrational beings, can change the past, present, and future of water. We can heal the water of pollution.

You have this gift of healing within you. I will show how you can access that energy and how you can accomplish healing through this book, which will offer you authentic methods that facilitate healing in safe and effective ways.

The realm of water beckons you. It is time to answer its call.

What You Will Find in This Book

This book explores, discusses, and brings awareness to the physical pollution and vibrational issues that concern our world's water supply. While there are a number of places and sources that are major contributors to water pollution, there are incredible nonprofit organizations working to protect water as well; I have shared a number of them in the appendix.

As you read this book, you will learn about the sacredness of water, why water is important to diverse cultures and traditions, a brief history of worldwide water pollution, and detailed practices to heal the water using multiple energy medicine techniques. Using energy medicine, you will learn how to raise the vibration of our sacred waters by creating positive vibrational healing frequencies.

Energy medicine is not considered a religious practice—you can be a part of any religion (or no religion) and still practice energy medicine. I have covered energy healing in a general sense so that it is accessible to everyone. You do not have to be attuned to any specific energy system to perform energy healing, though I have included Reiki options for those who are attuned because I use Reiki in my personal practice.

This book is not based on witchcraft or paganism; it is based on energy healing and connecting to the element of water. However, I have included methods that you can use to personally connect to our sacred water if you wish to do so. These practices include water rituals, ceremonies, blessings, and prayers in addition to the method of energy medicine. Each of the practices that I have included can be altered to fit your own personal beliefs so you can connect to the water in your own way. This book is meant to be inclusive and available to anyone, anywhere.

Water Healers, This Book Is for You

Who is this book for? For whomever the water calls upon, from its deepest depths, to all who feel a connection to this sacred essence. *Heal the Water* is for the physical healers who contribute their time and energy to assist in cleaning pollution out of the water and its miles of shoreline. This book is for the families who want a better future for their children, one where they have access to clean water; for those who are sensitive to vibration and can sense the water's dangerously low vibrational frequency; for the environmental advocates and tribal members who spend thousands of hours advocating for legal, permanent modifications to the ways we use water; for all the witches, pagans, and priestesses/priests/priestex; and for all who want and are demanding change.

This book is for healers, regardless of religious background, because the essence of our water is life-sustaining for all; whether you have certain religious beliefs or not, you can honor and respect the water. Water does not discriminate: it lives deep in our cells no matter who we are, where we have come from, or what path we follow. We have been created in the same image as the flowing shape of water, full of differing emotions and capable of incredible transformation.

On the outside, our human bodies seem to be quite physical, but on the inside, we are literally made of water—up to 70 percent! Some stories suggest that humanity was created within the womb of the deep sea. To say that we depend on water to survive is an understatement—we cannot go more than three days without drinking water or we will die.

Our bodies demand water, and each day we physically thirst for it. You cannot deny that water exists within you. Humanity has been heavily dependent on our water to survive, but now the roles have reversed: water has become dependent on us due to the alarming rate at which we are changing its genetic structure and energetic frequency.

The world's water—formerly healing and life-sustaining—is becoming angry and toxic, more like the humans that pollute it and less like itself. Within the past one hundred years, humanity has overflowed the planet's water with plastic and toxic chemicals. Our planet, which is also about 70 percent water, has more water than it does land! Humanity needs to realize what we are doing to our water before it becomes too late.

Me and My Story

I am guessing you are reading this because you feel called to heal our sacred water, just as I do. You may not know me, but my name is Cat. I have Huntington's Disease, and I am considered terminally ill. I am sharing this medically sensitive information with you because this is the reason I began my energy medicine journey and why I became a Water Priestess. Explaining my connection to the water requires us to take a deep—yet brief—look at my life.

I have been an introvert since birth. From a young age, I was drawn to witchcraft, paganism, nature, and energy work, but my small Indiana hometown did not really encourage those sorts of interests. When I was growing up, my grandparents used to live by the Yellow River in Plymouth, Indiana. The gray, speckled house that I practically grew up in was a century old. I loved that house, and I spent my summers underneath the registered historic bridge across the Yellow River, located about one hundred feet away from my favorite childhood home.

Underneath this bridge was a huge rectangular rock formation that I spent hours on, reading with my bare feet in the cool water and watching the sun-glistened river sparkle like thousands of diamonds as it flowed past me. I remember being mesmerized by how beautiful the water was underneath that old rickety bridge, full of slick rocks, slimy frogs, fish, plants, and other organisms that floated by. I went to that spot underneath the bridge every day, until one day the rock formation broke away and I no longer had that place of solitude that I had enjoyed for so long. I lost my beloved safe space, and I was devastated.

Years later, I was diagnosed with Huntington's Disease. When I found out that I had a rare genetic neurodegenerative disease, life did strangely continue. The clock continued to inch forward, although I did not want it to because, according to my genetic makeup, I am a ticking time bomb. I am absolutely terrified of dying; my worst fear in the world is death. This is ironic to me now that I am a healer for the water because water represents change and transformation, and death is likely the biggest transformation of all.

When I heard that I have a higher chance of dying young, it really kicked me down hard. Then I was told that there was no cure, that there was nothing that could be done to make my lifespan longer. I did not like that answer—honestly, who would appreciate that kind of finality? Being told by medical doctors that there is *nothing* that anyone can do is the worst statement I have ever experienced in my entire life.

After a year of procrastinating, of being depressed, crying, and telling myself that I could not pursue my personal goals because I was going to die sooner rather than later, I decided to change my negative attitude toward my diagnosis into a positive one. I decided to stop wallowing in self-pity, which is exactly what I was doing. I was pretty good at self-pity, but I came to the decision that I did not want to live that way any longer. I would not continue to let my diagnosis break my spirit and control my life.

As life went on and I grew into adulthood, I more actively pursued my interests, though many people were not aware of them. I started reading about the different options that were out there, slowly researching the benefits of holistic health, energy medicine, affirmations, yoga, and essential oils. I was willing to do almost anything to make my life longer. I refused to give up because it was the only thing I could control in my life at the time. During this learning phase of my life, Usui Reiki was the first energy healing system that I came across. I loved the energy, and I had seen positive outcomes for others who used this type of healing energy for physical, emotional, and mental ailments.

During this journey of learning how to channel and heal myself through Reiki, I got better. Not physically—it did not make my terminal illness go away—but my negative attitude and mentality toward the illness did. The invisible energy flowing through and around my physical body started to change. My vibrational energy started changing, though not much at first. It was a slow process, but it gave me the positive energy boost that I desperately needed to continue with my own energy healing journey.

I wanted to learn more about other energy healing systems, so I studied how to heal myself—mind, body, and soul—through chakras, crystals, mindfulness meditation, yoga, positive thoughts, and intentions. I have always been interested in metaphysical exploration and the subjects that naturally come with it. Throughout the years, I became certified in reflexology, chakra healing, mindfulness meditation, Usui Reiki, tarot, yoga, and metaphysics. After a couple of years practicing and experimenting with different methods of energy healing for myself, I realized that I wanted my life to mean something, to be more, and to be an advocate for our sacred water.

During this path of self-discovery, I found that when I was near the water, I felt very strong emotions deep down in parts of my soul that I had not explored myself. It was as if the water was singing my song, a song only meant for me, but I did not know the lyrics. I could feel the whispering melody, arising from within the watery depths that pulled at my skin, causing sensations that made me want to dive deep into the water and never resurface. Because of this water lullaby I had been hearing for years, I knew that the water had been calling me to heal all along.

It took me months to come to the realization that I have been connected to the water for so many years. I realized that I was being called to the water as a young child, sitting on that rock formation, back before I really knew what that meant. As I continued to try to figure out who I was, I came across Annwyn Avalon's water witchcraft, and I was stunned. While I knew there were different magical traditions, I did not know that a whole world of water magic existed, and it ignited a spark within me that was so strong that I decided I needed to learn more about it.

I started researching water magic, as well as water witchcraft and mythology. While I did enjoy performing water witchcraft, it was not my focus. I was more focused on the way water was being treated by people—not the people who are working diligently to heal the water, but the other people, the ones who treat water like it is their own personal trash can. Now, I understand that we are only human and that everyone, including myself, has made choices at some point of our lives that have harmed the environment. I am not going to lie and tell you that I have never littered because a long time ago, I was that person, and I tolerated that kind of behavior from people that I cared about. But once I started researching water magic, I could not help but notice how unfairly humans were treating water, as if they had no need for it. I was so focused on seeing trash, plastic, and filth in the water that I could not focus on anything else. The intense rage I felt about the treatment of the water drew me to Water Priestess work. I wanted to do the hard work of working for the water, and I was willing to do anything.

I decided that if I wanted to create change, I needed to get hands-on experience. I learned how to get involved with water conservation and participated in river cleanups in my local area, starting with the Kalamazoo River that runs through Battle Creek, Michigan. I continued to recycle as much as I possibly could. I began to purchase all my household cleaners from an organic plastic- and chemical-free company. I contacted the local environmental departments to inform them of areas that are in desperate need of a group cleanup. I joined

Alliance for the Great Lakes as a team leader to facilitate water cleanup events on the Great Lakes. I began to volunteer as a clean water ambassador for the Michigan Department of Environment, Great Lakes, and Energy. I took multiple courses on water conservation and management. Still, I felt I could do more to give back to the water that has given so much. I contemplated how I could give back to this sacred substance for a long time. One day, while I was performing energy work on myself, I was struck by the idea that if I could use energy medicine on myself, then I could use it on water too.

Of course, I am aware that other practitioners do use energy medicine on water. However, it is mostly used on water for other purposes, such as using that water in magic to heal the body. When I use energy medicine on water, I am *only* healing the water and not using it for myself. I am giving back to the water without asking for anything in return.

After I spent some time working with the water through energy healing, I began to listen for any messages it might wish to communicate with me. It was around this time that I started having vivid dreams, dreams telling me that it was time for me to step up, to become the queen that I was meant to be. I spent many days in solitude with the water while it nurtured and guided me, and it led me on this path. The water brought the people that I needed into my life so I could eventually become what we *both* needed, and I have been on this path ever since.

This was the path that led to my work as a Water Priestess. Now it is time for you to discover your own path. However, as this story of water is a long one, we must start at the very beginning, when the era of pollution began. We will explore the human history of pollution, discuss the beauty and struggles of water, and discover the power of energy medicine, the magic of ceremony and ritual, and the love that we as healers can give to the water.

Chapter 1
THE POWER OF WATER

Water is the source of all things.
—Thales, the first Greek philosopher

Water is a wild, mysterious, loving, conscious, living, and magical composition without human intervention. It is a vast realm of diverse emotions, consciousness, and a purifier of the human body, mind, and soul: the purifier of all life. Water sustains our mother, planet Earth. It is both a mesmerizing spiritual essence and a physical medicine.

The symbolism behind water is deep and ancient, and it offers us wisdom, healing, transformation, and peace in times of suffering and vulnerability. This divine, ever-flowing water carries the blood of the earth's most ancient secrets, giving us the briefest glimpses of the ebbs and flows and cycles of life, death, and rebirth before it fades again, leaving us in awe-inspiring wonder.

Water has always managed to captivate us. It draws us in with its magnetic, seamless curves, fluidly and effortlessly changing form. It always catches us off guard, bringing us to a halt because we are one with the water, and it is natural to be mesmerized while gazing at our true home. We are created in water, sustained through water, born through water, and when we die, the water that animated our bodies returns to the land and to the sea. When water suffers, we suffer, because we are it and it is us.

Our emotions match the fluidity of water, expressing love, anger, hate, fear, peace, and joy. Water can be vicious, dark, and unwavering. It is incredibly powerful, fierce, and deadly; it is capable of modifying rock formations and any other physical obstacle in its path, capable of instilling fear and destroying the lives of millions. Yet it is also quite precious, gentle, loving, and nurturing.

Water is in everything that we do in our daily lives—we cannot hide from water. Physically, the water that lives within us has the power to create life, sustain that life, and then destroy it. Without water, there is no life. Without water, all life would cease to exist. As humans, we are consciously aware that we cannot survive without water; our bodies are our daily reminder that we desperately need water to survive, making us physically thirst for this liquid substance. We have a sacred connection to the elixir of life, and though this is a well-known fact, we continue to willingly destroy Earth's nourishing waters.

Water can remember physical substances that it has been exposed to and can energetically hold negative and positive frequencies for a significant amount of time—I've seen this in my own work. Water will always return the energy that it has previously received. If we do not take water pollution seriously—if we continue to take without making change—within the near future, water will not replenish our bodies with life. Instead, it will poison us in the same ways that we have so thoughtlessly corrupted it.

Not So Pure

I live in a state that consistently informs the public that we are surrounded by the greatest freshwater lake basin in the world on all three sides. Michigan may be nestled intimately within this watery embrace, but the Great Lakes, while remarkable and irreplaceable, are not our only major water resource.

Michigan has an overabundance of water throughout the state. In fact, we have eleven thousand inland lakes and hundreds of rivers flowing across the state. We have more freshwater coastline than any other state in the United States with tens of thousands of miles of water. Also within this enchanting state are numerous natural, mossy-green swamps, rich with algae and illuminated from within. There are thousands of murky, multicolored ponds, displaying hues of gray, deep green, and blue. Iron red, blue, and green churning rivers twist through the natural landscapes of mist-filled forests.

Michigan is a magical place full of life. Green plants and sunbaked, whittled, bark-covered trees grow wild, and heavy heads of blossoming flowers hang down and gently caress the nourishing soil of the earth. Hidden within the thousands of native sugar maple, aspen, and pine trees are the bare, bone-white, curved branches of the trees that have been lost to the natural cycles of death, dotted sporadically across the lush, hilled land, twisting toward the continuously changing sky, dancing between sun blue and thunderous.

About twenty million acres of forests are home to ancient trees, mushy marshes, and wetlands that allow a wanderer to follow and explore this region; Michigan is indeed a natural and mystical place of pure natural resources. As you enter, the state signs that welcome visitors along the border are titled "Pure Michigan." This description of Michigan is not completely correct. There are environmental issues within this beautiful state that you may not be able to see at first glance. Michigan is not pure anymore; it has been used for personal gain and fallen to the greedy, becoming highly polluted in the aftermath.

My first reaction when witnessing this state was one of wonder, as I was not born here. Being from Indiana, a state of flat lands and cornfields, I had intense feelings of awe and bliss. I really did feel as if I had landed in a mystical fairyland. I had heard that Michigan was wildly beautiful, but I did not know how magical it was, nor did I expect that it would pull at my heart and soul, making me feel as if I had been pulled back into the ancient past when nature, water, and life were not generally misused and taken for granted. It was nothing like I had felt back in Indiana; I finally had a soul connection to a place that made sense.

The vast, delicate ecosystem of water that we live off of was pure in the past, but many events leading up to modern day have changed that. When I looked deeper, underneath the glossy face of Michigan, I saw that the Great Lakes and our natural forests, lakes, wetlands, and rivers are coated with the remains of oil, plastic, microplastics, chemical pollution, bacteria, and trash. Aquifers are being drained and rivers are being dammed. The lives of freshwater aquatic species have been destroyed due to more than 180 nonnative, invasive species being introduced into the Great Lakes. Of the hundreds of rivers in Michigan, 95 percent are too polluted for swimming and recreation. That does not sound pure to me.

My deep love for the state that I call home (Michigan) and the Great Lakes has been the passion behind my motivation and has inspired me to see past the glamour that our government has used to distract us from significant impurities and water pollution. I discovered that almost all of Michigan's water has been polluted and that this is a continual problem. Because I have a spiritual connection to water, I knew that I needed to work to give back and inspire change; I knew that I could not ignore these issues any longer.

While I am speaking about my personal experiences in the state of Michigan, pollution is a worldwide environmental problem, and it has been for quite some time. Environmental issues are a problem wherever you live. If you can, take the time to dig deeper, and take notice of local environmental issues, water pollution or otherwise; then, take small steps to assist in helping the environment. While the contents of this book are about assisting with our water, you can give back to any of the earth's natural elements, since they are all polluted.

At one point in history, the earth's water was pure in every aspect. While I was not alive then, I can still see and feel the remnants from that antiquated time. When I first saw the waters of Michigan, I saw sapphire-blue hues streaked with hints of emerald green, as if splashed along the edges with a paintbrush carrying beautiful colors that glisten and shimmer in the sunlight like a precious diamond. I saw awe-inspiring beauty. Witnessing the water is an experience that words do not fully describe; you have to feel it. This is something that I want future generations to have the opportunity to witness for themselves, that sense of soul-awakening peace and purity. However, this experience is only possible in a future without pollution.

Journaling Your Experience

Keeping a journal allows you to reflect on and navigate a previous experience that you may otherwise forget in this busy and chaotic world. The art of writing down your feelings and thoughts amidst ritual or ceremony allows you to create a time capsule of honest and raw reflection on your internal state of mind and of yourself that you can experience again at a later time. You may not be able to make sense of previous events (and the emotions attached to those events) if you don't preserve your experiences in a journal.

Of course, it is not a requirement that you journal, but I strongly recommend developing a journaling practice if you don't have one already. Journaling will help you explore your thoughts and emotions as you progress through this book. You will be experiencing plenty of differing emotions as you work with energy, vibration, and water. Journaling will help you deeply connect to the energy work that we will perform in these pages, as it will allow you to remember those practices more clearly in the future. I want you to be able to have clarity as you learn, grow, and evolve as an individual on a sacred path while overcoming challenges and accomplishing your goals. At the end of each chapter, I have included a set of questions that will guide you on your path.

You do not need anything fancy to get started: a notebook and pencil will suffice. When I started journaling, I would write on small scraps of paper. I did not write every day, only when I wanted to preserve special memories to retain my intense feelings. My practice of writing has since evolved and developed over the years, just as yours will. Your experience of journaling after the practices and essential information here will be your intimate connection to the wonderful magic of water and energy.

Journal Prompts

1. What does water mean to you? How has water benefited your life and practices?
2. What is your favorite body of water? Can you explore it and describe why it calls out to you?
3. If you had the chance to address water pollution globally, what would you say to others? What would you do?

Chapter 2
ANCIENT SACRED WATER SITES AROUND THE WORLD

All water is holy water.
—Rajiv Joseph

For generations, humans throughout the world have been visiting sacred water locations such as holy wells, rivers, lakes, springs, and oceans as a tool for their own spiritual practices, as well as for practical intents. In this chapter, I will share how water was—and is—a way of life for various countries, cultures, and religions.

Over the next several pages, I have attempted to section off geographical areas of sacred water sites into groups based on the location of the people that used these water locations in their practices. I will speak in depth about the sites and practices that I have included to help you understand why certain bodies of water were used as they were, which will include the pagan ancestors of the past as well as modern usage of water in ritual and religion.

Sacred Water in Europe

We will begin with Celtic traditions, hidden in the woodlands of the United Kingdom, filled with wells, springs, and long-told stories that are heavy with a sense of meaning and tied to the ancient waters. I am beginning with the religious practices and beliefs of the Celts because water lore and spiritual practice in this culture have a long, rich history that spans thousands of years. This is due in part to the thousands of healing holy wells throughout the United Kingdom and the British Isles, which includes Ireland, Scotland, Wales, England and the islands of Great Britain, and the Isle of Man.

The British Isles

In the past, worshiping wells was a large part of Celtic religion. Wells are a fascinating and unique water source that have been popular places of worship since before pagan times. Wells were used for their curative medicinal abilities to heal a variety of illnesses, which is due in part to the certain types of minerals that have been found in these water sources. In ancient times, this was not a known fact, but knowing how a place of water is able to cure does not change the magical aspects or spiritual meanings behind it.

In northern Scotland, in the village of Munlochy, a sacred natural healing well is surrounded by a grove of trees. This mystical well, called a clootie well, is said to have healing properties. For generations, it was said that the well cured sickness and disease for those who performed a ceremony to the water spirits who resided within the well. For hundreds of years, starting around 620 AD, people who practiced pagan religions would come to this magical place to perform their healing rituals. The rituals involved circling the well three times, then sprinkling water from the well upon the ground and the participants. After officially beginning the ceremony, participants would take either whole articles of clothing or strips of cloth and dip the cloth into this well, soaking it with the healing powers of the water while speaking their prayers. Then, they would tie or hang the cloth on a tree near the well. The cloth was left to rot away on the tree and as it did, so too would the person's illness rot away with it; it was considered to be bad luck if the cloth was removed before it disintegrated. In 1581, pilgrimage to holy wells throughout Scotland was banned, but the practice still carries on to this day.

Scotland's beautiful neighbor, Ireland, has approximately three thousand sacred and holy wells. On the west coast of Ireland, in between the Cliffs of Moher and Liscannor, sits one of the oldest sacred wells with immense healing power. St. Brigid's Well is dedicated to the Celtic goddess Brigit (and after Christianity became the dominant religion of the region, Saint Brigid). Fifteen of these sacred wells have been dedicated to her, according to a nineteenth-century survey.[1]

---

1. Ohaire, "St. Brigid's Well."

In Celtic mythology, the goddess Brigit, whose name translates into "the exalted one," is a goddess of multiple different roles.[2] This goddess is highly venerated for her knowledge, her ability to inspire creativity for the written words of others, her incredible healing capabilities, her invention and blacksmithing skills, as well as protecting domesticated animals. She is a goddess of opposite domains: she yields fire as a sun goddess, yet rules over waterways as a water goddess of the rivers and wells. As Christianity increased in popularity in Ireland, because Brigit was a well-known figure, this Celtic goddess was overtaken by the church, and many of the ancient healing sites that the Celts had dedicated to Brigit were reassociated with the Christian Saint Brigid as well.

Since antiquity, St. Brigid's Well has been a very spiritual and mystical place. To this day, people from all religious faiths and backgrounds visit Brigit's sacred healing waters and honor the version of the goddess that pertains to their own spiritual practice. Thousands of votive offerings (personal and beautiful objects that have strong intentions behind them) such as prayers, feathers, coins, rosaries, and mementos have been left at this well. These offerings are left for distinct reasons by people who believe in the power of this sacred place, the benevolence of this goddess/saint, and the benefits of participating so that they may be healed from their ailments.

In addition to wells, hot springs are also known for their healing properties. Legend has it that in 863 BC, healing mineral hot springs were discovered in Somerset, England, by Prince Bladud. The story goes that Prince Bladud had an incurable skin condition called leprosy. He was banished from the royal court due to this contagious illness and became a swineherd, and his pigs contracted the same skin condition. One day the prince found his pigs rolling around in hot, steamy, sticky mud that had been created by the hot water from the springs. Shortly after this event occurred, Prince Bladud noticed that the pigs were cured! The prince curiously immersed himself in this mud as well, which ended up curing his leprosy. He returned home, and his royal status was restored by the court, and he eventually became king.

King Bladud went on to build a temple over this hot spring so that others could be cured from physical illnesses and spiritual sufferings in its healing water, founding the city of Bath. The temple was dedicated to Sulis, the

---

2. "Bridget."

Brythonic goddess of healing, sacred water, and curses. Since the construction of this first temple dedicated to this water goddess, millions of people have come to bathe within her sacred waters. While there is no historical evidence that King Bladud ever existed, he was mentioned in a text by Geoffrey of Monmouth's *History of the Kings of Britain*, which was written in the twelfth century, and he is still honored today at the hot springs, where a statue overlooking the King's Bath has been constructed in his name.

Originally, the Celts worshiped these divine hot springs and the goddess Sulis, who presided over the healing waters at Bath. She would be willingly offered coins, gems, wooden and leather objects, and jewelry as votive offerings that her worshipers would throw into her springs. Eventually, after thousands of years, the Celts' natural place of worship and Sulis's ancient springs were discovered by the Romans who invaded Britain. When the Romans arrived, they overtook and rebuilt the hot baths, temples, and courtyards, and a new (Roman) city was born around the springs. The Roman city became known as *Aquae Sulis*, Latin for "the waters of Sulis."[3] However, the Romans dedicated the hot springs to their own goddess, Minerva, who had a different image than the Celtic goddess Sulis. But, being that the Celtic Sulis was quite popular, the Roman goddess Minerva ended up being known as Sulis-Minerva, a combination of the two.

After some time, the Romans stopped maintaining the healing baths, and they fell into disuse. Certain pieces of these buildings were partially destroyed. In the regency period, baths came back into style, and the architects of that time remodeled the city of Bath and created new buildings in a neoclassical design around the original baths. People from all over the world would bathe in these healing hot springs, but in the 1970s the water was stated to be unsafe to be within.[4] Today, over six million people visit Bath per year, many of them to tour the Roman Baths and its ancient hot springs. As of July 2021, the hot springs in Bath, Somerset, were officially declared a UNESCO World Heritage Site, and Bath is also a UNESCO World Heritage City.

Also in Somerset, England, is the town of Glastonbury, a place of magic and legend. Glastonbury is home to the Chalice Well (also known as the Red

---

3. Milligan, "Aquae Sulis – Roman Bath."
4. "Why Swimming in Roman Baths Can End Badly."

Spring), which has been releasing twenty-five thousand gallons of water per day for at least two thousand years—including times of drought—while maintaining a steady temperature of 52 degrees Fahrenheit. The iron deposits are quite rich, leaving these waters a muted reddish color, where its other name, the Red Spring, gets its title from. This sacred healing well is located near Chalice Hill, which is a small hill near Glastonbury Tor. This puts the springs relatively close to the hot springs of Bath.

People from all over the world travel to visit these sacred waters for healing. The Chalice Well has deep roots in history and mythology, living on within pagan practices and the Christian religion. In ancient pre-Christian mythology, Celtic pagan wells were seen as a gateway into the spirit world by some; thus, these wells were an ancient source of wisdom and power. One pagan tradition with roots in Glastonbury is the Avalonian tradition, which is a spiritual, goddess-based tradition inspired by the myth of Avalon. Thus, Glastonbury is a place where the old pagan ways have never truly died, and all pagan paths continue to honor the gods, land, spirits, water, and ancestors of the land.

The Chalice Well is home to the Lady of Avalon, who appears to those in need of spiritual healing as the "White Lady of the Mists."[5] According to Christian faith and mythology, the Chalice Well is the site where Joseph of Arimathea buried the chalice that he had used to catch the blood of Christ during his crucifixion, which ties this well to lore about the Holy Grail. Members of this faith travel from different countries to drink from the Chalice Well's flowing waters because they are believed to contain the blood of Christ. It is also stated that the red waters represent the rusty iron nails that were used to hold Christ to the cross during his crucifixion.

In Northern Wales, surrounded by woodlands, the ancient well of St. Cybi sits in tranquility, protected by an old, crumbling cottage amidst blooming wildflowers. For centuries this particular well has been used as a place to cure many different ailments. Some stories report that this healing well was capable of reversing blindness; other sicknesses that were cured by St. Cybi's Well are scurvy, lameness, warts, and rheumatism.[6] Remedies consisted of giving the ill a mixture of well water and sea water twice a day for up to ten days. After they

---

5. Gully-Lir, "Lady of Avalon."
6. Thomas, "St. Cybi's Well."

successfully completed this portion of the ritual, they then had to bathe in the well water once or twice a day. After these healing immersions, the ill could toss copper pennies and silver pieces into the water as offerings. Before they went to sleep, they were to drink a cup of healing water. The person being treated would then either become too cold or too warm in bed, which would indicate whether or not this treatment was removing the illness or disease. Once they were cured, the person could take bottles of well water away with them.

Another rag well, located in Denbighshire, Wales, is the well of St. Elian. This well offered healing for those who washed in its healing waters, rubbed a rag upon the diseased area of the body, and then tied the rag to a tree using natural wool. Corks with pins were also left at the well, often tied in the bushes; some were found to be left floating in the water of the well itself. This well was also well-known for bestowing and removing curses.

—

An old proverb states that running water is a holy thing, and as you can see, water is well-known to carry healing properties throughout the United Kingdom and the British Isles. While I have only shared a few sites for you to discover, there are thousands of sacred wells and springs throughout this region of magic and mystery.

Each well possesses unique, strong healing properties. Our ancestors from thousands of years ago would visit these ancient places, mostly in search of physical healing. Their physical ailments included a range of issues that varied in severity: broken bones, leprosy, skin diseases, lameness, insanity, illnesses of the eye, and infertility were common problems. Many requested healings from the miraculous, medicinal waters. These magical wells were seen as living shrines and had deep roots in local history and lore.

It is not only wells that were (and are) honored in the United Kingdom—rivers and springs were quite sacred as well. There were many goddesses and gods in Celtic culture that were associated with various forms of water, either in relation to rivers, springs, wells, or the ocean. Each deity had their own function, and some had multiple. In chapter 8, you will find a goddess ritual that I have created that allows you to embody rivers and other waters of the Celtic lands.

It is unfortunate that over the years, many sacred healing sites were ruined either partially or completely by human and animal activity. Still, there are thousands of natural healing wells and springs hidden throughout the rugged landscape of the UK; granted, some of these sites are visited more often than others. When wells, springs, and rivers are visited, they are used in many of the same ways as our pre-Christian, pagan ancestors used them thousands of years ago. People visit wells for divination, spiritual healing, blessings, worship, and ritual in honor of the deities, spirits, or water nymphs that preside at that specific location. Celtic deities were and still are believed to dwell within or in proximity to sacred healing wells, springs, and rivers. Votive offerings are made during ritual or left as an offering, usually in exchange for a healing request or to show respect and gratitude to the water or to deity. Offerings include herbs, food, beads, coins, crystals, art, and sculptures; at times, the offerings are removed once the healing request is granted.

The wells of the United Kingdom have the liquid of life within them, imbued with amazing healing energy. They give thousands of people who are sick, hurt, or emotionally distressed hope and healing during times of desperation.

Other Regions of Europe

The ancient Greeks used water in their religious practices. Springs represented water nymphs and were dedicated to female deities, so caves that had springs or pools of water were seen as divine. Structures were built around the springs. One, the Life-Giving Spring in Athens, located in the Acropolis caves, dates back to the sixth century BCE. Ancient Greeks worshiped at this spring, building shrines and leaving offerings. As centuries passed, the practices at the springs were influenced by Christianity, and most caves with divine water were transformed into churches.

Today, the Life-Giving Spring is referred to as "the oldest church in Greece" by some, and the sacred spring is now dedicated to the Virgin Mary.[7] It is still a gathering place; many local worshipers have visited the caves since childhood. The cave is said to have miraculous healing capabilities. Visitors wash in the spring's waters and then take a drink after bathing. Silver- and gold-plated items representing people or body parts that need healing are left as offerings in the

---

7. Håland, "The Life-Giving Spring."

hopes that the spring's water will offer a miracle. Flowers and candles are also left as offerings, and bottles are filled with the spring's holy water to take home.

The Life-Giving Spring was sacred to Christians and pagans alike, and a yearly ceremony dedicated to the spring united both groups. Today, a modern version of the Festival of the Life-Giving Spring is held each year. People of all ages participate, bringing offerings of special breads, including holy bread and sweet bread. A priest holds mass, distributing pieces of the blessed breads to the attendants. After the ceremony, some attendants wash in the spring and drink the water. Others fill bottles with the spring's water. Centuries ago, only women were permitted to retrieve the springs' holy water and perform rituals. Now, everyone can interact with these sacred waters.

The city of Lourdes, France, attracts over six million people a year, many of them visiting the city's healing waters. In the Sanctuary of Our Lady of Lourdes—a Catholic shrine and pilgrimage site—people bathe, drink, pray, and hope that a miracle will be bestowed upon them. They visit the sanctuary's waters for medicinal, spiritual, and moral healing. The sanctuary is open to the public, and people line up in the Lourdes Grotto, strip naked, and dunk themselves in the icy water to be healed.

This sacred spring was discovered in 1858 by a young woman named Bernadette, who had started seeing multiple apparitions and discovered the water's healing properties when she drank a mixture of mud and water. Over the last few decades, at least seventy people have been miraculously healed by these springs. The water here is easy to access, as water taps labeled in six different languages flow freely. People fill up bottles of water to return home with.

Water is also collected from waterfalls found in Norway's fjords. The word *fjord* comes from the Old Norse *tjǫrthr*, meaning "to travel across."[8] Norway has hundreds of fjords, which are long, deep, narrow, and majestic valleys carved out of the surrounding bedrock by glaciers, creating steep mountains. These valleys are filled with massive waterfalls, slanted mountains, and idyllic, fairy-tale scenery. The waters within the fjords range from a serene blue to a brilliant emerald green. Hundreds of thousands of people visit Norway each year to see its fjords, mountains, and waterfalls, taking in the mystical quality of these beautiful bodies of water and the rugged landscapes that surround them.

---

8. "Sound vs Fjord – What's the Difference?"

Nearby Sweden is home to a sacred spring called St. Olof's Well in Väster-landa. The spring was around long before Christianity, though in the 1100s, it was dedicated to Saint Olaf. This spring was known to cure eye conditions, with the first recorded cure in 1693. Pilgrims visiting this sacred spring left offerings of money or meat. Another well-known site in Sweden is the Fagertofta Spring. On the night of Midsummer, people visited the spring to drink its water and bathe in it to maintain their health.

On Midsummer in Mogenstrup, Denmark, locals who were ill visited St. Magnus's Well, believed to cure cancer as well as other physical and mental conditions. Visitors brought offerings of animals, swords, or jewelry in the hopes that they would be healed by the water. To make sure the water was effective, visitors approached the well in silence.

Iceland, about one thousand miles east of Scandinavia, is an island in the middle of the Atlantic Ocean, so it is no surprise that Iceland's culture and life-style revolve around water. In addition to being surrounded by the salty ocean, Iceland boasts an abundance of river systems and is home to over ten thousand waterfalls. The water is so pure that you can safely drink straight out of almost every river and stream. There are geothermally heated pools all over the island. People can immerse themselves in these warm waters, known as "healing water cures."[9] These pools are available to swim in year-round. In Iceland, water is honored, as it is the holy source that can give life and take that life away.

Another holy source of water can be found in northeastern Italy. Two mes-merizing springs come together to create the Livenza river. These springs trans-port pure, surreal, translucent waters from deep underneath the ground to Earth's surface. The first spring, *La Santissima* ("the very holy"), was a sacred place of worship and devotion for local pagans; for generations, members of the pagan faith visited this magical spring to honor water goddesses through ritual and ceremony. Eventually, a Christian church called the *Santuario Della Santissima Trinita* ("Shrine of the Most Holy Trinity") was built beside the Livenza springs.

In Latvia, spiritual practices connected to sacred wells and springs are similar to those found in the British Isles. Like the "clootie well" in Scotland, Latvia has its own rag well, the Bolenu Spring. Ribbons given as an offering are tied to trees around the spring. The Baltic goddess Laima is associated with this spring

---

9. Kois, "Iceland's Water Cure."

in particular, and it is said that her tears created the spring, making it highly medicinal for the eyes. In fact, some call this the Bolenu Eye Spring.

Another body of water steeped in lore is the Green Spring in Eastern Europe. The waters of this mystical Russian spring do not freeze even in the coldest winter months. According to the legends of the people, a green-haired *rusalka*, a "mermaid-like demon," was transformed into the Green Spring by her father as punishment for marrying a local Mari man.[10] To this day, the sacred waters of this spring are used in ritual and ceremony by one of the last surviving pagan communities in Russia, the Mari people.

As you can see, Europe is a land of living water full of wells and springs that nourish the land they sustain with waters so pure that you can immerse yourself in them and even drink from them. These ancient bodies of water are located throughout the continent. With thousands of wells in Europe, it is impossible to share each of them here. It is my hope that you will be inspired to seek out other water sites surrounded by mystery, miracles, and ancient lore.

—

While Christianity is the dominant religion of Europe, many of the pagan practices found in Europe continue to this day; just because the pagan community is not as obvious in certain areas does not mean it is not there. Christianity does, however, have its own water practices throughout Europe. There are a variety of rituals connected to water, specifically springs and wells. These curative water sources were once dedicated to water nymphs, spirits, and deities, though many of these waters have been rededicated to the Virgin Mary. Perhaps the most obvious connection to pagan practices is using holy water during ceremony. This is a tool not only in Europe, but all over the world. Holy water is used in baptisms, blessings, and church services. Sometimes it is given to the faithful to take home so they can drink it or bless their homes with it. Holy water is meant to visibly represent God's presence and work in their lives.

10. Clifford, "One of the Last Surviving Pagan Communities in Russia."

Sacred Water in Asia

Asia is home to the Ganges River, considered to be one of the most spiritually pure and beloved rivers in the world. This purifying river travels 1,560 miles southeast through India, Bangladesh, and into the Bay of Bengal. In Hinduism, this river is the most sacred river because it is seen as the living body of the Hindu goddess Ganga, a deity who descended to earth to purify souls, then release them from the endless cycle of death and rebirth (*samsara*).

In the traditional practices of Hinduism, it is believed that this cleansing river will bring good fortune, cure ills, and wash away impurities in those who perform rituals in its revitalizing waters and on its riverbanks. Offerings are left to this watery outdoor temple in the form of flowers and *diyas* (floating clay lamps, filled with oil and a lit wick), given with love for the river. This river and the beliefs that it carries are strong. For example, a recently deceased person may be cremated in the city of Varanasi, near the Ganges; if their ashes are placed in the water of the Ganges, it is said that their soul will receive instant salvation.

In western Tibet, near Mount Kailash, is Lake Manasarovar, a sacred fresh-water lake that is considered the most transparent lake in China. Surrounding this lake were eight Buddhist monasteries, but time and the elements have taken their toll on these holy temples, and only two are well restored. According to one Tibetan legend, the mother of the Buddha took a bath in these waters before giving birth to her son.[11] It was also said that the god Shiva and his wife bathed together in this lake. Hindus consider this lake to be a symbol of purity and believe that drinking its holy water can cleanse one of every sin in each of their lifetimes. For generations, Hindus have traveled from far and wide to ritually bathe in Lake Manasarovar's icy water. Many pilgrims walk the fifty miles around the lake, taking four to five days in the process.

In Kyoto, Japan, the "Pure Water Temple" (also known as the Kiyomizudera Temple, or Kiyomizu-dera) was founded in 780 CE among the wooded hills of Mount Otowa within the Higashiyama Mountain Range. This sacred Buddhist temple received its name due to the waterfall that flows underneath the floors of this sanctuary. The waterfall has three separate streams of water that flow into a pond. It is believed that these clear mountain waters have the power to make wishes come true, leading visitors from all over the world to hold cups

---

11. "Manasarovar Lake."

underneath a stream to catch its water. As they drink from the sacred flow, they make their wishes known. It is stated that these three streams each have different benefits: one for a long, healthy life, another for success at school, and a third for a happy love life. It is seen as greedy or desperate to drink from all of the streams, so visitors should choose carefully. People from all over the world visit this temple due to its wish-granting powers, lore, and natural beauty. This temple has been a UNESCO World Heritage site since 1994.

In Bali, water is a sacred aspect of culture and religion. It is a symbol of strength, purification, and prosperity, and water is such an integral part of Balinese life that holy water is included in every spiritual ceremony—it would not be a ritual without it. *Tirta* (holy water) is seen as "a doorway to God," and it ensures that blessings are able to be received.[12] Priests and priestesses infuse water with flowers and holy blessings, chanting sacred mantras, so that the water may effectively carry deity's blessing. Balinese Hinduism is sometimes referred to as *Agama Tirtha*, the "religion of the holy water."[13]

There are a number of water temples on the island of Bali, accompanied by water from rivers, waterfalls, springs, and streams. One of these, the Tirta Empul temple, was founded in 926 CE around a natural spring. This water site draws devotees who come with prayers and offerings to immerse themselves in the sacred waters. Tourists from all over the world also visit this temple to replenish themselves on both the physical and spiritual planes.

At Tirta Empul, Hindus and non-Hindus alike partake in the traditional Balinese *Melukat*, a water ritual and blessing that is performed for purification of the body, the heart, and the soul. Water represents the spiritual flow of energy, so it makes sense that chanting, meditation, prayers, blessings, and holy baths are included in this sacred practice.

—

The countries, cultures, and traditions found in Asia realize the sacredness of water, and many incorporate honoring the water into their lives. Here in the United States, on the other hand, I come across many people who rarely drink water or take water for granted, not acknowledging its sacred uses.

---

12. "Water – The Sacred Element."
13. Indosphere Culture, "Agama Tirtha."

Asian water traditions are very spiritual and connect people to the source of existence. I have created rituals that I will share in chapter 8 with the hope that you will be able to experience a sense of that divine, soul-restoring connection to water and to your own personal gods, whoever they may be for you.

Sacred Water in North America

Indigenous peoples have honored the water for longer than any other group in North America. You will notice as you read that Indigenous peoples are an integral part of the history of each body of water in this section. For thousands of years, Native Americans have believed that water is alive and that spirits live within that water; they have known for a long time that water should never be taken for granted.

Long before the United States was established, Indigenous peoples located and revered sacred waters, many of which were believed to have healing properties. One such spring can be found in what is now recognized as South Carolina. Local Indigenous people believed that these healing waters were a gift from the great spirit. During the American Revolution, it is said that Natives came across a group of badly wounded soldiers and led them to these secret sacred waters, and a few months later, the wounded were miraculously healed.

Now, those same springs are known as God's Acre Healing Springs, and they can be found behind a Baptist church in Blackville, South Carolina, on land that has been, interestingly, deeded to God. The healing potential of these springs has become a local legend that is still well-known today. Lines of people who believe in the mystical power of the Healing Springs wait for their turn to collect the holy water, storing the water in jugs that they return home with. Modern analysis of the water has verified that the water is pure and filled with healthy minerals.[14]

Thousands of miles away, the state of Hawaii has plenty of legends surrounding water as well. The people of these islands recognize that water is indeed life itself, which is evident in the legends and stories passed down. One legendary Hawaiian location is the coastline of Waikiki, on the island of O'ahu. Here, visitors can find a sacred stretch of beach known as Kawehewehe. The word *Kawehewehe* translates into "the removal," as in the removal of disease.[15]

14. "God's Acre Healing Springs."
15. Prats, "Kawehewehe."

Kawehewehe has been a place of healing for hundreds of years. For generations, people visited Waikiki to bathe in its healing water. Sometimes, the sick wore seaweed leis; they asked for forgiveness from their sins and wrongdoings, if they believed that their past mistakes caused their current sickness. After bathing, they would duck beneath the water's surface and remove the lei, releasing it out to sea. It was customary to remain looking forward as they returned to shore, as this would put an end to their illness.

During this period, people from all over the world traveled to Waikiki to bathe in the waters near Kawehewehe and experience the miraculous healing of physical and spiritual ailments. Using the sea to heal is still done to this day, but Kawehewehe is now known as Gray's Beach, and this specific area is not as well-known for its healing capabilities as it used to be.

In western New Mexico, there is a body of water that is unique for several reasons. Zuni Salt Lake is a high desert lake, located approximately 6,220 feet above sea level. This lake is also a classic maar, a lake or pond that has formed in the low region of a volcanic crater. Because of the way the lake formed, it is very shallow—during the wet season, the lake is only about four feet deep.

But Zuni Salt Lake is perhaps best known as a sacred being: Salt Mother, the mother deity of the Zuni people. Salt Mother is honored by other Indigenous peoples as well, including the nearby Navajo and Apache tribes. For thousands of years, Indigenous peoples have journeyed to this lake to connect with Salt Mother; to this day, the Pueblo people of the southwest make an annual pilgrimage to Salt Mother, as do other Indigenous people. Once they have journeyed to Salt Mother, she is offered respect and worship via ancient ceremonies. Ritual bathing may take place, as well as gathering of salt from the lake, known as the Salt Mother's "sacred flesh."[16] During the dry season, when the water in Zuni Salt Lake has evaporated, a layer of salt remains; this salt is ceremonially harvested by Natives, who may then use this salt in their cooking or in religious ceremonies.

There have been numerous attempts to develop the land near Zuni Salt Lake, most notably an attempt to build a coal mine in the late 1990s. The Zuni vehemently opposed any development in the area, specifically noting that the mining process would disturb thousands of sacred sites. There are approximately

---

16. "Zuni Salt Lake."

five thousand archaeological sites near Zuni Salt Lake, including shrines placed all around the lake as offerings to Salt Mother, and over five hundred human burials. That coal mine was never built, but decades later, the Zuni are still working tirelessly to establish protections for Zuni Salt Lake, the home of Salt Mother.

About one thousand miles northwest, in California, are two hot springs heated by volcanic activity. Naturally reaching temperatures of up to 115 degrees, these mineral-filled, medicinal waters are very potent. These springs, now known as Harbin Hot Springs, were referred to as *Eetawyomi* by the Miwok people, which translates into a "hot place."[17] For hundreds of years, these million-year-old springs were a sacred healing ground for Indigenous peoples. The Miwok believed that *Eetawyomi* was a pathway to ancient spiritual realms. The sick were brought here to experience the healing power of the springs, and shamans could enter a trance state to communicate with the spiritual realm, then share that knowledge with the tribe. Indigenous peoples gathered here to honor the land that produced these magical waters.

Eventually, colonizers took over the land, and they too believed in the sacredness of the healing springs. Over the years, the land changed ownership several times, and the springs were part of a Victorian resort, a hunting lodge, a boxing camp, and even a university. Now, these miraculous waters are part of a health resort, and for a fee, visitors can enter the waters to heal ailments such as nervousness, kidney disease, and rheumatism.

In the Huron National Forest, along Michigan's River Road Scenic Byway, sits one of the state's many hidden gems: the Iargo Springs. Filled with large, crystal-clear pools (one spans over fifty feet across!), these beautiful springs are not a well-known spot. It is thought that the word *Iargo* means "many waters," which perfectly describes these four-hundred-year-old springs.[18] Natives believed that these gorgeous waters held mystical healing powers. The babbling spring water and the sanctity of this place make visitors feel as if they have traveled to another world.

The deepest lake in the United States can be found in Oregon. Crater Lake is a spiritual place of immense power and danger. For thousands of years, the

---

17. Marinacci, "Harbin Hot Springs and the Heart Consciousness Church."
18. Mossolle, "Iargo Springs Is a Michigan Hidden Gem That's Worth a Road Trip."

Native people who worshiped the water called it *Giiwas*, "a sacred place."[19] Legends passed down from the Modoc and Klamath tribes tell of an epic battle between two powerful Spirit Chiefs that resulted in the formation of Crater Lake. The Klamath tribes managed to keep this holy lake secret for over seven thousand years.

It is said that those who visit Crater Lake will "always remember the beauty and sacredness of such a place."[20] Although Crater Lake is widely known for its beauty, it was also a location for underwater spiritual quests, even though the lake was feared to have dangerous spirits living in the sacred water. Those who swam in the lake at night hoped to experience visions of the supernatural beings that lived in this lake. The people that did so were considered very courageous for exploring this watery portal between the human and spirit worlds.

Another lake with roots in the Native American community is Lake Tahoe, situated on the borders of the states now recognized as California and Nevada. Lake Tahoe has been the homeland of the Washoe people for over two thousand years. Washoe legends mention mystical "Water Babies" that inhabited bodies of water, including the waters of Lake Tahoe. Water Babies were believed to be quite powerful, for better or for worse: they were occasionally a good omen, though they could also cause illness or death. The Washoe would offer the Water Babies pine nuts, corn, and bread before traveling across the lake in hopes that the spirits would not become angry and instead allow them to cross without being harmed.

Across North America, Indigenous groups have honored the water for thousands of years. In Canada, a country filled with an abundance of sacred places, one unique body of water is Spotted Lake, located in the Okanagan Valley, within the desert of British Columbia. This lake, which the First Nations people called "kłlilx̌ʷ," was sacred to the Indigenous people of the Okanagan Valley.[21] The mud and water were used for therapeutic purposes, treating headaches, wounds, and other ailments.

Spotted Lake is most famous for its appearance. Spotted Lake is an endorheic lake, which is a lake that does not flow outward to rivers or the ocean. These lakes receive their water supply from the rain, which washes an abundance of salt

19. Peters, "Origin Stories of the Lake."
20. Peters, "Origin Stories of the Lake."
21. "Exploring the Mysteries and Scientific Wonders Behind Canada's Spotted Lake."

and minerals down into the lake from the surrounding land, and in the summer, the rainwater eventually evaporates. As the water evaporates, it leaves behind about three hundred mineral deposits of assorted shapes, sizes, and colors, in vibrant and muted hues of yellow, green, and blue; the color of the deposits varies depending on the amount of minerals in each pool. It is believed that this lake has the highest natural concentration of magnesium sulfate (Epsom salt) in the world.

Over the years, businessmen talked about establishing a spa at Spotted Lake, which had become privately owned. In 2001, the Okanagan Nation Alliance purchased the lake and the surrounding property to protect it from development and preserve it for future generations. The lake is now on private tribal land and is surrounded by a fence to keep others from polluting or disrupting this sacred water.

This is only a brief overview of sacred bodies of water in the land now recognized as the United States. There are countless bodies of water and beliefs in this region; for example, the Blackfeet believed that water was home to divine beings and divine animals; the Cherokee that lived amongst the southern Appalachians believed that a nearby river was a spiritual entity whose waters could heal and nurture the Cherokee people; the Taos Pueblo believed that New Mexico's Blue Lake was the source of all creation, where birth and death existed together. For thousands of years, First Nations people have believed water represents purity and life itself; it is also an important element on the Medicine Wheel. "Water Is Life" is a popular refrain: it connects all living beings and is seen as "the blood of Mother Earth."[22] Many Indigenous tribes, including the Anishinaabe, raise women to be water carriers. Women are revered as the leading protectors of water because of their natural ability to create life.

To this day, there are a variety of practices that worship water in North America. Water is used for religious and spiritual purposes by different cultures and faiths. However, not all water rituals connect to the land. For example, Christians use holy water in baptism to bless people, places, or things; *tevilah* is a Jewish purification ritual that involves fully immersing oneself in a *mikveh*, a dedicated ritual bath. While water is honored in these rites as well, I find it

---

22. "Water in First Nations Ceremonies."

unfortunate that water is only seen as a carrier of the holy and not necessarily sacred itself.

In chapter 8, I have included rituals that honor water as a sacred gift from the land. For now, though, we will journey south and explore Mexico's ancient waters.

Mexico

In the northern Yucatán Peninsula is an ancient site called the Sacred Cenote, which is located at the archaeological site Chichén Itzá. Chichén Itzá translates into "at the mouth of the well of the Itza," referring to this cenote.[23] Cenotes are sinkholes with a pool of water at the bottom. They are created by water that has managed to flow through the limestone bedrock, creating small caves. Eventually, the cave's roof collapses, exposing a pool of groundwater underneath. While there are various cenotes in the Yucatán, the Sacred Cenote was especially revered.

Pre-Columbian Maya believed the Sacred Cenote was a portal to the underworld and used it to connect to the other side. The Maya used this cenote as a tool in their own spiritual practices. They believed that Chaac, a rain god who was feared and worshiped, lived at the bottom of this cenote. Thus, the Sacred Cenote was only used for ceremonial purposes, which involved water ritual, worship, and human sacrifice. During times of drought, the Maya sacrificed an individual to the cenote as a form of worship before praying to the gods for good rain, harvests, health, and fortune. They also sacrificed their possessions by throwing them into the cenote. The offerings at the bottom of the cenote—found centuries later by archaeologists—included gold, jade, incense, pottery, and many human skeletons. Chichén Itzá was declared one of the new seven wonders of the world in 2007.

Many ancient Maya rituals and ceremonies took place near sacred bodies of water. One such ceremony, the Kay Nikte' Ceremony, was performed on the full moon to celebrate and honor love, fertility, the moon, and water. This ceremony was predominantly performed by female Maya priests. Fresh cenote water was gathered in a clay pot, which symbolized Ixchel, a goddess of fertility, midwifery, medicine, and rain. The water was then chanted over and blessings,

---

23. Bell and Bell, "Chichén Itzá – The Sacred Cenote."

prayers, and mantras were said. To finish the ceremony, attendees danced inside a circle of candles underneath the moonlight. Some of the water was given back to the earth, and some was used to bless attendees. Today, descendants of the Maya still perform this enchanting ceremony to connect themselves and others to water, the earth, and the universe.

Rituals to appease the rain god in times of drought or to prevent drought from occurring were highly common, and this spiritual practice continues to this day in certain locations. In some areas of Mexico and the United States, shamans called *graniceros* facilitate rain rituals passed down from their ancestors, a tradition that dates back thousands of years. These *graniceros* are priests with a direct lineage to Tlaloc, the Aztec rain god. Many of these rituals are performed during the month of May.

Decades ago, blessed water was an important part of the Christian Holy Week in Mexico. On Glory Saturday, the day before Easter Sunday, locals threw buckets of water on each other to represent purification and baptism. This practice is now penalized in Mexico City, where participants can be fined for throwing large amounts of water.

Sacred Water in Central America

In north Guatemala, over five hundred artifacts and offerings were found at the bottom of Lake Petén Itzá. The Maya in this area also made sacrifices to the water, which included skull-shaped incense burners, shells that were likely used as musical instruments, ceremonial bowls, and knives and other blades, some made from obsidian and volcanic rock. Several of the knives were believed to have been used in human sacrifice during rituals asking for rain and other blessings.

More Maya artifacts can be found in southwestern Guatemala, where a preserved city lies underneath Lake Atitlán. Lake Atitlán used to be a much smaller lake on an island, but sometime between 250 and 300 CE, the island was impacted by a volcanic eruption. The eruption blocked off the lake's drainage, and the island's water level began to rise, completely enveloping the Maya city that had been built on the island. For centuries after, people believed Lake Atitlán was simply a breathtaking body of water. Then, in 1998, a scuba diver discovered the Maya's lost city beneath the surface of the lake.

This sunken city, which the diver named Samabaj, was full of undisturbed artifacts. "Sweat baths" were also found beneath the water. Sweat baths, which are similar to saunas, induced sweating with hot moisture and very little ventilation. Sweating removes toxins from the body, making it a purifying experience. These findings are significant since these sweat baths would have been used prior to worship so that the Maya could spiritually purify their bodies.

Sweat baths have also been found in Belize. At the Cara Blanca pools in central Belize, sweat baths were found near a cenote. The Maya believed that cenotes were portals to the underworld, so rituals and offerings were often done near cenotes. At a water temple near the Cara Blanca pools, the Maya left offerings for their rain god, Chaac, including pots, jars, bowls, teeth, and claws.

Sacred Water in South America

The largest high-altitude lake on earth, Lake Titicaca, can be found in South America. This lake is 12,500 feet above sea level in the Andes Mountains. Covering 3,200 square miles and straddling Peru and Bolivia, Lake Titicaca was the birthplace of the Inca. The Inca people had several spiritual practices and beliefs that were connected to Lake Titicaca. More than eighty temples were built in the southern part of the lake on *Isla del Sol* ("Island of the Sun") for worship and ritual. This lake was the integral to the Incan creation myth, with the creator god emerging from its waters. According to legend, the god Con Tiqui Viracocha emerged from Lake Titicaca, bringing a few humans with him.[24] Then, after creating the moon, the sun, and the stars, Viracocha created more humans out of rock. He sent these people off and instructed them to populate the earth. Since Lake Titicaca was the origin of life, the Incas believed that it was also a place of death. Upon dying, the spirit was believed to leave the human body and return to its original home, the lake.

Thousands of fragments have been found on the bottom of Lake Titicaca, originally part of an offering to the lake. Offerings included carved llamas, human figurines, golden pins likely used on Inca shawls, and silver and gold jewelry. Some offerings, placed inside boxes, likely also contained the blood of sacrificed children or animals. It is believed that by making offerings to Lake Titicaca, the Inca were praying to the creator god for fertile land, bountiful

---

24. Crystal, "Inca Creation Myths."

harvests, and/or rain. They may also have been requesting fertility for their llamas and alpacas, animals that were said to originate from lakes.

Another deity that is revered in South America is Iemanjá, the Afro-Brazilian goddess of the sea. This African goddess made her way across the Atlantic Ocean and settled into hearts of thousands of people in South America. Sometimes depicted as a mermaid, Iemanjá represents water, fertility, and abundance. She protects mothers and children as well as fishermen. Each year, several South American countries honor this deity with a Iemanjá festival on the second day of February. Hundreds of sand altars are built on beaches, overflowing with statues, perfume, lipstick, mirrors, candles, jewelry, flowers, white foods such as coconut pudding, fruit, and plates of food, all given as offerings. Performances of song and dance last throughout the day. After the sun has set, gifts for the goddess are released to the sea. If an offering washes back upon the shore, it is believed that the offering was rejected, but if it drifts out to sea, then it was accepted by Iemanjá, who will provide her blessing. In Montevideo, Uruguay, cleanup crews visit the beaches the day after the festival to pick up nonbiodegradable items left behind. Many religious leaders are now urging participants to make eco-friendly offerings that will not harm our waters.

In Brazil, people travel from across the country to the city of Rio de Janeiro to celebrate Iemanjá on the first of January. Her annual festival (*Festa de Iemanjá*) brings together a variety of practitioners, all dressed in white. They throw themselves into the waves of the sea in dedication to Iemanjá. Offerings are made as practitioners ask the goddess for blessings. The South American festivals for the sea goddess showcase the dedication and love that these people have for their water deity and the environment that surrounds them.

In the mountain ranges of Colombia, the Arhuaco people are concerned about the local water supply. Environmental dangers such as unregulated agriculture pose serious threats to the freshwater ecosystems in Colombia. In an effort to protect the water, the Arhuaco regularly pray for water conservation. They perform smoke rituals in the hopes that their pleas will be heard.

As in many areas of the world, Christianity is a popular belief system. Holy water is used in blessings and prayers, and it can ward off evil. Attendees can dip their finger into holy water placed at the threshold of the church, then bless themselves with it before entering.

Sacred Water in Africa

The Semuliki National Park in western Uganda is a place filled with rich cultural history. Inside the park are the Sempaya Hot Springs, two springs that are a sacred water site for the indigenous Bamaga people. The Bamaga know the two springs as the Male Hot Spring (*Bitente* or, less commonly, *Mubungu*) and the Female Hot Spring (*Nyansimbi*). The Bamaga people have a creation story for the springs, and they believe that their ancestors reside beneath the spouting water of the springs, with male ancestors connected to the Male Hot Spring and female ancestors connected to the Female Hot Spring. Bamaga women visit the Female Hot Spring to enhance their own fertility or to pray for safe deliveries during childbirth. Bamaga men visit the Male Hot Springs and ask for wealth and blessings. Each year rituals are performed to appease the ancestors, and coins are sacrificed to the springs as an offering. It is believed that these sacred hot springs can cure illness and disease, especially skin problems.

For the Ba Tonga people, the Chibwatata Hot Springs near Binga, Zimbabwe, have been considered sacred for generations. The Ba Tonga associate these springs with rainmaking. For many years, only the Rainmaker was allowed to visit the hot springs. The Rainmaker visited the hot springs when they wanted to ask the gods for rain. But first, a Rainmaker had to prove that they were no ordinary person by standing in the springhead's scalding water; if they were burned by the water, they were seen as an imposter and deemed not worthy of rain.

Now, the Ba Tonga people can visit the water and even swim in it as long as they are further downstream. Water from the springs is thought to grant good luck and remove misfortune. The Ba Tonga sprinkle water from the hot springs around their homes to deter evil spirits and prevent mental illness. Some families keep spring water on hand to use as curative waters for stomach pain, digestive disorders, and discomfort caused by teething. It has other uses too: for women who are struggling to conceive, a mixture of spring water, tiger fish bones, and dried spring materials can be drank to "unblock" the woman's womb.[25]

Non-natives have begun to encroach upon the Chibwatata Hot Springs, and the Ba Tonga people are working to establish the Chibwatata Hot Springs as a

---

25. Parish, "An Abecedary of Sacred Springs of the World: The Hot Springs of Yemen and Zimbabwe."

national monument so that the area may be fenced off and protected from out-siders in the hopes that it will prevent desecration of their sacred springs.

Many indigenous people in Southern Africa see water as a living force that has the ability to purify and heal both the physical and spiritual form. They believe that water improves communication with the spirit world, and snakes and mermaids (who reside in or near the water) are seen as ancient wisdom keepers who can teach people how to use medicinal plants for healing. It is said that these spirits of the water decide which individuals should be "taken under the water," indicating that they have been called to become healers.[26] The water spirits choose the healers, not the other way around.

Sacred waters are revered and feared in southern Africa. Common people are forbidden from entering sacred pools, as it is believed that mermaids, snakes, and other water spirits reside in these spaces. Only healers associated with the water are allowed to approach. Legend states that if one enters a lake, river, or sea without being summoned by their ancestors, the water will keep them forever.[27]

Mami Wata (Water Mother) is one water spirit who is worshiped in much of Africa. She is described as a mermaid: half-woman, half-fish. A variety of spir-itual practices surround her, all honoring the sacred nature of water. Another sacred female water deity is Osun, the Yoruba goddess of fertility, love, and water. In Nigeria, the Osun-Osogbo Sacred Grove holds the river of Osun, which is named after this orisha. This river has deep religious significance to the Yoruba people. Devotees of Osun live near the river and perform daily wor-ship. The devotees—all women, most between ages thirty and sixty—oversee sacrificial offerings to the river, usually beverages or live animals. They engage in cultural activities, not limited to singing, dancing, and healing ceremonies, which are performed within the river itself. Devotees also utilize the river's sacred properties by drinking from or bathing within the river in the hopes that the goddess will heal afflictions, offer wealth, or improve fertility. Once flowing with clear, pristine waters, this sacred river (and World Heritage Site) is now a lifeless, murky shade of brown. The water has been contaminated by miners in search of gold and other minerals. Recently, authorities have ordered people to stop drinking the water, which has high levels of mercury and lead.

---

26. Bernard, "Sacred Water Sites and Indigenous Healers in Southern Africa."
27. Bernard, "Sacred Water Sites and Indigenous Healers in Southern Africa."

Another revered body of water is Egypt's Sacred Lake of the Temple of Karnak. This manmade lake was a place of purification created by King Thutmose III around 1450 BCE. The sacred lake is the largest of its kind, and it was filled with water from the Nile River. Priests visited this lake prior to entering the temple to ritually bathe.

Sacred Water in Australia

Australia is known to be a dry and barren country, having little to no rain each year in much of the region, so it is not surprising that water has been spiritually sacred for eons. Australia faces many of the same challenges as other countries: water resources are scarce, and they are being affected by pollution. However, for generations, the Aboriginal peoples of Australia have continued to honor the water.

In Queensland, Australia, the Ban Ban Springs are sacred to the Wakka Wakka people. The Wakka Wakka associate Ban Ban Springs with Dreamtime, the time of creation. Legend says that the Rainbow Serpent—the symbol of creation in Aboriginal mythology—surfaced at this spring.[28] For hundreds of years, the Wakka Wakka people traveled to the Ban Ban Springs for a variety of reasons: to get married or trade goods, for example. Before entering a river, pond, lake, or the sea, people informed the Rainbow Serpent of their presence, promising to do no harm. This was done because if the serpent was lying at the bottom of a waterhole, resting, and was suddenly disturbed, the consequences would be dire.

Ban Ban Springs was the first site in Queensland to be formally recognized as an Aboriginal cultural site. In 2022, the Wakka Wakka people received native title for land that includes the Ban Ban Springs, meaning the Wakka Wakka are now federally recognized as having rights and interests in the land.

In the Kimberley Region of Australia, in a rugged and remote national park, sits Mitchell Falls. The waterfall is 260 feet tall, reportedly the second tallest in Western Australia.[29] While this waterfall is difficult to access, it is beautiful: the waterfall has four levels that flow over the sandstone and into a freshwater lake, and the surrounding area is home to hundreds of species. Mitchell Falls is

---

28. "Gayndah-Biggenden Loop."
29. Cheng, "Mitchell Falls."

sacred to the Wunambal people, who were granted native title over this land in 2011. No one is allowed to enter the waters of Mitchell Falls, as the Wunambal Gaambera people believe that snakes with mystical powers reside in its waters.

For hundreds of thousands of Aboriginal Australians, water is a sacred element and the source of all life. Feasts that include ceremonies of dance and song are performed close to the shorelines. Art, carvings, and figures made of clay are offered to the water, as well as drawings in the sand. Cleansing water rituals are performed to remove unwanted spirits. Aboriginal Australians engage with their sacred water sources in deeply spiritual and healing ways.

One powerful, moving event that took place on February 16, 2019, was the Blessing of the Rivers ceremony in Wentworth, New South Wales, at the junction of the Murray–Darling rivers. People of all faiths and practices were invited to honor the water in hopes of drawing attention to the health of the Murray–Darling Basin, which is Australia's largest and most diverse river system. Participants were asked to bring a bottle of water to use in ritual.

First, a Barkandji Elder cleansed all participants in a smoking ceremony. The origins of the event were explained, the current state of the water was addressed, and a statement of purpose was shared. Next, a prayer for healing was chanted by the hundreds of attendees. Scriptures were read. Then, everyone lined up along the river. Once everyone had a bottle of water, the Ritual Blessing and Pouring of Waters took place. Participants stated where their water was sourced from, then poured the water from their containers into the rivers, expressing solidarity through symbolic action. Afterward, individuals offered their own prayers, which they shared with the rest of the group. The ceremony ended with a call to action and a "Final Prayer of Blessing."[30]

—

As with the Australian Blessing of the Rivers ceremony, I too hope that efforts to protect our waters do not go unnoticed in this modern age. In chapter 8, I have created my own river blessing to show the water that we have not forgotten it even if those with higher authority have lost their way, and we will continue

---

30. Howard, "A Mercy Prayer Ritual for a Local Blessing of the Rivers Ceremony."

to persevere in the water's name until all of Earth's waters are fully protected by law.

Journal Prompts

1. What practices in this chapter did you find most interesting? Why?
2. Do you think these practices will affect your personal relationship with water? Why or why not?
3. Were you drawn to a certain region while reading? Which one, and why?

Chapter 3
THE POLLUTED
HISTORY OF WATER

When the well's dry, we know the worth of water.
—Benjamin Franklin

Note: This chapter talks about issues with water pollution worldwide, and even though it is essential information, it does read a bit heavy considering the overall theme of this book. However, while this chapter may be difficult to read for some, knowing about water pollution issues firsthand is essential to becoming a healer and advocate. To create change, you should know what you are fighting against.

Since the beginning of human history, water has been our most precious and vital resource, yet it has been abused on a global scale. Many have fought over this life-giving substance. And yet, for hundreds of thousands of years, humans have been contaminating water. Even though humanity is highly dependent on water to survive, we are the number one cause of the world's water pollution.

Our early ancestors did not understand the importance of clean water and the consequences of their unsanitary habits. For centuries, water was polluted by humans who used their local rivers, streams, and lakes to dispose of trash, dead animals, and human waste. They then used these polluted water sources as their drinking water supply, since our ancestors did not have the resources or knowledge to maintain water safety. This led to outbreaks of life-threatening diseases such as typhoid and cholera, and many people became ill and died after drinking from these polluted, diseased water sources.

As time went on, large numbers of people started leaving their rural homes for more conventional lives in the city. They still did not have proper sewage systems, so the practice of throwing animal and human waste into vital water sources continued. Civilians threw feces, urine, and trash into the street, where rainwater caused this waste to flow into the local rivers, lakes, and groundwater. Unknowingly, the people of this time were contaminating local water sources with pollutants.

The Industrial Revolution

With the arrival of the Industrial Revolution, water pollution intensified, causing long-term damage to our waterways. In the beginning of the Industrial Revolution, people wanted to advance humankind's way of living as quickly as possible; they were not thinking about the impacts their factories would have. Factories were not set up to manage waste products, so they were releasing toxic chemicals directly into natural streams, rivers, lakes, and oceans. Companies also began creating products such as plastic and inorganic pesticides, which have been found in a large amount of our waters. These toxic pollutants would later be linked to health issues such as cancer, birth defects, and organ damage.

The Clean Water Act

On June 22, 1969, in Cleveland, Ohio, the Cuyahoga River caught on fire when floating debris that was covered in oil was ignited by sparks from a passing train. The fire grew to over five stories high and burned for almost thirty minutes. This river had caught on fire previously (at least nine other times since 1868) and was considered one of the most polluted rivers in the United States at the time. However, the 1969 fire on the Cuyahoga River caught the attention of *Time* magazine, and it went on to serve as a major event that motivated thousands of people to protect the environment. This caused a huge uproar that the United States had never seen from its citizens. The government knew they had to institute some kind of water regulation.

The 1969 river fire inspired Congress to enact the National Environmental Policy Act, which was signed into law on January 1, 1970. This act helped to establish the Environmental Protection Agency, created later that year, which was given duties to manage and regulate environmental risks. One of the first legislations that they put into action was the Clean Water Act of 1972, which required all waterways in the United States to be clean enough for safe fishing, swimming, and drinking by 1983. While this act has helped extensively over the years, it did not reach its goal in time.

Life Since the Clean Water Act

Even after the creation of the Environmental Protection Agency and the signing of the Clean Water Act, multiple majorly destructive events have occurred that have negatively impacted our water sources. Here are just a few of the occurrences that indicate the damage we have done to our water.

Exxon Valdez Oil Spill of 1989

On March 24, 1989, a few minutes after midnight, an oil tanker named Exxon Valdez—which was carrying fifty-three million gallons of crude oil—hit a local reef and spilled eleven million gallons of crude oil into Alaska's Prince William Sound. This oil spill polluted over thirteen hundred miles of coastline and killed an estimated 22 killer whales, 250 bald eagles, 300 seals, 3,000 otters, and 250,000 sea birds.

Over eleven thousand Alaska residents worked together to clean up the oil spill and to rescue animals that were trapped in the oil. Later, it was revealed that the ship's captain had been drinking and allowed an unlicensed person to take control of the ship. Exxon ended up paying about 2 billion dollars in cleanup costs and 1.8 billion for habitat restoration and personal damages, but the economic impacts on Alaska's small coastal towns were extensive.

This oil spill caused significant issues for the local fishing industry during the 1990s as salmon and herring supply plummeted. This event that happened in a matter of moments had years-long effects. In 2001—twelve years after the spill—studies showed that over half of the affected coastlines were still contaminated with oil. The number of herring, once a prominent source of income for Prince William Sound fisherman, has still not recovered from the spill.

At the time, this was the largest oil spill in United States history. It was due to this event that the United States Congress decided to take action for our water.

Oil Pollution Act of 1990

After the Exxon Valdez oil spill, Congress passed the Oil Pollution Act of 1990, and President George H. W. Bush signed it into law that same year. This act was intended to streamline and strengthen the Environmental Protection Agency's power to prevent oil spills. This act also increased company penalties for oil spills and required that all oil tankers in US waters have a double hull—the Exxon Valdez was a single-hulled tanker, and requiring tankers to be double-hulled decreased the likelihood of a collision causing another oil spill.

Grand Rapids, Minnesota, Inland Oil Spill of 1991

On the morning of March 3, 1991, the largest inland oil spill occurred in Grand Rapids, Minnesota, when an underground pipeline owned by Enbridge ruptured onto sixteen acres of wetland. Following the rupture, oil exploded forty feet into the air and coated aspen trees that were in the area. This rupture spilled over 1.7 million gallons of oil, and much of the crude oil from this spill flowed into the Prairie River, which is a tributary of the Mississippi River. However, the river was frozen over with ice eighteen inches thick at the time of the spill, so much of the oil sat on top of the ice. If there had not been ice on the river, the oil spill would've traveled from Prairie River into the Mississippi River, the second-largest river in the United States. While some oil did flow under the ice and into Prairie River, the ice ultimately prevented an even larger disaster.

The operators for Line 3 were aware that the pipeline's pressure had dropped significantly, but it took some time for them to respond appropriately. According to the National Oceanic and Atmospheric Administration, it took over an hour for them to shut down the pipeline.[31]

The delay in shutting down the pipeline according to policy caused an oil spill of 1.7 million gallons and has cost the company at least 1.2 billion dollars in cleanup costs. This same pipeline spilled over 1.3 million gallons of crude oil in Argyle, Minnesota, in 1973.

Deepwater Horizon Oil Spill of 2010

On April 20, 2010, an exploratory oil drilling rig called Deepwater Horizon exploded. The explosion killed eleven people working on the rig and injured

---

31. "Lakehead Pipeline Company; Grand Rapids, Minnesota."

multiple others. After the Deepwater Horizon was evacuated, it took thirty-six hours for the wreckage to sink to the seafloor. Over the next eighty-seven days, four million barrels of oil (168 million liquid gallons) spilled into the Gulf of Mexico, just south of Louisiana. After multiple attempts to close the oil well, it was stated to be effectively sealed on September 19, 2010.

During the weeks that oil continued to spill, many people worked to protect the coastline, wetlands, and estuaries from the oil spreading. However, despite their best efforts, extensive damage was done to the environment. After all, this was the largest marine oil spill in history. In 2013—three years after the oil spill—Louisiana reported that 4.9 million pounds of oily material was removed from their beaches alone. Dolphins and other marine life were also dying at a much faster rate than normal, with some fish developing deformities.

In 2011, a report by the United States government blamed the spill on the well's defective cement, an inadequate safety system, and "cost-cutting decisions."[32] The company that owned the rig, BP, pled guilty to eleven counts of felony manslaughter, two misdemeanors, and a felony count of lying to Congress. BP agreed to have its safety practices and ethics monitored by the government for four years.

The cleanup costs of this devastating oil spill were well over 65 billion dollars. In 2014, a judge determined that BP was primarily responsible for the oil spill, and in 2015, BP agreed to pay 18.7 billion dollars in fines, which is the largest corporate settlement in United States history.

Kalamazoo River Michigan Inland Oil Spill 2010

On the evening of July 25, 2010—just a few months after the Deepwater Horizon explosion—an Enbridge pipeline burst. (If this sounds familiar, it was also an Enbridge pipeline that burst in the Grand Rapids, Minnesota, oil spill of 1991.) According to the Environmental Protection Agency, an estimated one million gallons of "DilBit," a heavy crude oil, spilled into the Talmadge Creek and the Kalamazoo River, a tributary to Lake Michigan. Over thirty-five miles of the Kalamazoo River became contaminated with oil. It took three days for the oil spill to be contained, approximately eighty river miles from Lake Michigan.

---

32. "The True Story of Deepwater Horizon."

During this event, Enbridge's employees were slow to respond to the rupture, even though they were notified with alarms. Pipeline operators were required to shut down a pipeline that had abnormal readings within ten minutes. However, operators did not identify the problem correctly, which resulted in the pipeline not being shut down for seventeen hours. Oil continued to flow through the ruptured pipeline during that time.

In the months that followed, several hundred people worked to remove oil from the river, the flood plains, and the marsh areas where the spill originally started. Later, investigators from the National Transportation Safety Board Investigation determined that the pipeline ruptured due to a flaw on the outside lining of the pipe, causing it to crack and, eventually, to break. In fact, Enbridge had been informed that the pipeline was wearing down five years prior to the spill, but they did not dig up the pipeline to inspect it. Enbridge paid over one billion dollars in cleanup costs and was ordered to pay 177 million dollars in penalties.

Water Today

While many of us feel connected to our sacred waters and respect them, others do not. There are multiple organizations that are working to save our water from industries that have shown they are not interested in keeping their toxic waste products out of natural water sources. The advantages of money and power have taken root in our society and instead of working toward helpful methods to protect the water, these beautiful water sources are being destroyed for personal gain.

It is not just corporations who are polluting water. Everywhere I go, I see trash in the water or lined up along the riverbanks. I've seen people throw their empty plastic food containers into the water. I see trash being tossed out of car windows almost every day. It is because of industrial companies *and* these kinds of people that water pollution has become a huge environmental issue.

Since plastic and oil are major contributors to water pollution, I wanted to focus on them in more detail.

Coal, Oil, and Gasoline

While we acknowledge that burning fossil fuels is a major threat to our water, we still actively use fossil fuels to meet 80 percent of our energy needs. When companies drill, frack, and mine for fossil fuels, they are risking the health and safety of our water sources. They then store their toxic waste either in underground wells or open-air pits, which leak into the groundwater and contaminate it with harmful pollutants that have been linked to serious health issues such as cancer.

When coal is mined, it creates an acidic water full of heavy metals and radioactive materials that runs off into local water sources. And in everyday life, oil and gasoline drip from cars, farm equipment, ships, and airplanes, and eventually this runs off into groundwater, rivers, lakes, and oceans.

When fossil fuels get into our water sources, they can contaminate the entire freshwater or ocean ecosystem. The ocean absorbs some of these manufactured carbon emissions and has become 30 percent more acidic since the Industrial Revolution. This increased acidity in our oceans is lowering the amount of calcium carbonate molecules in the water, which are needed for shells, skeletons, and coral reefs to grow properly. The ripple effects of decreased calcium carbonate molecules could damage food chains and ecosystems.

Plastic Pollution

Plastic pollution has been a problem for decades, and it is actively causing damage to water all over the world. Plastic makes its way to our water sources because of improper management, littering issues, and poor recycling systems. Worldwide, 380 million tons of plastic are produced each year, and 50 percent of this plastic is produced for single-use items such as straws, trash bags, plastic cups, plastic bottles, and food packaging.

Plastic has been in production for decades, and since plastic never fully decomposes, every piece of plastic that has ever been produced is still in our environment. For example, plastic water bottles are made from a chemical called PET (polyethylene terephthalate) that natural bacteria cannot break down. It takes almost 450 years for a plastic water bottle to break down in a landfill via a process called photodegradation; ultraviolet radiation from the sun breaks down plastic into much smaller pieces over time. The problem is that plastic in landfills is covered by dirt, so it cannot get the UV radiation that it needs to break down. When photodegradation occurs in the ocean, it can break down plastics faster—but at the very high cost of marine life, as small plastic particles are mistaken for a food source.

As much as 80 percent of the ocean's pollution is plastic, and each year, up to ten million metric tons of plastic end up in the ocean. Every year, thousands of marine animals such as whales, fish, and turtles are slowly starving to death because they have stomachs full of plastic that they cannot digest. In the 1960s, less than 5 percent of birds were found to have plastic in their stomachs; twenty years later, over 80 percent of birds had plastic in their stomachs. Around one million birds die each year from eating plastic.

Plastic is not just a problem for our oceans. The Great Lakes in the United States are the largest freshwater system in the world, with more than twenty-two million pounds of plastic ending up in their waters every year. Researchers have found an exceedingly high amount of microplastics (small, broken down pieces of plastic) in all five of the Great Lakes, which is concerning because these lakes are a source of drinking water for an estimated 40 million people.

There are multiple organizations that have volunteers who clean these lakes. Of the tens of thousands of garbage removed from the Great Lakes each year, about 85 percent is plastic. As beautiful as the states that are surrounded by these amazing sources of water are, their waters have become very polluted. Microplastics have been found in oceans, beaches, rivers, fish, bottled water, drinking water, and even beer. Recently, microplastics were discovered in human blood. It is estimated that every week, we each consume a credit-card-sized amount of plastic.

Water Pollution around the World

Pollution is a global issue. According to a report in 2016 from the World Health Organization, water pollution is costing thousands of lives, killing an estimated 842,000 people each year.[33] It is imperative to be knowledgeable about this issue to know what actions to take to heal the water. While I have provided a lot of information in this book, I am barely scratching the surface of the issues facing our waters. It is my hope that I can motivate you to create change.

Water Pollution in the United States

The United States is the world's largest generator of plastic waste. While China is the world's largest manufacturer of plastic, the United States has twice the

---

33. "Running Out of Water."

amount of plastic waste. In 2016, the United States produced an estimated forty-two million metric tons of plastic waste.

This plastic penetrates the environment, pollutes local water sources, and eventually ends up in the ocean. In 2020, 2.6 million pounds of trash were collected along US coastlines. Littering and illegal dumping cause trash and plastic to build up each year. As much as 1.25 million metric tons of waste can be attributed to littering and illegal dumping. According to researchers, if Americans continue to produce and waste plastic at this current rate, by 2030 an estimated fifty-three million metric tons of plastic could end up in the ocean *each year.*[34]

It is not only plastic that is polluting water in the United States. An estimated 1.2 trillion gallons of untreated sewage, storm water, and industrial waste are dumped into United States water every year.

United States Great Lakes Oil Pollution Crisis
The United States is home to enormous amounts of oil pollution, and the Great Lakes are currently at high risk of a major oil spill. A pipeline known as Line 5 was built in 1953. Owned by Enbridge, Line 5 was only intended to last for fifty years. Almost twenty years after their expiration date, this pipeline has been dented and cracked from multiple anchor and cable strikes. One anchor strike was as heavy as twelve thousand pounds! Line 5 also suffers from corrosion issues and extreme stress caused by strong underwater currents. This pipeline that is over seventy years old pumps twenty-three million gallons of oil underneath the largest freshwater system in the world.

This aging pipeline runs from Superior, Wisconsin, through Michigan's Straits of Mackinac, and under the St. Clair River to Sarnia, Ontario, Canada. Since 1968, Line 5 has failed at least thirty-three times and has spilled no less than 1.13 million gallons of oil. If this pipeline bursts, the Great Lakes would turn into an oil-covered wasteland. These beautiful lakes are irreplaceable and much too precious to continue taking such a hazardous risk. A large oil spill poses significant risk to over 450 miles of shoreline and 100,000 acres of water, as well as the forty-seven different species that rely on the habitat for survival and the forty million people who rely on the Great Lakes for drinking water.

---

34. Root, "US Is Top Contributor to Plastic Waste, Report Shows."

In July 2019, the Bad River Band of Lake Superior Chippewa filed a lawsuit against Enbridge, requesting that Line 5 be removed from the Bad River Reservation. In 2023, a federal judge gave Enbridge three years to shut down the section of the pipeline that crosses through the reservation. The company was also ordered to pay the tribe over five million dollars for trespassing, as the land agreements between them ended in 2013.

In November 2020, the Governor of Michigan gave Enbridge six months to shut down the Line 5 pipelines under the Straits of Mackinac in an effort to protect the Great Lakes from a potential oil spill. Enbridge missed the deadline, refusing to shut down their pipeline, and a lawsuit was filed. The legal battle is ongoing, with many environmental activists and organizations calling for the federal government to shut down Line 5. Unfortunately, at the time of this writing, Line 5 continues to transport oil.

Water Pollution in Russia

Russia has over two million lakes and over two hundred thousand rivers, but over eleven million people in Russia do not have access to safe drinking water. Many of Russia's water treatment facilities are in poor condition, and many of their water pipelines are heavily corroded. Sewage and industrial, nuclear, and chemical wastes are dumped into rivers, bays, and lakes.

Over 75 percent of Russia's surface water is polluted, and the majority of Russia's water does not meet quality standards. In Moscow, substantial amounts of heavy metals pollute the water supply, as well as local soil and groundwater. Major rivers in Russia (including the Volga, Don, Kama, Kuban, and Oka) have up to one hundred times the allowable levels of viruses and bacteria in the water.

Lake Baikal, the Caspian Sea, and the Black Sea are all suffering from water pollution caused by chemical waste, sewage, carcinogens, pesticides, and more. A large paper mill built in the 1950s dumped industrial waste into Lake Baikal for years, twenty-four hours a day—the mill closed in 2013. The Caspian Sea is the largest inland body of water in the world, but it has no outlets, meaning it cannot flush out pollutants like other bodies of water. While some of the factories that polluted the Caspian Sea have shut down in the last few decades, the water is still dangerously polluted. The Black Sea has extraordinarily little oxygen left, and the sea contains excessive amounts of lethal hydrogen sulfide, a poisonous gas. Because the Black Sea is depleted of the oxygen needed to support life, environmentalists believe this sea could die off completely due to the severity of its pollution. Already, there are only five species of fish remaining in the Black Sea, down from twenty-six.

Water Pollution in Italy

According to the European Environmental Agency, less than half of Europe's lakes, rivers, and coastal waters met ecological standards, and only 38 percent met chemical pollution standards. The majority of Europe's surface water has been polluted by chemicals, pesticides, mining operations, and agricultural run-off, with mercury being the most common pollutant found.[35]

The Sarno River is thought to be the most polluted river in Europe due to industrial and agricultural waste being dumped into its waters. This river, which is the primary waterway of Southern Italy, used to be safe to drink from, but now it is full of chemicals, fertilizers, sewage, and other waste. At one time, the Sarno was a source of fresh water for animals, plants, and people, but now it is full of litter and bacteria. This contaminated water flows into the Tyrrhenian Sea in the Gulf of Naples.

Water Pollution in China

China has about 6 percent of the world's freshwater, and over half of China's population does not have access to safe drinking water. The water supply in China has been contaminated by human and industrial waste. Toxic levels of fertilizer, pesticides, arsenic, sulfates, and fluorine have been found in China's water sources. One study found that approximately 70 percent of China's lakes and rivers are not safe for human use; lakes may have a bright green surface due to algae blooms caused by intense pollution.[36] In addition, 90 percent of China's cities were found to have contaminated groundwater.[37]

Two major rivers in China, the Yellow River and the Yangtze River, are the most polluted rivers in the world. These rivers flow from east to west along the

35. Ochs, "Many European Lakes and Rivers Have Water Quality Issues."
36. Buntaine, Zhang, and Hunnicutt, "Citizen Monitoring of Waterways Decreases Pollution in China by Supporting Government Action and Oversight"; Gibson, "Water Pollution in China Is the Country's Worst Environmental Issue."
37. Gibson, "Water Pollution in China Is the Country's Worst Environmental Issue."

industrial belt and because of this these rivers must be extensively treated before being used for human consumption.

In Southeastern China, black wastewater the size of fifty Olympic swimming pools was discovered off the coast of Shishi. This oil spill—so large that it was visible via satellite imagery—came from a wastewater treatment plant that served nineteen of the city's textile dyeing companies. Because of poor environmental regulations, corruption, and limited enforcement, companies are able to dump their toxic waste into lakes and rivers without consequence.

Many of China's factories are located near rural villages, and those that live in the area must rely on contaminated water for cooking, drinking, and washing. In addition to dealing with severe water pollution, most rural villages do not have a proper wastewater management system. Chinese villages near factory complexes are known as "cancer villages" because of their high rates of cancer and death.[38] Water pollution in China kills an estimated one hundred thousand people each year.

Water Pollution in Africa

In Africa, an estimated 115 people die each hour because of diseases caused by contaminated water and poor sanitation.[39] Water sources are polluted by industrial waste, agricultural waste, and sewage, but they are also affected by foreign industries that ship their plastic waste to Africa and dump it into local rivers, lakes, and dams. African shorelines are full of plastic, and beaches and forests are covered in disposed single-use items. Coal mining and deforestation are also contributing to water pollution issues in Africa. Coal mining is a huge source of economic activity, but it creates toxic water as a result of acid mine drainage; mining also results in high amounts of salt and mineral content, which find their way to water and affect its pH levels. Deforestation has led to a decrease in tropical rainfall, which negatively impacts bodies of water as well as plants, animals, and people.

In Egypt, water poverty is a serious issue. The Nile River, which supplies 97 percent of Egypt's water, has been significantly impacted by pollution and climate change. More than 165 million tons of industrial waste are dumped into

---

38. Gibson, "Water Pollution in China Is the Country's Worst Environmental Issue."
39. Paul, "Sanitation Woes Cost Africa 115 Lives Every Hour."

the Nile each year. Due to the contaminated water supply, over 38 million Egyptians drink polluted water—close to the population of the entire state of California. With a population of over 110 million people, Egypt has high demand for fresh water, but according to UNICEF, the country may run out of clean water entirely by 2025.[40]

Water Pollution in Brazil

Brazil has 12 percent of the world's available freshwater resources, largely due to the Amazon region. At least ninety-four million residents of Brazil do not have access to sewage networks, and in larger cities such as Rio de Janeiro, coastal waters are full of untreated human waste. The waterways are plagued by "black tongues" of sewage, though from a distance, the waters may appear blue and beautiful.[41] However, studies have shown that viral levels in the water are up to 1.7 million times what would be considered concerning in the United States.[42] Rio de Janeiro does not have proper water systems or sewage treatments and due to this, 70 percent of the city's sewage ends up in the water and on beaches, filled with viruses and bacteria that can cause multiple health issues.

It is not just waste that is to blame for water pollution in South America. Medications are also contributing to water pollution, as they were recently discovered in major rivers in Brazil's Amazon Basin. Waterways that feed into the Amazon River were deemed "highly contaminated" with pharmaceuticals.[43] Fishermen have stated that there are no longer any fish near the city of Rio.[44] Sugar cane plantations are also causing water pollution, with runoff from fertilizers and herbicides entering local water sources.

Brazil is the world's fourth largest producer of plastic waste. An estimated 11.4 million tons of plastic waste is generated each year, with only 1.28 percent of that plastic waste being recycled. That means that each year, around 7.7 million tons of Brazil's plastic ends up in landfills and, ultimately, rivers, lakes, oceans, and beaches.

---

40. Hughes, "Effects of Water Pollution in Egypt."
41. Barchfield, "Study."
42. Barchfield, "Study."
43. Gonzales, "Pharmaceutical Water Pollution Detected Deep in the Brazilian Amazon."
44. Phillips, "The Lagoon in Front of Rio's Olympic Park Is So Filthy the Fish Are Dying."

Water Pollution in Tasmania

Australia is the driest inhabited continent on Earth, so it makes sense that water should be Australia's most valuable substance. However, water pollution is a topic of concern here just as it is in other countries. Australians use an estimated 324 pounds of plastic per person each year, but only 14 percent of Australia's plastic is recycled. Hundreds of thousands of pounds of plastic end up in Australia's waters, and once at sea, plastic becomes deadly. Turtles eat and choke on plastic bags, mistaking them for jellyfish in their environment. Whales can starve to death after eating plastic because it gives them a false sense of fullness and obstructs their bowels, interrupting food digestion and causing death. Around one million Australian seabirds are killed by plastic pollution each year, either due to eating plastic or becoming entangled in plastic, which can lead to drowning, infection, or an inability to fly.

Agriculture runoff, animal waste, and chemical waste also flow from the land into the water, reducing water quality and creating dangerous algae blooms. Another pollutant is mining waste, which has contributed to the devastation of the King and Queen Rivers in Tasmania. For over one hundred years, these river systems were used as a dumping ground for waste materials from copper and gold mines. Today, the rivers are orange in color, and there is little natural life found in or near these acidic waters.

Journal Prompts

1. What sensations, emotions, or thoughts did you experience as you read about the problems that water faces due to worldwide pollution? Did you feel angry or upset?
2. Do you have the desire to create change?
3. In the appendix, there is a list of water organizations that you can become involved with. Which one are you most likely to get involved with, and why does that particular organization's mission speak to you?

Chapter 4
HOW TO GET INVOLVED

A river cuts through rock,
not because of its power,
but because of its persistence.
—Jim Watkins

In 2020, there were 785 million people without access to clean drinking water. Experts have estimated that by 2025, half of the world's pollution will live in an environment that does not have full access to water.[45] Water pollution is a serious problem. Water is a universal dissolvent, and it dissolves more substances than any other liquid, which can make it easier for water pollution to occur. When water is contaminated by harmful substances, it becomes unsafe for drinking, cooking, and bathing. The pollution that we are seeing in our waterways is increasing due to the larger population, inadequate waste management, improper disposal of toxins, and a general discard of water by many. Salt pollution is also a contributing factor in damaging our waters' fragile ecosystem, as it runs off into our waterways. This is not an issue created by table salt or ritual salts. For instance, residents of regions that experience freezing temperatures are likely familiar with de-icers, products that are sprinkled onto icy roads to melt away the ice and enhance driving conditions in winter weather. Many de-icers are full of chemical salts. These salts are then washed away by rain or melting ice, ending up in the groundwater and local bodies of water.

Over the last few years, more ways to get involved with water pollution and conservation have become available. How you decide to give back to our sacred

---

45. Haghighi, "What Effects Does Water Pollution Have on Human Health?"

water is a personal choice. You can focus on magical energy work by offering a revitalizing ritual or participating in a ceremony. You choose to only perform desperately needed physical tasks to honor the water. Or you can do magical *and* physical work, as many water advocates and waterbearers do. There is no right or wrong way when it comes to working to heal the water.

Healing the Water Locally

Believe it or not, you can have a massive impact on the ecosystem in your area. From small lifestyle changes to cleaning debris from local waterways, here are some ways to get involved.

Create a Plastic- and Chemical-Free Household

One way to change the amount of pollution and toxins that you may be releasing into the environment is to practice mindful shopping. Many popular products are dangerous. There are a variety of companies online that offer organic, biodegradable, and nontoxic cleaners that are all chemical- and plastic-free. Your local store may even carry some, depending on your location. If you can, keep water pollution in mind to motivate yourself to select environmentally friendly products.

When shopping at local stores, usually the store will have plastic-free, reusable shopping bags for purchase. These are made with environmentally friendly products that will not harm the water. Reusable shopping bags are a great investment because you can bring them back to the store the next time you visit.

It is not just cleaning supplies that contain toxins. Other everyday purchases such as paint, gasoline and motor oil, and prescription medication can have toxic properties. To find out how you can dispose of these contaminants properly, contact your local waste department—they will have specific resources for your area, which may be different from mine. Never pour contaminants down any drain or dump them in the toilet. Studies have found that fish have been absorbing these toxins via their environments' polluted drinking water, leading to deformities and reproductive issues; contaminated fish are obviously not safe for human consumption as a result.[46]

---

46. Collier, "Swallowing the Pharmaceutical Waters."

If you plant flowers or a garden each year, try to reduce fertilizer usage, or choose fertilizers that are less toxic; you can find organic fertilizers online and at your local growers. Fertilizers can create run-off and pollute your local water sources. Another simple way to reduce pollution is to inspect your vehicle on a regular basis to make sure that oils are not leaking from broken seals or gaskets.

Report Illegal Water Pollution Activity

If you witness what you believe to be illegal dumping of hazardous waste, you can report it to your local authorities. If it is safe to do so, write down a description of the person or company performing the illegal dumping as well as a description of any vehicle used. This information may be helpful.

Respect Wells and Storm Drains

As water travels, untreated, into storm drains, they should only be used for rainwater. Avoid putting grass clippings, oil, or fertilizer into storm drains to prevent rainwater from becoming contaminated.

Research Your Local Watershed

A watershed is an area of land where all of the rainwater, melting snow, and other water run-off drains into a common body of water, such as a nearby river or lake. This water eventually flows to water reservoirs, bays, and the ocean. In Michigan, my watersheds connect to the Great Lakes and the underlying groundwater. All of us live in a watershed, though they can range from a few miles long to thousands of miles long. Maintaining our watersheds is essential for healthy aquatic ecosystems.

A healthy watershed should have a natural, intact habitat with native vegetation, unpolluted water, and natural hydrology. Healthy watersheds maintain clean drinking water and water quality as well as providing habitats for animals and fish. According to the Environmental Protection Agency, "More than $450 billion in food and fiber, manufactured goods, and tourism depends on clean water and healthy watersheds."[47]

Locate and research your nearest watershed. There should be a website for your local watershed that shares information on the condition of its water and

47. "Addressing Water Quality Challenges Using a Watershed Approach."

how you can get involved. These websites also offer tips and advice for maintaining water quality. If you cannot physically volunteer, you can make a financial donation to your local watershed to support the work that they are doing.

Volunteer for Cleanup Events

You can offer your time in service to the water. Volunteer for cleanup events near your home. If you've located your watershed, that would be the best place to start to look for an official cleanup event; the website for the watershed in my area has information on when, where, and how to get involved. However, you do not need to wait for a cleanup event to start picking up plastic, trash, and other litter near your local river or lake. All you need are trash bags, gloves, and protective clothing to begin this physical ritual. Make sure that you are mindful of protecting yourself when picking up items that may be hazardous, such as glass and other sharp objects.

Conserve Water

Another great way to get involved is by reducing the amount of water that you use each day. By using water mindfully, you can save thousands of gallons each year. You can start conserving water quite easily by making some simple changes to your daily routine.

There are many methods to conserve water, so I will only share a few household habits that you could change.

- Do not use your toilet for anything other than its intended purpose. Each time you flush, you are using at least one gallon of water. Also, double check your toilet for leaks. A leaking toilet can waste more than one hundred gallons of water each day.
- Take shorter showers, only showering the length of time that it takes to wash yourself. At least two gallons of water are used for *each minute* that you are in the shower.
- Turn off the sink while you are brushing your teeth; only have the water on when you are using it.
- Don't use your dishwasher or washing machine unless it is full, as a complete cycle can use up to thirty-five gallons of water.

- If you drink your tap water and enjoy it cold, instead of grabbing a cup and leaving your faucet running until the tap water is cold enough, fill up a couple of bottles with room-temperature tap water and put them in the fridge to cool. In the long run, this can save hundreds of gallons of water.
- Every so often, walk through your home to make sure that none of your pipes are leaking, as this can waste hundreds—or even thousands—of gallons of water a day.
- If you wash your car by hand, fill a pail with water and soap, then use the soapy pail to clean your car. Do not leave the hose on while doing so; instead, turn it back on to rinse your car when you are ready. This will save hundreds of gallons of water.

By being self-aware and facilitating a few lifestyle changes, you can make a difference for our water supply and reduce pollution in the process.

Purity Healing Ritual

In many cultures, purification of the body was required before entering a sacred space or performing a sacred ritual. This was done via a special rite to remove negative energetic and physical pollutants.

I have chosen to include a purity healing ritual in this chapter. This ritual will draw out the negative impurities in polluted water. Remember that the rituals in this book can be modified in any way. Though they are not formally a part of the ritual, you can include gods and goddesses, angels, or any other aspect of your religious practice. The rituals in this book are meant to be a basic introduction to healing energy and water that you can easily customize. Before you begin this ritual, you will need to gather a few items.

Ritual Tools
- Large stainless steel or glass bowl
- Healing herbs (I recommend dandelion, rosemary, and palo santo)
- Spring, creek, or sea water
- Three chime candles (one white, one black, one silver)
- Candle carving tool
- Matches

- Healing crystals (I recommend smoky quartz, black obsidian, clear quartz, garnet, and selenite)
- Glass jar
- Piece of solid silver or moonlight

To proceed, you will need to choose a location to perform this ritual. This ritual should be done outdoors by a body of water. This ritual can also be done at an altar, if you have one; if you are working at your altar, you will still need to choose a location to direct the magical energy to.[48]

The day before your purity ritual, collect spring, creek, or sea water in a jar. (I suggest these types of water because they have magical purification qualities.) Make this water sacred by setting it underneath the moonlight overnight or by immersing solid silver in the water overnight. Both are easy and effective methods for sanctifying water.

Cleansing your crystals before use is highly recommended to clear them of negative buildup. You can do this in a variety of ways, though the easiest way to do so is to place the crystal in sun- or moonlight for a supercharged vibrational cleansing. You can also smoke cleanse crystals with a purifying herb or spray.

On the day of the ritual, place your large bowl on the ground at your chosen location, as close to the water's edge as you can. Later you will be placing candles around the bowl, so make sure you leave enough room for them.

Pick up your candles and carve symbols into each of them to magnify their energy. White candles are symbols of purification and cleansing, so I recommend etching a dove, a lotus, or a lily, and perhaps a flame. Black candles are for releasing and banishing, so I would suggest carving symbols of your faith to banish negative energy, such as a pentagram, a witch's knot, a hammer, mistletoe, Brigid's cross, or the Christian cross. Silver candles are for healing, and there are so many powerful healing symbols in various traditions. Etching a caduceus or the Celtic Ailm symbol would work well, as they are both highly recognized symbols of healing.

Once you have finished carving, place the three candles around the bowl in an upside-down triangle, which is the alchemical element for water. The three candles serve as the angular points of the upside-down triangle.

---

48. More information about creating an altar can be found in chapter 6.

Then, fill your bowl with crystals that are associated with purity. (I have recommended crystals for this purity ritual, but you can add or replace crystals to your preference.) Smoky quartz and black obsidian effectively neutralize negative vibrations. (Be careful with black obsidian, as it can break when immersed in water that is either too hot or too cold.) Clear quartz is a universal healing crystal. Garnet, the stone of health, purifies mind, body, and soul. I also recommend using selenite, as it dissolves negative energy and cleanses spiritually and physically. However, this crystal is considered a "soft crystal" due to its chemical structure, which allows it to dissolve in water, shedding flakes into the water when immersed. Because the crystals in this bowl will be covered with water, do not place the selenite inside the bowl. Instead, place this crystal next to your bowl, which will offer healing vibrations to the water contained within, as water absorbs energy.

Take your sacred water and pour it into your bowl filled with crystals. As you pour, visualize bright white, purifying energy flowing from the sacred water into the bowl. Then add dandelion, rosemary, and palo santo to the bowl to promote purification and to dispel negative energy.

Sit in front of the bowl. Using a match, light the black candle. While lighting the candle, state your intention to remove negativity from the water. For your intention, you could state, "Water, I banish your negative impurities with the power of myself and the universe."

Place your hand above the bowl of water. Visualize the universal energy that sustains you flowing out of your hand into the bowl of water. If you are attuned to Reiki, draw the Power Symbol, or "Cho Ku Rei," in the air above the bowl, as it will add more power to your ritual.

Now that you have banished negative energy and physical impurities from the water, it is time to light the silver candle for healing. While lighting the candle, state your intention to heal the water from unwanted painful or harmful emotions. For your intention, you could state, "Water, I heal your soul and rejuvenate your aura with the highest vibration. I heal you from pain, hate, anger, trauma, and fear with the power of my myself and the universe."

Place your hand over the bowl of water. Visualize the universal energy that sustains you flowing out of your hand into the bowl of water. If you are attuned to Reiki, draw the Master Symbol, or "Dai Ko Myo," in the air above the bowl, as it has the highest vibration and the power to heal the soul and aura of the water in your ritual.

After healing the water from long-held negative emotions, you can light the white candle, which corresponds to purification. While lighting the candle, state your intention to permanently purify the water. For your intention, you could state, "Water, you are pure once more. Your DNA is pure once again, and the purity of your soul has been revived."

Place your hand over the bowl of water. Visualize the universal energy that sustains you flowing out of your hand into the bowl of water. If you are attuned to Reiki, draw the Harmony Symbol, or "Sei He Ki," in the air above the bowl, as it has the power to assist in the purification process.

Sit with your bowl until all three candles burn out. After the candles have burned out, clean any dirt off your hands and remove the crystals from the bowl. Then, pick up the bowl and pour it into the body of water that you have chosen. If you are performing this ritual at your altar, you can either store the water and bring to a body of water at a later date, or you can take the bowl to your yard and pour it over Mother Earth; the water will seep through the ground back to its natural home, and it will spread healing, pure energy on its journey.

To finish your ritual, you can meditate near the water or offer prayers, blessings, or mantras.

What We Can Do through Vibration

We can revitalize and rebalance water's energy by offering positive healing vibrations to our sacred water. This is possible because we are vibrational beings, constantly in motion, and our vibrations can affect other energy fields. Our vibration generates electromagnetic energy waves, causing a disturbance in matter. Negative vibrations can harm physical substances, but on the other end of the spectrum, positive vibrations can heal.

Since everything in this universe is interconnected, we can use vibration to release underlying energetic imbalances in water by offering positive higher frequencies. We can change water's vibrational frequency so that it may function at its best just by using our voices, thoughts, visualizations, and intentions. We can heal the water at any location, at any time, through the power of positive vibration. We now know that vibration has the power to change everything.

May There Be Peace: Water Pollution Apology Ritual

Throughout history, our water has fought many battles, as you learned in chapter 3. For generations, water has been defending itself against humankind's corruptive activities, and it seems that we are not learning from our previous mistakes. I created this apology ritual in the hopes that the water recognizes that not all people are at fault, and that there are thousands of waterbearers around the world who are in support of healing and protecting our water. This ritual soothes the water and clears any negative emotions held within it, including anger, fear, and anxiety.

Ritual Tools
- Lavender, lemon balm, and chamomile (herbs or essential oils)
- Large glass or crystal bowl
- Crystals (black obsidian, aragonite, amethyst, citrine, moonstone)
- One ammonite fossil
- A cup
- Polluted (but safe) water
- Gloves (optional)

Make sure that your crystals have been cleansed of all negative energy before using them in ritual. This can be achieved by leaving them under the moon's light, preferably during a full moon. You could also safely pass the crystals through the flame of a candle while envisioning purifying light energizing your crystal. Another option for cleansing your crystals is to light a healing herb bundle and pass them through the smoke.

Once your crystals are cleansed, find polluted water near you. With that being said, do your research and do not attempt to work with water that may physically cause you harm. If you would like to work with water on private property, always ask permission first. Once you have located the water you would like to work with, transfer some of that water into a bowl using a cup until the bowl is half full. Always use a cup when handling water that is polluted; you can even wear gloves to protect your skin. Be respectful to the water and speak your intentions aloud. As you work, tell the water what you are doing and reassure it that you will return the water at a later time.

Decide if you want to perform your ritual near the body of water or at home. If you would prefer to perform this ritual indoors, transport your cup and half-full bowl of water back home. Set aside the cup, remembering that you used it to collect polluted water, so take note that you should not drink out of it; use it only for ritual collecting purposes.

Next, place the bowl on a safe surface. If you are outdoors, walk a ways away from any contaminated ground before setting down the bowl. If you are at home, you can place the bowl on the floor or a table. Position yourself directly in front of the bowl with your crystals and herbs beside you.

Before you can offer the water peace, apology, and rejuvenation, you first need to cleanse it of the heavy negative vibrations that it carries. Hold the black obsidian in both hands and bring the stone directly in front of your heart. Say aloud, "Water, I draw out the deep infection of pollution that resides in your DNA, bursting forth with the explosive strength of magma being released from a volcano, from the pure, loving energy of my heart and into this crystal."

Place the black obsidian into the bowl of water and say, "Water, you are cut off from the negative connection that drains you."

Pick up the aragonite crystal and cup it in both hands. This nurturing stone can provide the water with balanced and peaceful energy. Bring the stone directly in front of your heart and say aloud, "Water, I give you balance and peace, from the pure, loving energy of my heart and into this crystal."

Place the aragonite into the bowl of water and say, "Water, your agitation is released. You are balanced and at peace once again."

Next, select the ammonite fossil. This will soothe the anger that polluted waters carry. Again, bring the stone directly in front of your heart. Say aloud, "Water, I give you calmness in times of turmoil, from the pure, loving energy of my heart and into this fossil."

Place the fossil into the bowl of water and say, "Water, you are free of your deep anger."

Hold the amethyst crystal in both hands. This crystal will relax the water's feelings of anxiety. Bring the stone directly in front of your heart and say aloud, "Water, I give you serenity when you are on constant alert, from the pure, loving energy of my heart and into this crystal."

Place the amethyst into the bowl of water and say, "Water, you have been released from your anxiety."

Now that the water has been cleansed of negative vibrations from pollution, anger, and anxiety, grab your citrine crystal. Citrine is a lightworker in crystal form; it carries the energy of the sun. We will be using this crystal to give the water a desperately needed boost of positivity. Bring the stone directly in front of your heart and say aloud, "Water, I give you positive energy. You are infused with the power of the sun's radiant light, from the pure, loving energy of my heart and into this crystal."

Place the citrine into the bowl of water and say, "Water, you have been given light and happiness as radiant as the sun."

Finally, hold your moonstone crystal. Bring the stone directly in front of your heart and say aloud, "Water, I give you a new beginning. With your ancient wisdom, begin anew. From the pure, loving energy of my heart and into this crystal."

Place the moonstone into the bowl of water and say, "Water, you have been given the strength to create a new beginning."

Next, place lavender, lemon balm, and chamomile into the bowl. If using essential oils instead of herbs, use three drops of each. Lavender represents undying love for water, lemon balm is for staying calm in trying times, and chamomile soothes the water's soul.

Place both hands over the crystal-filled bowl and offer a heartfelt apology for water pollution and disrespect. You can share any personal statement that aligns with your intentions. Here is a recommendation: "Water, I am sorry for the water pollution that I and humankind have caused you, whether it was intentional or not. We have taken your life and corrupted it with plastic, chemicals, oil, and hate. I love you, water. I respect you, water. Be at peace, water."

When you are ready, hold the bowl of water that is now free of pollution due to the healing vibrations of the crystals and your healing mantras. Remove your crystals. Then, pour the contents of the bowl back into the polluted water source that you retrieved the water from. This pure elixir will flow through the polluted waters and heal the water from within, restoring its peace.

Journal Prompts
1. If you choose to assist in physically healing our water, which practices interest you? Are you drawn to water conservation, volunteer work, or swapping your cleaning supplies for nontoxic products?

2. If you are unsure where to start healing the water, you can choose something easier to break down. What are three small steps that you can take toward healing and protecting our water? How will you put these steps into action?

3. How did you feel while performing the Purity Healing Ritual? Do you believe that your ritual was successful? Why or why not?

4. How did you feel before, during, and after the Water Pollution Apology Ritual? Observe your physical, mental, and spiritual states.

5. How did you affect and heal the water through the Water Pollution Apology Ritual? Did you feel that it was successful? Why or why not?

Chapter 5
ENERGY, FREQUENCY, AND VIBRATION

If you want to find the secrets of the universe,
think in terms of energy, frequency, and vibration.
—Nikola Tesla

To improve your understanding of how energy healing can create change in water with human consciousness, I would like to briefly explain how certain laws of the universe have built the foundation of the practice of energy medicine. I am only going to introduce eight of the twelve universal laws; these laws are relevant to the practice of energy medicine, other forms of metaphysical healing modalities, and this book. These laws are the rules that control universal manifestation, with each of them magically intertwined, coexisting and collaborating with each other to create desired change. It is important to remember that these universal laws were not invented—they were found by our ancestors, who experienced them firsthand.

The first law that lays the foundation is the Law of Divine Oneness. This law recognizes the energetic interconnectedness of all that exists within the universe. It illustrates that everything is connected in this world and that every thought, word, or action influences all others because we are not separate from each other. There is no difference between us because we are all one. This first law allows us to create change vibrationally in bodies of water because water is energetically intertwined with our own energetic bodies.

The second law is the Law of Vibration, which may be more familiar. This law states that everything in this world is made up of energy that is constantly vibrating at specific frequencies. The thoughts, feelings, and emotions that make

67

up human consciousness are all several types of energy that never stop vibrating. Our personal vibration can produce effects in our own lives. All that is physical and nonphysical in this world vibrates all the time, every minute of every day, nonstop. Nothing stands still. So, to manifest your desires with this law, all you need to do is find the vibration that you are wanting to match, then continuously raise your own vibration until you match it. The higher your vibration is, the faster you will receive the results that you want. You will be able to identify as a person with a higher frequency if you have these traits: you have positive thoughts and emotions, such as love and joy; you experience empathy, compassion, confidence, and enthusiasm; you have healthy relationships and a healthy spiritual lifestyle.

The third law is the Law of Correspondence, which states that the vibration that you dwell on will become your reality. For example, worrying about a negative event occurring will send out negative vibrations and can bring negativity into your life. Your natural vibration tells the universe how to communicate to you.

The fourth and most popular law is the Law of Attraction. This law is widely used for manifestation, and for good reason. What you focus on—whether it is a want, need, or desire—the universe will reflect back to you. You truly need to believe that the Law of Attraction works, or it won't. You have to put what you want out for the universe to grab. You have to vibrate at the level that you want to attract—no doubts allowed. And I know firsthand that belief can bring your innermost desires into reality. When I desperately wanted my desired outcome, I had no shame. I would yell, chant, and sing to the universe as loud as I could manage. I was extremely focused. I told the universe that I would be an author, that there was no other option. That I would be a successful writer, energy medicine practitioner, and Water Priestess. There was no other path for me—only this path. I would not take no for an answer. When manifesting a desired outcome for the water, this law can help us stay positive and focused on the change that we are visualizing.

The fifth law that needs to be physically enacted for your manifestations to become real is the Law of Inspired Action. You have to put in the work to receive your manifestation. You cannot just believe that your goals will completely manifest and then sit on the couch. I had wanted to be an author since I was a young girl, but when I reached a point in my life where I had something to say to the world, I had to take the necessary steps that were required for me to achieve my goal: I had to start writing. When working with water, this law is self-explanatory. If you are manifesting pollution-free waters, then you have to either do the physical work of getting your hands dirty, or you have to perform that ritual, or both.

The sixth law of the twelve universal laws is the Law of Perpetual Transmutation of Energy. This law states that on an energetic level, the universe is constantly fluctuating, with every action preceded by a thought, and that thought will one day manifest into physical reality. High frequencies will transform lower frequencies into higher ones when they are applied with intention. This also works the other way around: lower frequencies can transform higher frequencies. When I am in the vicinity of a person who gives off negative vibes, I can feel their energy lowering mine at times. It leaves me feeling mentally exhausted and depleted. If you are naturally a person with a higher vibration like me, you probably can feel the difference in people's energies too.

The seventh law is the Law of Cause and Effect, which displays the connection between actions and events. You may not notice the energetic effects of your actions or thoughts immediately, but in time they will become more apparent as they bounce back to you. However, effects can return to you positively or negatively, depending on the energetic action that you sent out previously.

The Law of Compensation, the eighth law, states that you reap what you sow. If you want something to manifest, you will need to contribute to your goals and desires in some way to receive benefits for your hard work. This will always come back to you in a positive way, never a negative one.

Energy and Consciousness

Energy is the origin and reality of the universe, and in many Eastern traditions, energy and consciousness are identical. For example, an ancient Taoist principle states that the mind creates energy and energy creates the mind. Mind and energy are viewed as one inseparable entity. While I believe that the energy contained in our mind generates our consciousness, modern science has not been able to prove where the energy of the mind comes from or how human consciousness is connected to the universe. However, science *has* shown that the body's natural processes are not responsible for our consciousness.[49]

What we do know is that our conscious mind generates self-awareness and contains all our perceptions, memories, thoughts, and feelings. When we intentionally use our self-aware human consciousness to manifest change in the physical world, the universe reacts to our conscious thoughts, feelings, intentions, and vocal vibrations, which then sets our desires into motion.

You are the engine that creates the spark. This spark ignites a chain of events that occur over time, leading you toward the reality you are manifesting. This process works for the positive *and* negative energies that you may or may not consciously release to the universe, so be mindful of your thoughts when you are working to facilitate positive change.

While working with energy, negative feelings such as fear, hatred, or doubt will lower your personal frequency, and instead of setting a positive manifestation, you may unintentionally set a negative one, thus receiving negativity in return. What you give to universal energy is exactly what you will receive back. As previously discussed, this is the Law of Attraction. Most of the energy-based practices in this book call on the Law of Attraction and positive manifestation.

Heal Water with Energy

The phrase *energy medicine* refers to energy that creates healing vibrations. An energy medicine practitioner uses this energy by locating the biofield, which is the large field of energy that surrounds and extends from the human body for around eight feet. The biofield can transform or "stimulate" negative energy to create positive healing on the atomic level. All biofields are connected and unified at the quantum level. That makes people—and everything else—connected to the quantum field of energy via the "Universal Field." The Universal Field is what allows energy medicine practitioners to connect and create changes in people, plants, animals, and water.

In the human body, we have an estimated thirty trillion electrically charged atoms. We are beings of pure universal energy able to access an interconnected web of electromagnetic vibrational frequencies while also being a physical living, breathing form. As a living energy field that is always vibrating, we can

---

49. Oberlander, "A New Theory in Physics Claims to Solve the Mystery of Consciousness."

manifest transformation within the physical and energetic world because we are all connected in the same vast Universal Field and capable of interacting with everything else.

There are various methods of alternative or vibrational healing practices that are typically used to cure the mind, body, and soul of physical and emotional illness by bringing all three aspects into balance. Water is sensitive to vibrational energy, so we can use these same metaphysical techniques on water to restore its physical and vibrational properties. When water receives an abundance of vibrational frequencies, it can facilitate a total healing transformation.

Our human vibrational energies have immense impacts on water because our bodies are living water—water within a physical form. As I stated in the introduction, the human body is up to 70 percent water, so we have the power to influence the physical and the vibrational properties of water within each of its three forms: solid (frozen water/ice), liquid (rain/room-temperature water), and gas (water vapor).

As a Reiki Master Practitioner, I can channel universal healing energy and transmit this energy to water through my palms, restoring balance within the water. However, you do not have to be a Reiki Master to heal the water. To be successful, you must fully shift your conscious thinking to a higher positive vibration so that you can positively affect the energetic frequency of the water. In my opinion, to heal through energy requires a practitioner to consciously control their thoughts. You must choose to have a positive mindset throughout the process; if you are thinking negative thoughts, then the energy you're transmitting could become unclear, so paying attention to your thoughts is important. Remember, negative energy attracts negative energy and positive energy attracts positive energy.

The Origins of Usui Reiki

Since I mention Reiki frequently throughout this book, I wanted to provide a brief history of Usui Reiki for those who may be new to this energy system. Reiki is a safe, beautiful, noninvasive form of Japanese energy healing. Universal energy has always been in existence; people have been tapping into this energy for eons. No human can claim rights to the energy itself because we did not create the vibrational energies—they have always been there. However, this particular energy method was developed by Mikao Usui (1865–1926), a Japanese doctor.

Dr. Usui had a special interest in healing, which led him to become a doctor. However, he also went on to work as a missionary and public servant, amongst other roles. One day while performing a sermon, a student asked him how the Buddha were able to perform the miraculous healings that he preached about, and if Dr. Usui himself could spontaneously heal as well. He was surprised to find that he did not have the answer to this question. While he understood the spoken word of his faith, he did not know how the healing process worked. He set out in search of the secrets of healing, traveling to America to become knowledgeable about psychology, theology, and philosophy.

Upon his return from America and after years of self-reflection, discovery, and study, Dr. Usui retreated to the mountains to fast and meditate for twenty-one days. On the last day, universal energy struck Dr. Usui's third eye, and he fell into a deep state of meditation. Sacred Sanskrit symbols were revealed to him while he was communing with the divine.

After his enlightenment, Dr. Usui awoke restored to full health after fasting for a long twenty-one days upon the mountain. Excited to share the news that his attempts to discover the secrets of universal healing had not been in vain, Dr. Usui began his descent down the mountain. While walking, he stubbed his toe, and as he reached for his toe, his hands became hot with healing energy. His pain and the bleeding immediately stopped. Dr. Usui had just experienced his own healing touch.

For years afterward, Dr. Usui used his newfound ability to facilitate healing in others. But he wanted to share the teachings of the sacred symbols and attunements so that others may experience the healing magic of this energy system as well. Due to this desire, the "Usui Reiki Spiritual Healing Method" was created. In addition, Dr. Usui trained others to become Reiki Masters.

Over the years, Dr. Usui spoke to countless people about the healing power of Reiki, and in the process, he met a naval commander and doctor named Chujiro Hayashi. Dr. Usui invited Dr. Hayashi to travel alongside him, teaching the word and power of Reiki to heal the world, and Dr. Hayashi agreed. After Dr. Usui passed away, Dr. Hayashi continued his work, opening his own clinic and devoting his life to Reiki.

Dr. Hayashi was an important part of Reiki spreading to the West. In 1935, a Japanese American woman by the name of Hawayo Takata had made an appointment for a Reiki healing session with Dr. Hayashi. By the end of this session, Mrs. Takata was quite impressed and demanded to be taught the healing practice of Reiki. In time, Dr. Hayashi agreed, and Mrs. Takata went on to become a Reiki Master, eventually opening her own Reiki clinic in Hawaii. During her lifetime, Mrs. Takata taught and attuned a total of twenty-two Reiki Master teachers who helped spread Reiki to the rest of the world.

The Power of Reiki

The word *Reiki*, which is pronounced "RAY-key," translates into "universal life energy."[50] Attuned practitioners use this energy system by transferring energy from the universe through the palms and into the recipient's aura/biofield/body (which can include the chakra energy system) to facilitate healing of the mind, body, and soul. This loving energy triggers the recipient's natural ability to heal themselves, removing negative energy from the biofield and creating balance and harmony on the physical, emotional, and mental level.

Reiki can be compared to a variety of other energy systems that work with chi, aether, prana, or spirit. At their core, most energy systems are working with the same energy, just using different words. Even Reiki itself has different systems. Over the years, Reiki has grown considerably, which means that there are a variety of Reiki methods and symbols that are separate from Usui Reiki. I am only attuned to the Usui Reiki System of Natural Healing, which is why this book focuses on that system; if you are a Reiki practitioner attuned to other symbols or systems, feel free to customize the ceremonies, rituals, and blessings that I have provided.

Before I began learning Reiki, I thought that it would be difficult, but it is quite easy. Reiki can be learned by anyone: neither the energy nor the Masters discriminate for any reason. You can be of any religion, race, age, or gender, and no prior experience is required. However, a person must become attuned to Reiki's energy system via a Reiki Master Teacher.

Traditionally, in the years before us, the Usui Reiki tradition was an oral one, passed from the Master Teacher down to the student. The Master Teacher

---

50. "Mrs. Takata Talks about Reiki."

also passed down the symbols used in Reiki. These symbols, while considered sacred, do not hold any special power themselves; rather, it is the practitioner who energizes the symbols with their focus and intention. After reaching the appropriate level of attunement, students had to memorize the symbols as well as the multiple hand placements utilized during Reiki, as writing the information down on paper was strictly forbidden. Students would then apprentice for years alongside their Master Teacher to become attuned to the first, second, and Master levels of Reiki. (While there are traditional Reiki practitioners who still follow this method, attunement to Reiki and its symbols are less severe today. More Master Teachers, including myself, are allowing our students to draw the symbols or save them digitally so that they can reference the symbol throughout their training.)

An attunement, a type of sacred initiation ceremony, is performed after successfully completing all requirements. An attunement connects your energy system to the vibrational frequency of Reiki energy. This connection opens a type of electrical, spiritual conduit that allows you to draw upon Reiki energy and effortlessly pull it through you whenever healing is needed. Once you have become attuned to each level of this system, you are attuned for your entire life; even if you stop using the energy, it will never leave you.

An attuned Reiki practitioner can channel loving and healing spiritual energy directly from the universe to their chosen recipient, stimulating the recipient's natural healing abilities. Reiki's unconditionally loving, healing energy can be sent from afar due to the vibrational field that surrounds us all, or it can be sent in person. In person, the Reiki practitioner places their palms either directly on or above certain areas of the recipient's body, allowing the healing energy to flow through the practitioner and into the recipient. Some practitioners can feel the energy of Reiki in their palms; however, it is not a requirement to be able to feel the energy during a healing session for it to work.

When I was first learning Reiki, I worried that I was not doing it properly, but with enough time and experience, it felt natural, and I realized that my worries were invalid. The energy of Reiki is something that you have to sacrifice your time for, because it takes a lot of practice and experience to learn how to feel and work with the energy. And while I absolutely love learning from books, I had to put the books down and get real-world experience too; I did not feel the hot, tingly sensation of pure universal energy radiating from my palms that

I do now from reading alone. After years of practice, I can simply think about Reiki with the intention of performing a healing, and my hands will immediately start to pulse or tingle with the hot, vibrant energy.

Reiki can be used on yourself and other people, and it can also be used on places, animals, plants, rocks, water, food, and past, present, and future events. When I perform a healing on a person, I always make sure that I have permission beforehand if they did not come to me directly. I personally feel that the energy flows better if a person is open and consciously willing to receive Reiki. While I understand that Reiki will still work without permission, I avoid doing so unless the circumstances require it. If you are a current or future practitioner, use your own judgment and do what makes you comfortable as an energy healer. Always keep in mind that Reiki heals for the highest good of the recipient, so it is not capable of doing harm.

The Usui Power Symbol Ritual

I feel connected to the founder of Reiki, Mikao Usui, when I work with water and energy together because it embodies me in the same way that healing embodied him with pure love, energy, and gratitude. As you learned in chapter 3, water all over the world is incredibly polluted and needs our help. With that in mind, this ritual can assist us in moving toward our common goal.

In this ritual, you will be filling a sacred object with beautiful healing energy via a purifying symbol. This sacred object will then be offered to the water. I recommend using the Reiki Power Symbol as your purifying symbol. This symbol, "Cho Ku Rei," is one of the first symbols taught to a Reiki Level 2 practitioner. Cho Ku Rei brings all of the power of the universe into a healing session, which is why it is called the Power Symbol. If you are a Usui Reiki practitioner and have been attuned to the Power Symbol, you can use it for this ritual.

If you have not been attuned to Reiki's Power Symbol, you can still imagine and visualize healing energy flowing into the body of water of your choosing. We are all born with energy within us, so you can send healing energy without using Reiki. Using your natural-born energy alongside your chosen purifying symbol can heal our sacred waters just as effectively as using Reiki and its symbols. Purifying symbols that you normally use for healing in your culture or personal practice can be used to clear the water that you will be working with. As long as you are visualizing positive healing, the symbol you use will not matter.

Any symbol that is sacred to you is healing because your belief gives it power. That is very powerful in itself.

Ritual Tools
- One crystal of your choosing (optional)
- A cup (optional)

Decide whether you would like to perform the ritual outside or indoors. If performing the ritual indoors, gather water in a cup and move it to a table or altar. If you are performing the ritual outside, simply stand near your local river, pond, lake, or ocean. You could also gather some of the water in a cup and remain outdoors, if you prefer.

Before you can heal the water, you must cleanse it of unwanted energies. Using your finger or a crystal of your choice, draw the Power Symbol over the water. If you are not attuned to Reiki, use your chosen purifying symbol. This symbol will remove any negative energy from the water and allow pure love to flow in.

As you draw the symbol, imagine bright white, purple, blue, or gold light flowing from your hand and into the water, creating a waterfall of dazzling rainbow prisms. State aloud that you would like the divine to fully cleanse the water from its negative imbalances. I make sure to ask, not demand, when I want a certain outcome from the universe—I want to be on good terms with the energies that I am working with.

Once the water has been purified from unwanted energy, hold your hands above the water. Using your finger or the crystal of your choice, draw the Power Symbol or your chosen symbol above the water once more. Imagine the full vibration of the universe flowing down through the symbol in the way that a waterfall flows; watch as it drips pure vibrational droplets into the water below. Chant, scream, or simply state with loving intent that you are giving the water the power of Reiki and its Power Symbol in an offering of love and devotion to the water. (If you chose your own symbol, state it instead.) Make your intentions clear.

Visualize the Power Symbol (or your chosen symbol) vibrating and glowing from within, then slowly sinking down underneath the surface of the water until it finally disappears. The water is now glowing from within, and it contains the energy of the entire universe. It is pure. You have given the water a rare gift of purity, which is quite a personal experience. You, the water, and the universe are now unified.

Seal the energy in. To end the healing session, draw the Power Symbol (or your chosen symbol) over your precious water source for a third time. Say aloud, "I seal this positive energy and love into this vessel of water." This step is done to keep negative forces from reentering the water.

After performing the ritual, sit with the water in meditation. Observe your thoughts and any sensations you may have experienced.

Journal Prompts

1. How do energy and vibration resonate with you?
2. Scan your own energy by holding your hands above your body for a few minutes. What do you feel? Is the vibration hot, cold, or tingly? Then, scan the water's energy in the same way. What do you feel? How is the water's vibration different?
3. Think about the Usui Power Symbol Ritual you performed. What sensations did you experience when invoking energy through your-self to offer healing? How did you feel as you worked with universal energy and water together? Document the body of water that you decided to work with, the date you performed the ritual, and the ritual's outcome. You may wish to repeat the ritual and reflect on your previous findings.

Chapter 6
SETTING UP YOUR PRACTICE

Magic is believing in yourself.
If you can do that, you can make anything happen.
—Johann Wolfgang von Goethe

In this chapter, I will be teaching you how to create an altar. I have included this chapter so that you may be able to practice your spirituality as effectively as possible while serving the water. While you can use an altar for any of your spiritual and religious practices, I have included guidelines and inspiration for creating two specific kinds of altars: a water altar and an energy altar.

An altar is your own sacred and private space that is deeply personal to you and your spiritual practices. It is a place where you can step away from the physical boundaries of daily life and connect to the divine. As a reflection of you and your personal energy and magic, your altar is a spiritual focal point where you can manifest transformation using its powerful energy, which grows with each use.

The practice of creating an altar actually dates back to prehistoric times, and it has continued to this day in many religious and spiritual practices. Most churches—whether Christian or pagan in nature—have some form of altar where the priest or priestess speaks and performs energetic and magical workings. You may not associate the word *magic* with religion, but in fact, Aleister Crowley's definition of magic simply states that magic is "the science and art of causing change to occur in conformity with will."[51] Another well-known occultist, Dion Fortune, stated that magic is "the art of changing consciousness at

---

51. Crowley, *Magick in Theory and Practice.*

will."[52] In my opinion, magic is simply sending energy with intention. An altar is a place where you can do just that.

Your altar is where you can offer worship, spell work, devotion, meditation, prayer, blessings, ritual, and ceremony to the universe and your deities and guides. You can perform magical workings for yourself, other people, places, and even the earth's elements—for our purposes, the element of water. Your altar can be elaborate, ceremonial, and complex, or it can be quite simple. Altars can be large or small, though they are normally found on a raised, flat surface such as the hearth of a fireplace, a windowsill, the top of a bookcase, on an end table, or on a shelf. Altars can even be placed outside; perhaps you have an altar in your yard, on your back porch, or out in your garden where you commune with nature and meditate.

Many of us have limited space, so a permanent altar may be difficult to maintain. You can always create a temporary altar that is easily dismantled and store it in a special container of some type when it is not in use. For example, you could use a ceramic, wooden, or silver tray as the base of a temporary altar. If you have children or pets, a temporary altar works well because it is easier to protect your items if you store them somewhere safe after you have finished your spiritual practices. Personally, I have built temporary altars on tree stumps alongside rivers and on sandy beaches for a variety of different ceremonies and rituals. I enjoy having a temporary altar because it allows me to be in close proximity to the water. However, I also have a permanent altar in my home. The beauty of building an altar is that there is no right or wrong way to do it because you are creating an altar that fits your practices. Let your imagination flow, be creative, and do what works best for you.

If you are on a limited budget or would rather find or create your own altar tools, many of the items found on water altars came from combing the sandy shores and caves of beaches, lakes, rivers, and swamps. In this way, I have found plants, herbs, rope, sand, stones, shells, pearls, devil's purses, and other natural materials. Keep in mind that your altar can change. You can add and remove items that no longer speak to you. Introduce new aspects to your altar and let it evolve as you grow. And don't forget to physically tend and clean your sacred space, keeping it free of dust that can clutter the vibrational energy of your altar.

---

52. Faerywolf, "Into the Realm of Enchantment."

Creating a Water Altar

Creating an altar based on water will give you a personal connection to water and enhance your energy and power during practice. A water altar allows you to connect with any body of water in the world, no matter where you are located, to perform distance healings, ceremonies, and rituals. A water altar is convenient if you are unable to physically travel to an outside water source or if you live in a dry area that has limited water resources.

There are a variety of tools and objects that can be used on an altar that is specifically for water-based practices.

Fabric

To begin shaping your altar, start with a piece of fabric that will lay flat on the surface of your chosen location. If you can, use fabric that has natural material to connect to the element of earth, which would include wool, linen, silk, cotton, hemp, and bamboo fiber–based fabrics. While using all-natural material is nice, it is not a requirement that you do so. You can use any fabric that you have available to you.

One of the fabrics that I enjoy using on my water altars is silk. Silk is a natural insulator, and it keeps the magical energy that it sustains and protects itself from outside energies. Silk gives off a watery appearance, almost like small waves or ripples. It expresses movement and both gentle and powerful energy. Turquoise, blue, aquamarine, sea green, purple, silver, ivory, white, or black would be appropriate colors for your water altar. These colors represent the many hues of water in all its forms: oceans, lakes, rivers, waterfalls, and more.

Tools and Objects

Statues, printed images or sketches, and carvings of water spirits, water deities, nymphs, mermaids, marine life, and freshwater animals and mammals would be appropriate for a water altar. Other objects that work well on a water altar include mirrors, shells, starfish, bones, hag stones, shark teeth, devil's purses, rope, netting, sand, seaweed, sea glass, herbs, pearls, coral, candles, crystals, glass bowls and jars, silver bowls, ceramic bowls, and singing bowls, as these magical items provide high vibrations and water representation. Driftwood can be used to handcraft a wand for your magical or energetic work. Drawing or painting the alchemical symbol for water, an upside-down triangle, on your altar draws in and contains the energy of water.

Water Itself

A key part of a water altar is water itself. When collecting water for your altar, I recommend using a glass jar.

Keep in mind that there are several uses for specific water types. Spring water facilitates new beginnings, growth, blessings, and healing. Storm water can be used for protection magic. Ocean water is full of magical energy and power that can be used for rejuvenation and purification, as it absorbs negative energetic residue and cleanses the aura. River water assists with moving forward. Creeks and streams offer harmony and cleansing properties. Lake water creates peace within one's self. Swamp water can bind others who have caused harm. Water from melted snow works well for regeneration, peace, and transformation. Ice curses and banishes. Some rituals require ice to remain frozen for the ritual to be effective, but there are always exceptions; for example, melting ice can encourage releasing a bad habit. Avoid using tap water on your altar, as it has been treated with fluoride and other chemicals.

For all of the rituals in this book, I have included the type of water that I recommend using. However, if you do not have access to that specific kind of water, I have offered alternatives. If you only have access to a certain type of water and do not have access to others, you can use whatever is available in your local environment; you can then use your local water source to connect to other bodies of water anywhere in the world. Remember, you can also choose to work with any body of water on Mother Earth.

The Elements

Even though this is a water altar, you should include at least one item for each of the elements (earth, fire, water, air, and spirit) to balance your altar. Each element is significant: The element of earth keeps us grounded and embodies nature's elements. Air represents movement and knowledge. Fire is creative energy, destruction, inspiration, and manifestation. Water represents power, flow, emotion, healing, and reflection. Spirit represents the infinite wisdom and the spiritual life force that moves through us all.

When selecting elemental items for your altar, keep in mind any spiritual meanings, energetic frequencies, or physical properties the item may carry. To represent fire, I recommend using a candle. Smoke from burning incense and/or feathers would work well for air. A bowl of water, shells, or a pearl can represent water. Earth can be represented with soil, crystals, or salt. For spirit, which is the element of pure energy, you can sketch or paint the Om symbol on a piece of paper or on top of your altar. Om is the universal symbol that represents the truth of all reality, our connection to the world, and our connection to each other.

Place the elemental items on your altar in the direction that corresponds with them. Earth is placed in the north, air in the east, fire in the south, and water in the west. You can place spirit anywhere on your altar, but some prefer to place it in the center.

Crystals and Stones

When choosing crystals for your water altar, you'll find that there are a variety of crystals connected to the water element. Here are a few of my recommendations.

Aquamarine, called the stone of courage, is used to calm one's inner thoughts and works to reduce fear and anxiety. Amethyst absorbs negative emotional energy and heals emotional wounds, healing one's heart in the process. Moonstone releases emotional trauma, promotes intuition, and offers feminine energy. Black obsidian effectively absorbs negative energy. Turquoise is connected to wisdom and living one's truth.

Larimar, a rare healing stone, assists with expressing emotion and is a powerful emotional healer. It is quite mysterious, with hidden realms and secrets that eventually become known. It is a Caribbean blue color with stormy gray spots. Larimar is connected to the sea and dolphin and whale energies. This is a crystal that attracts people who have a strong connection to water. Personally, it is one of my favorite stones.

Selenite is another stone that has more than one role. It serves as a vibrational bridge to the universe and is associated with protection, harmony, femininity, and motherhood. Selenite can be used for psychic protection, soul healing, releasing negative energies, and so much more. The possibilities with this crystal are endless! This divine crystal is also associated with the Greek moon goddess, Selene, and the moon directly influences the tides of the ocean. Just like the cycles of the moon, this wonderful crystal gently reminds us that everything changes, and that while we cannot change our past, we can learn from it—we can move forward and build a better future for ourselves and for our watery mother. I use selenite in a variety of rituals. However, a word of caution: do not immerse this crystal in water, as it is soluble and can be damaged easily.

All of the crystals I've listed here are connected to the water element in some way. However, there are a variety of other crystals that could be used on your altar. Feel free to experiment.

Herbs and Plants

You can decorate your altar with magical concoctions, such as herbal charm bags or vases of fresh herbs or plants. If you wish to store herbs or plants, you can place them into sealed glass jars with sweet oils to preserve them. You can place dried herbs on your altar, or near it, to cleanse the area of negative energy. There are a variety of herbs and plants that would work well on a water altar. Here are a few of my favorites.

Aloe brings protection and good luck. Apples can create love and facilitate healing. Birch can be used to protect and purify. Elder increases wisdom, protects against negativity, and offers prosperity and peace. Gardenia protects from outside influences and assists in spiritual connection. Lilac drives away evil. Lily represents renewal and rebirth. Myrrh will enhance your rituals or ceremonies if you burn it as incense, and it will lessen the pain of tragedy. Sweet pea increases courage. Violets create a state of tranquility. Willow assists in overcoming sadness.

Many practitioners prefer to use incense in their practice rather than dried plants and herbs. Incense comes in the form of sticks, cones, and loose powders that are specifically blended for a certain purpose. They burn slowly and emit a strong smell. When working with the water element, I like to use incense that represents a variety of aspects, mostly scents for love, healing, purification, and rebirth.

Candles

Candles reflect different energy, depending on their color. Red candles can be used for action, motivation, power, strength, and survival. Orange candles are associated with creation and connection. Green candles can be used for healing the heart and soul of the environment, harmony, and abundance. Blue reflects healing and acceptance. Purple is for spiritual awareness, wisdom, and power. Black is associated with psychic protection and justice. Pink candles are used for love and compassion. White candles can be used for new beginnings, peace, and serenity. Silver candles are a good option when working with feminine energy and fertility. Gold candles represent positive energy, happiness, and abundance.

Color is not the only thing that influences candle work. Candles come in different shapes and sizes that you can choose from. I work with a variety of candles, depending on the type of ritual I am performing. For most of my practices, I use chime or pillar candles. These candles are longer, so I can etch symbols on the side to enhance the magical power; I then roll them in sweet oils and attach herbs to them. If you are looking for a candle that has a faster burn time, tealight or votive candles work well. These candles are shorter and take less time to burn down.

Personalization

This is your altar. Feel free to include aspects of your faith on your water altar since it is a representation of yourself, your spirituality, and your needs. Place items that are meaningful to you. For example, if you are Christian, you can place a cross on your altar; if you are Wiccan or pagan, perhaps you would enjoy including an athame or a cauldron on yours.

There are countless items that could be placed on a water altar. Make sure that you create your altar mindfully and with intention, as that is a sacred activity in itself. You can find many items for your altar out in nature. Browse wooded areas and wander along riverbanks, lakes, and beaches. Check out local antique shops or thrift stores for mirrors, bowls, and other items; you may be surprised at what you find.

Finishing Touches

Before adding anything new to your altar, always energetically cleanse the altar's surface and the objects that you have chosen to place upon it with sacred smoke. To do this, you will need to take a match and light a bundle of purifying herbs. (Lavender, palo santo, rosemary, frankincense, and myrrh herb bundles effectively remove all unwanted negative energy.) Waft the smoke from the bundle around your altar space and any objects or tools. I recommend holding a fireproof plate or bowl underneath the lighted bundle to catch any hot ash while you are smoke cleansing an area. You can either let the bundle burn down or extinguish it and save what is left for another time and purpose.

When you have finished setting up your altar, you can call in additional protection by placing an energetic protective shield around your altar to protect it from unwanted negative energies. There are instructions on how to do this later in the chapter.

Constructing a Reiki/Energy-Based Altar

This section provides instructions for creating an altar that reflects Reiki and alternative forms of energy healing—without water. I decided to include this altar separately for a few reasons. This altar may appeal to someone who practices energy medicine but does not want to create a water altar for their rituals and ceremonies, or to those who would prefer to facilitate an energy-based altar without a focus other than energy. Of course, you can combine the two themes together to create one beautiful altar that reflects both water and energy if that appeals to you.

An energy-based altar is a wonderful addition as you work to heal the water through vibration. This sacred place of vibrational energy can be used daily, or you can use it for remote distance healings, communing with the divine, meditation, spiritual and religious practices, or your personal energy work. As with any altar, this altar should be a reflection of your personal vibration, the modalities of energy healing that you offer, and your intentions and focus. An altar is an extension of your energy and a sacred space where you can manifest your desires into reality.

Energetic Noise

First and foremost, choose a location for this high-vibrational altar. It should be in your home on a flat surface. I recommend placing this altar as far away from digital activity as possible, so do not place it beside your television, cell phone, or other electronics. These can disrupt your energy.

Herbs and Plants

Once you have chosen a location for your altar, burning herbs or incense will cleanse the energy from this sacred space and allow high vibrations to manifest.

I have included a few recommendations here, but there are endless options when it comes to using herbs.

Lemongrass works wonderfully to remove negative energy from a space. Palo santo does the same, and it also attracts positive higher energy. Frankincense enhances the healing capacity of energy work. Lavender will protect the space after all negative energy is dispersed and replaced with higher vibrations. Eucalyptus is known for its healing and purification properties. Burning cedar will declutter any lingering energy.

If you prefer not to use dried herbs and plants, you could use essential oils instead. Essential oils have multiple uses, and they are very potent. A few drops of essential oil are all you need. Place a couple of drops of essential oil on a crystal to add additional healing properties. You could also add essential oils to a diffuser to assist in releasing negative energy. When working with essential oils, keep in mind that they should always be diluted with a carrier oil such as jojoba oil. Essential oils can also be diluted with water. You can take oils, herbs, and sacred water, place them in a spray bottle, and then spray this essence on your tools and altar space to cleanse, purify, heal, and release negative energy.

Fabric

Once you have cleansed your altar, you could lay down an altar cloth. Any type of fabric of any color will be effective. I believe that purple, blue, white, yellow, and gold represent and introduce higher vibrations, so I use those colors on my energy-based altar. Be mindful of using eco-friendly fabrics if you can, such as hemp, silk, cotton, linen, or wool.

If you prefer not to use an altar cloth, that is fine too. You can skip this step.

Crystals and Stones

Any type of crystal is useful on an energy-based altar, and I keep a variety of them on hand. Using darker crystals is especially beneficial, as they absorb negative energies and unwanted toxins; I always have one placed on or near my altar. On the other end of the spectrum, I also keep light, high-vibrational crystals on my altar to enhance the positive energies. It is good practice to have an energetically balanced space.

In addition to balancing physical, spiritual, and emotional energies, Himalayan salt lamps continuously absorb negative energy and emit gentle energy that is grounding and centering. I have one in my home, and it creates a very peaceful atmosphere.

Chakra stones can be placed on your altar. I was taught that there are seven main chakras, and these chakras represent certain areas of the body. When a chakra is unbalanced, an individual may show signs of disease in that specific region. Similarly, a body of water's energy may become unbalanced. One simple healing method is to place a chakra stone into a bowl of water and imbue it with healing energy. Then, state your healing intentions—this will allow the universe to determine exactly where the energy from the chakra stone needs to go.

Healing Grids

I have a crystal grid on my energy-based altar, which is a sacred tool to promote healing. These powerful grids can be used for in-person or distance healing, and they work for any purpose. I normally use crystal grids when promoting healing or offering protection to the water. (Keep in mind if you are sending healing to a person, you should be respectful by asking for permission first, unless it is an emergency and they cannot give you permission.) A crystal grid is composed of charged crystals that are laid out in a variety of formations, depending on the intention. A crystal grid can be elaborately arranged on cloth, or it can be simply arranged on pieces of paper. It is up to you.

Before I make my crystal grid, I first choose crystals that align with my ritual intent. Then, I cleanse the crystals. Using my intuition, I arrange the crystals in varying shapes and patterns. After they have been placed, I activate the grid and create an energetic connection between the crystals using a clear quartz point. I create invisible links between the crystals by tracing the crystal point from one crystal to the next, tapping each crystal lightly. Then, I charge the crystal grid with universal healing energy. Sometimes I drop eucalyptus or lavender essential oil onto my crystal grid for an added boost when sending healing.

Charge the crystals each day so that the grid will maintain its power. If you are attuned to Reiki, simply keep these crystals energized by drawing your selected symbols over each crystal and infusing them with Reiki. If you are not attuned to Reiki, you can place your hands upon each crystal and imbue them with your own personal energy. Be mindful to only send positive intentions while doing so, because if you are upset or agitated before infusing this grid, you will send that agitation to whatever you are attempting to heal.

Singing Bowls

In addition to healing grids, you may wish to add singing bowls to your energy-based altar. Singing bowls are usually crafted out of a combination of different earth-based metals that align with the seven main chakras of the human body. However, there are a variety of singing bowls; some are fabricated with crystal, though these sound very different from metal singing bowls. Medicinal singing bowls—metal or crystal—are crafted for different illnesses and diseases and have multiple frequencies, so do your research and find the best singing bowls for your needs.

Singing bowls are beautiful healing tools, and it is easy to learn how to use them. Typically, you take a mallet (usually included with the bowl) and then circle the bowl while pressing inward along the bowl's edges. This creates a healing frequency that radiates from the bowl. I have a handmade Tibetan singing bowl with the Om symbol etched inside, and the healing frequency is astounding.

When I am using singing bowls in my own practice, I prefer to use these frequencies: 174 hertz removes pain from the sufferer, 205 hertz influences energetic fields, 417 hertz facilitates change, 528 hertz encourages positive transformation and rebirth, and 639 hertz releases negative emotions. These numbers reflect the bowl's tonal capability—they do not reflect size. However, keep in mind that smaller bowls usually have higher-pitched sounds, while larger bowls typically produce deeper sounds.

Candles

Candles may be burned on your energy-based altar during healing sessions. Choose the candle's color based on your desired outcome. When I perform energy work, I usually use one of these colors: gold, which offers positive energy; purple, which imparts wisdom and power; or blue, which promotes healing. Sometimes I include extra colors, depending on what my goal is at that time. To make your candle magic stronger, you can etch sacred symbols into the sides of your candles.

Adding herbs to your candle can also enhance magical energy. You can place select herbs on the top of your candle as well as the base using a carrier oil such as almond oil, jojoba oil, or olive oil. Before lighting the candle, rub carrier oil on your candle, then roll the candle through the herbs or press the herbs onto the candle. It is best to do this right before lighting the wick, as this method does not always firmly attach herbs, and they may slide off with time. Keep a close eye on any candles you add oil or herbs to, as they are even more of a fire hazard.

Reflection
Mirrors are an easy way to contain the positive energy that you create in your space. They maintain a constant flow of high-vibrational frequency. However, if you are feeling negative and allowing negative thoughts and actions into your space or practice, a mirror will amplify negativity as well—you may unintentionally send negative vibrations if you are not careful.

Tools and Objects
While this is meant to be an energy-based altar, you may include items related to your personal practice, spirituality, or belief system. If you are a practitioner of Reiki or any other healing practice, you can include symbols of that practice that you feel drawn to. If you will be using your energy-based altar to send healing, include a photograph, painting, or drawing of what you are intending to heal; this gives you a physical item that you can use to focus on where you are sending healing. If you are intending to heal the water, you could also place a bowl of water or a photograph of your favorite body of water somewhere on your altar. However, it is important to avoid physical and energetic clutter on this type of altar, as clutter will disturb the energies.

Finishing Touches
Once your altar is complete, cast a circle of protection around your space to contain the energy you are working with. Keep this high-vibrational space maintained and free of dust, candle wax drippings, dirt, and pet hair. You should perform either an energetic or herbal cleansing prior to doing any energy work at your altar, as well as at the close of a healing session.

A Note on Plastic
As we are collectively working to manifest positive change, love, and healing in our beloved waters, please, if possible, refrain from using plastic in all water ceremonies and energy-based rituals. I do not recommend using any form of

plastic in your practice. I do understand, however, that plastic products may be the only option available to you currently. Instead of using plastic in my work, I use reusable items made of glass, crystal, silver, porcelain, or clay. I have found many of my sacred vessels at local thrift shops and antiques stores for very reasonable prices.

Creating Circles of Energetic Protection

At the end of each altar section, I mentioned that creating a circle of protection around your sacred space to protect your magical and energetic workings would be useful. While this is not a requirement, I wanted to provide specific direction on how to cast this circle. Not only will the circle protect your altar(s) and yourself, but you can also use it to contain and build your energy during rituals and water blessings if you choose to do so.

The practice of casting an energetic or magical circle has been around since prehistoric times. For thousands of years, people gathered in magical circles under the sun, moon, and stars, or amongst the waves of the ocean. Casting a circle is the foundation of ritual, as it creates an energetic sphere that allows you to practice magic and healing in a safe, protected space.

When working with any type of energy, it is important to keep out unwanted energies, and that is where this circle becomes useful. I say "useful" because if you do not cast a circle, you may be so focused on your ritual that you do not notice outside energies making their way in uninvited, which can leave you vulnerable. Casting a circle protects you and allows you to practice undistracted.

Cleansing the Space

Before casting a circle, you must first cleanse and purify the space you will be using for your ritual or ceremony. Whether you are performing a rite in your home or outdoors, negative energy has built up from the surrounding environment and must be cleansed; otherwise, it will disrupt your work. There are a number of tools for cleansing before casting. I have decided to share a few of my favorites, but remember that this is your circle, and cleansing can be adjusted for your own personal preferences.

The first tool that I use to cleanse a space is a ritual broom. I use a ritual broom to energetically sweep the area of negative energies. This broom does not need to touch the floor, as it is a symbolic gesture. While sweeping, I visualize bright energy flowing from the end of the broom and evaporating the negative energies that it sweeps away. When I use this method, I chant whichever mantra comes to mind—it is never the same. During my last ritual sweeping, I chanted, "Be gone, negative energy, and leave this sacred space to me. It is done; we are now in peace and harmony." However, you do not have to chant anything; chanting is not required for this cleansing tool to work properly.

Another tool that I use for energetic purification is a bell. Bells have been used for purification since ancient times. They have powerful energetic properties and can cleanse a ritual space and keep negative entities away. Resonant bells are preferred for cleansing, but any bell will do; bells with a bright, clear tone work best. You can either strike the bell or shake it at the beginning of your ritual to promote a harmonious energetic environment.

A third tool that I use often is as easy and effective as the last two: I use the smoke from incense to dispel negative energy from my work space. Any smoke will do, though I have found myrrh, frankincense, palo santo, and rosemary to be particularly effective.

My fourth tool for cleansing is, of course, Reiki. I send healing energy throughout the space, visualizing the purifying energies of the universe sweeping across the floors, walls, and the ceiling to release all negative vibration.

The four tools that I have listed are not the only options for cleaning, though these are the ones that I prefer to use in my practice. Feel free to explore other options and use what works best for you.

Grounding

Once you have purified your sacred space, you need to sit and ground yourself before invoking the elements. Grounding yourself ensures that you are not distracted during your casting. Take a few moments in silent meditation, along with a few deep breaths.

Place your hands on the floor or the earth. This allows you to connect to the energy of the earth. Allow your mind to relax and envision yourself as a plant on the earth, such as a tree with twisted roots embedded deep in the soil. Continue with your breathing and imagine the energy of the earth flowing up toward your core through your feet. It holds you in place, steady and strong, filling you with the magic and power of the earth's frequency.

If you would rather feel free and flowing before casting a circle, you can sit with your feet immersed in water. Then, during meditation, envision yourself as a gentle waterfall. Envision that the life and magic of water is flowing through your energetic body, calming your mind and imbuing you with the power, love, and strength of water.

Invoking the Elements and Casting the Circle

Casting a circle usually requires calling upon the elements of nature. I have included an example of what this looks like. However, if you are only working with water, you can choose to only invoke that element; I will describe that process in the next section.

Before invoking the elements, some people prefer to start by taking a ritual knife or wand and creating a physical circle on the ground, which they will stand in while they do their magical and energetic workings. This is optional.

To cast your circle, begin by invoking nature's five elements. While calling upon each element, you can place corresponding objects in the appropriate direction for an extra boost of energy.

Start in the east, with the element of air.[53] Speak aloud to air—the controller of the wind, the master of hurricanes, the breeze in your hair—with the power of your breath so that your voice invokes air to come into and hold your circle. When calling on air, you could place burning incense, a purple crystal such as an amethyst, or a purple or yellow candle in its corresponding direction.

Turning toward the south, invite the blazing element of fire—the sustainer of the sun, which carries the energy of passion—to come into and hold your circle. You can place a red or orange candle or a pyrite crystal in the corresponding direction.

In the west—where feeling, emotion, and transformation thrive—the element of water flows into and holds your circle. Place a moonstone crystal, shell, pearl, dish of water, or a silver or blue candle in its corresponding direction.

In the north sits Mother Earth on her throne of dirt—she who carries the ancient, deep energy of the land. Ask her to come into our circle and complete

---

53. When invoking the elements, it is not necessary to begin in the east. The direction that you begin with is based on your own tradition and is not set in stone. Some start in the north and others prefer to start in the west.

it. Place soil or salt in the corresponding direction, or place a green or brown candle.

Next, stand in the center of the circle. Visualize the energy of each element swirling around the bottom of your circle, close to the ground. This energy is the element of spirit—the fifth element, invisible yet felt in each magical working. It is what binds all of the elements together.

See the energy rising higher, building up speed and energy, until it encloses you in a sphere of brilliant protective, healing light. You are now in a safe space of containment. When you are ready, state, "This circle is now cast," then begin your magical or energetic work.

Uncasting the Circle

After you have finished your work, you will need to release or uncast the elemental circle. This allows the contained energies to dissipate and returns the area to its pre-ritual state. To do this, perform the circle casting in reverse. If you ended in the north, start with the north, the direction of earth. Blow out any candles, remove any crystals, and clear the corresponding point by stating, "I release the energy of earth." Then move on to the west/water, the south/fire, and the east/air, repeating the process until every physical object has been removed and the elements have been revoked. Visualize the energy of the circle dissolving while uncasting your circle to assist in the process.

Casting a Water Circle

Now, I want to share how to cast a circle based only on the water element. If you are casting your water circle outside near a shoreline of some type, such as a beach, a riverbank, or the edge of a lake, then I recommend that you start by drawing the physical boundaries of your water circle on the ground using a stick, a ritual knife, or a wand. Next, take a pinch of salt (sea salt or Himalayan salt) and sprinkle it over the border of your circle. After placing your salt, collect water from the source that you are casting your circle next to. Pour a small amount of water around the edges of your sand and salt-based border. You can also place pearls or shells around your physical outline; cowrie shells are associated with manifesting our desires, clam shells with healing energy and love, and scallop shells with birth, transformation, and spirituality.

If you are casting your water circle at home, determine whether or not you will be performing the ritual outside or indoors. If you are outside, stand on the earth and proceed as described previously. If you are indoors, instead of drawing a circle on the ground, you should take sand and create a circle on the floor of the area where you are working. Then, instead of pouring water around the outline of the circle, fill a chalice, an upside-down seashell, or four glass, silver, or ceramic bowls with sacred water. You could also use water that you have brought back from an outside source, such as water from a spring, well, or ocean. Place one vessel in each of the four directions.

Cleansing the Space
Ritually cleanse the space before facilitating your personal practice. One of my favorite tools is a conch shell, as it will cleanse unwanted negative energy from your ritual circle. To disperse energy, you can either blow the horn of a conch shell, or you can place water on the shell and then sprinkle the area.

Another tool that I enjoy cleansing with is incense. The act of burning incense is an easy and effective way to remove unwanted energy. I recommend using lavender, myrrh, or rosemary incense.

Grounding
Like a standard circle cast, ground yourself and meditate before casting this magical circle. Once you have mentally and spiritually prepared yourself, you may continue to the next section.

Invoking the Elements and Casting the Circle
Invoke the element of water into your circle. Start in the west, the direction corresponding with the element of water. Using a sacred pitcher, collect water from your chosen source. If you'd like, you can then pour the water into a chalice or bowl.

Place your chosen container in the corresponding direction of west. Then, place a fingertip into the water and begin to trace a spiral on a sandy beach, the ground, or your altar.[54] Start in the west, then move down to the south, up to the east, and around to the north. Continue back toward the west, retracing your steps and making the spiral smaller as you continue inward. Spirals are associated with water, as they represent change and transformation. You are manifesting intention into reality by building energetic spirals, bringing positive energy back to you in ritual. Continue tracing a spiral in the water until it is complete.

Say aloud, "Mother Water, hear my plea. Send me your sacred energy. Cleanse and protect this sacred space for me. I invoke the life and magic of your flowing entity into this circle. Gradually fill this space with your essence."

Visualize water rushing into the circle around your feet, splashing and rising around you to enclose you in an impenetrable sphere of churning water. I often visualize a thunderstorm (I was drawn to them while growing up and still am) full of lightning and angry water swirling around me in a protective embrace, shielding me from outside elements.

Finally, state, "This ritual circle of water has been cast."

Uncasting the Circle

Once your sacred practices have been performed, you will have to release the circle and allow the energy that you have built to dissipate. To uncast your water circle, begin by removing all physical objects that are not natural to the environment, including any ritual tools. Return any water that you have borrowed from a water source to its original home. This shows the water that you are trustworthy and builds a healthy relationship with water. Finally, say, "I release the element of water. Thank you, water. This circle is now uncast."

Other Metaphysical Healing Practices

In addition to Usui Reiki, there are other metaphysical healing practices that we can use to give back to our sacred water. You may have heard of other practices or even received treatments yourself. One of these practices is sound therapy, also known as sympathetic resonance. It has been used in many cultures throughout its history; ancient Greek, Egyptian, and Indian peoples used sound

---

54. Please note that if you would prefer to use sand, seashells, or sea glass in place of water to trace this outline, you may do so. Even changing the symbol is okay, as everything in this book is adaptable to your preferences. I recommend using a symbol of your faith that is connected to water, waves, or marine life.

therapy to heal the human body of physical, mental, emotional, and vibrational imbalances.

Sympathetic resonance occurs when the vibrations from one object produce vibrations in another. When one object is not at its natural vibration, sympathetic resonance can try to restore the vibrational imbalance. This method illustrates why water will vibrate at the same vibrational frequency that it hears from the healing tools used in sound therapy.

Frequencies of different variations will cause matter—such as the human body and water—to resonate to the frequency that it is receiving. The vibrations then interact with the cellular structure, and depending on the frequency of the sound being received, this could produce negative or positive effects.

Practitioners perform sound healing in the hopes of releasing blockages and resetting the flow of energy throughout the body. They use a variety of tools to create their desired frequencies. To heal the water, I recommend using sound to raise its vibration. In addition to the singing bowls that were discussed previously, other tools used in sound healing consist of tuning forks, gongs, shamanic drums, chimes, bells, and of course, singing and chanting using the human voice.

Another healing practice that I want to highlight is using crystals to work with and facilitate healing within the water. I included crystals in the rituals in this book because of their powerful ability to affect the energy fields around them. You can include water-safe crystals in ritual to enhance the water via their healing vibrational properties.

In addition to being incredibly beautiful, crystals have many beneficial uses, and they have been used as a healing tool for centuries. In ancient Greece, soldiers rubbed ground hematite on themselves for protection during battle. Ancient Egyptians used crystals to enhance the health of the living and protect the souls of the dead.

Finally, I have included symbols and drawings in some of the rituals in this book. Some symbols, such as Reiki symbols, pertain to a specific spiritual practice. Others are provided for those who are not attuned to Reiki as options to use in rituals and ceremonies. Of course, you can always use your natural-born energy instead.

A Simple Ritual: Creating Energy-Charged Water

Creating a water infusion is the simplest water healing practice. I do consider this to be a rite, as I perform this every day as an offering to the many water sources that I have here in Michigan. However, water infusions are now widely available, and I have found that practitioners perform this energetic work to enhance health, as an offering, and during Reiki healing sessions. The idea behind this water infusion is to clear the water of negative energy, activate it, and then recharge the water with healing energy before offering it back to the water in some way.

To perform a water infusion, simply place water into a vessel of your choice. I prefer to use glass containers because of plastic pollution issues; however, you can use what you have available. Then, place your hands on the container, wherever you feel guided to. You may choose to hover your hands above the container or along the sides.

Once you are in your preferred position, envision your own beautiful energy flowing into your chosen vessel. Hold your position for several minutes; you will feel the energy shifting when the water has had its fill. Choose a symbol to make the energy that you are offering to the water stronger and more effective. Then, you can either visualize the symbol, trace it in front of you with your finger, or draw it on the vessel you have chosen to contain your water. I also enjoy giving positive affirmations to the container as I work. If you feel inclined, share positive and loving words with the water. For example, I make gentle statements such as "Thank you for giving me life" and "I love you water." These are simple yet effective affirmations.

If you are attuned to Reiki, let the Reiki energy flow into the water for as long as you deem necessary. When I create Reiki water, I normally hold my position for two to three minutes, though I have held my position for fifteen to twenty minutes as well. You will feel the energy shifting when the water has had its fill. While you are performing the water infusion, you can incorporate any of the Reiki symbols that you are attuned to. I use the Power Symbol quite often to enhance the power of Reiki.

When you have finished infusing your water with positive energy, you can save the water to use in water rituals, ceremonies, or blessings. You could also keep the water infusion on your water altar to receive healing and loving benefits. I prefer to take my charged water and offer it to a sacred watery place nearby.

Healing Crystal Water Elixir

This elixir is a stronger variation of the water infusion with more elements added to it. I call this a high-vibrational healing tonic with dashes of love and positive energy thrown in, which makes it perfect for any occasion.

Ritual Tools
- Glass container, preferably blue or sea green
- Spring, rain, or snow water (avoid tap or distilled water)
- Four crystals (amethyst, clear quartz, black obsidian, and rose quartz)[55]

Gather amethyst, clear quartz, black obsidian, and rose quartz crystals. Amethyst decreases stress and anxiety and promotes personal healing. Clear quartz brings positive energy in. Black obsidian blocks negative energies and removes fear. Rose quartz has the energy of pure love.

Place all four crystals into a glass container. Then, pour your water into the container.

Next, send your universal healing energy into the water. As energetic beings, we are all born with the natural ability to sense and send universal healing energy; you do not have to be attuned to Reiki or any other modality to do so. Then, add power to your elixir using symbols. I recommend tracing the Om symbol, which is known for its connection to the universe, onto the sides of your vessel. You could also trace the letter *p* for "power" or a lightning bolt, as lightning bolts are considered a sign of power. If you would like to do both, first trace the Om symbol on your vessel, then follow that symbol with a lightning bolt or the letter *p*.

If you are attuned to Reiki, you can infuse your crystals with Reiki energy or draw symbols on the crystals before adding them to the healing elixir. I have found that tracing the Power Symbol on the crystals and the jar gives the elixir a punch.

For the next fourteen days, keep this container in an area where it will not be disturbed and where it cannot absorb negative energy. For fourteen days, send healing energy to your elixir every day. Make your healing intentions known in

---

55. This crystal elixir can be easily customized depending on your needs. You can choose not to use all four crystals I've suggested, or you may wish to choose different crystals completely. That is totally okay. Your intentions may need a distinct set of crystals.

this healing jar; in your mind's eye, visualize the water being revived. You can also offer blessings, prayers, and devotional words of love or gratitude to your healing elixir.

After the fourteenth day, choose a local water source, ideally one that is polluted or carries toxins. Remove the crystals from the jar, then lovingly offer your healing elixir to whichever body of water you have chosen. Empty the contents of your vessel into the water source of your choice to assist the water in transforming back to its original state. Your healing energy, your love, and the healing vibrations of the crystals will raise the water's vibrational frequencies to match the highest healing power in the universe. This gives water a chance to rejuvenate and to heal.

Journal Prompts

1. Are you more drawn to using an energy-based altar or a water altar in your practice? Why?
2. If you cast a circle of protection around your space, describe how you did it. How did the circle assist with your ritual?
3. What crystals and symbols did you use in your own crystal elixir? What did you create it for?

Chapter 7
EVERYDAY ENERGY
HEALING RITUALS

Healing is an art. It takes time, it takes practice. It takes love.
—Maza Dohta

Ritualistic healing practices produce a high-vibrational energy that offers a degree of reassurance during times of unpredictability, especially in our modern world, where things can change in an instant. Rituals direct us to bring our purpose, attention, and awareness into the present moment so that we can focus on the desired result. Daily ritual work encourages us to embrace our conscious energy and move forward to act on our goals.

It is not necessary to have a daily practice, but I strongly encourage you to. When rituals are performed each day, they become intentional practices that facilitate sacred healing vibrations; they also allow you to redirect and focus on energy, love, and gratitude. Having a daily commitment to the water is a ritual in itself, one that will make you and the water stronger. It allows your connection to the water to become intimate, with depth and intense spiritual meaning.

Water, in each of its forms, has various types of energy. In this chapter, I will provide an overview of how you can use the spiritual and physical traits of specific forms as well as how to offer them healing. The everyday healing rituals found in this chapter are simpler than the other ceremonies and practices throughout the book, making them faster and easier to perform, with less tools required. As with all the practices in this book, you can perform these rituals in any location and at any time that is convenient for you. You do not need to be near a physical body of water to perform any of these practices.

Healing the Ocean

For as long as humans have been in existence, we have felt a longing for the sea. Its rhythmic motion has drawn us in for centuries. Our ancestors were unconsciously aware of the therapeutic properties of seawater long before modern scientists. There is an immersive detox that only the sea can offer us, from the physical advantages of the mineral-rich water to the negative ions found in the ocean breeze, which can increase serotonin and promote feelings of happiness and positivity.

The sea reenergizes me in a way that nothing else can. It inspires a relaxed, meditative state and sparks creativity. As of late, I feel that the ocean has been calling for healing. The sea wants us to offer ourselves to it, to energize and love the water with all of its current flaws. Each day the ocean is exposed to pollution caused by boat and ship activity, oil leaks, and toxic runoff from the mainland. We can offer the ocean healing in the hopes that it will experience the same happiness and positivity that we do in its presence.

You can send healing and love to the seawater. Return the spiritual cleansing that the ocean offers us by reviving its healing waves. The following practices can be performed near the ocean, but even if you are not in proximity to the sea, the first technique is just as effective when done at your water altar.

To begin, envision a flood of golden cosmic energy flowing toward the water, streaming down from the universe and merging with the waves of the sea. See this light filling up the water you are healing. Watch as the crests of the waves become gold, lined with pure, radiant energy. Continue flooding the water with golden energy for as long as you feel is necessary. If you feel called to do so, chant or think positive, soothing statements that are intended to calm the ocean's waters. This helps prevent the ocean from experiencing intense waves in the midst of healing.

Another way to send healing to our sacred ocean is to offer energy and magic through the sand. Simply draw symbols of healing, love, tranquility, and protection in the sand. For example, draw a symbol of love in the sand, such as a heart, roses, or a dove, and as you do so, envision manifestations of true love. When the sea washes away your drawing, your manifestations will be offered to the sea.

Similarly, you can collect physical items that are naturally found in the ocean, such as seashells. Then, you can leave these items on the shore, along with your intention, for the sea to reclaim. Driftwood can be left for the sea as well; etch symbols on its surface with intention. There are many symbols and intentions that can be gifted to the ocean. Returning natural items to the water in this way is a beautiful counterbalance to all that humans take.

Healing Freshwater

People use freshwater every day for bathing, ritual bathing, swimming, aquatic therapy, and more. Freshwater sources all over the world—including lakes, ponds, rivers, springs, waterfalls, and more—have been exposed to pollution as well as invasive species that spread disease, eat native plants, drive out aquatic life, decrease the flow of water, and threaten the underwater food web. Offering energy to freshwater every day can enhance the spiritual and physical quality of our freshwater, and it allows us to connect with its refreshing qualities at the same time.

Freshwater sources can benefit from energetic gifts of healing. One of my favorite ways to send healing energy to my local freshwater is to take a singing bowl and sit beside the water's edge. I play my singing bowls, which emit healing vibrations, to the water while singing songs that are positive. Note that I sing positive songs—I feel that singing a sad song to a body of water that you want to give a refresh only does the opposite.

There are many other ways you can offer healing to freshwater:

- Gather a natural item (such as a stone, a piece of driftwood, plants or flowers that you have grown, or a dish of water) and imbue it with your natural healing energy, then find a local freshwater source and toss that item as far into the water as you can; this will assist in raising the vibration of that source.
- Offering healing herbal teas will aid in transformation; make sure that you are using high-quality, organic herbs if you make your own tea.
- Place your hands on the edge of the water and send positive vibrations for the water to enjoy. Trace symbols on the surface of the water with your bare hands; this is a beautiful way to physically connect yourself to the water.

Regardless of which healing method(s) you choose, make sure to put your own energy and attention into your creative offerings.

Rain Barrel Ritual

Rainwater is a type of freshwater, and rain barrels are a practical and spiritual tool. If you do not have access to a rain barrel, feel free to use a bucket of some type to collect rainwater.

Rain barrels are environmentally friendly because they capture and contain water, which prevents runoff and effectively reduces water pollution. Rainwater is considered to be one of purest forms of water due to its natural buildup of natural minerals and ions, and it normally has very few contaminants. In my opinion, as long as the rainwater that you are collecting does not run off roofs or buildings, which may introduce glass or chips of paint, the fresh rainwater that a rain barrel gathers is a safe choice for everyday ritual.

Ritual Tools
- One rain barrel (or bucket) filled with rainwater

Standing near your rain barrel, place your hands above the water, palms face-down so that energy can flow from the universe through your palms and into the water. Hold this position for a few minutes while envisioning healing, loving light extending its rays and imbuing the rainwater.

When you are ready, state your blessings for the water aloud. Say, "I bless this water with my hands. May your clear, honeyed waters be imbued so that together, you and I will cleanse, heal, nourish, and protect this land and all who live here. I send healing energies of love, positivity, and light." If you would like to include healing or protection symbols, you can draw them on your rain barrel or trace them in the sand, grass, or soil around your barrel. This is an added benefit for your water blessing.

Next, remove the sacred water from the rain barrel. Give that liquid love back to the environment by pouring some water on thirsty plants, at the base of trees, or into a birdbath. If you have a safe way to pour the blessed water onto the leaves and branches of a tree, that will cleanse, reenergize, and protect the areas where birds, squirrels, and other creatures reside. Sprinkle some newly blessed water on your lawn, whether it is lush and green, dry, cracked, or sandy. Your indoor plants would love to be included in your watering activities as well.

If you live in an urban area and do not have plants, trees, or even soil to water, you can pour this sacred water into flower boxes or pots near your home.

If there is a park nearby, you can take your blessed rainwater there and offer it to the plants and animals. City rivers, lakes, and ponds are usually polluted, so they would also appreciate a dose of the liquid love that you are offering.

Healing Rural Water

Those who have grown up in the vicinity of farmland know all too well the impacts that daily agriculture activity has on water. Manure, unsafe nitrates, and other toxic chemicals enter the groundwater through runoff. This runoff makes its way into rivers, streams, and shallow wells and can affect surrounding water resources for several miles. Polluted water in rural areas affects the animals, the land, and people who depend on these water sources, wreaking havoc in the countryside. Daily energetic healing can work as preventive medicine to ward off unwanted events.

If you live in a rural community, collect the rainwater from your rain barrel and use it to bless all the water on your property. Bless the water troughs that livestock drink from as well as any ponds or rivers that run through your property. If you have a well, you can offer blessed water to that as well.

If you live downriver from farmland, you can imbue healing energy directly into the river. The healing energy will flow to the source of the agricultural pollution, and it will infuse healing throughout the land to reduce the negative effects. Another option is to place a protective shield around the river, which can prevent agricultural runoff from being absorbed by the water as it flows through farmland.

Drawing symbols or visualizing a barrier of energetic protection over rural water sources will offer protection. Visualizing an ironclad bubble or shield can keep toxins, manure, and other chemicals from actively causing further harm. See any negative energy in your rural water sources being released and then push it away, far from your groundwater and into the universe.

City Water Ritual

In my opinion, city water is the most contaminated freshwater. When it rains, droplets mix with the fumes, gasses, and oils from vehicles, factories, and businesses. This runoff makes its way to surface water and is then collected. Water is chemically filtered before being sent through pipelines that may be aging and in need of repair. To offer positive vibrations to city water and encourage healing, we can target the contaminants that are poisoning our sacred water.

Ritual Tools
- Glass bowl
- Tap water

To perform this energy visualization technique, fill a bowl with tap water. Start by scanning the energy field of the water. Place your hands, palms facing down, over the bowl of water. Close your eyes and slowly move your hands around the bowl. Observe any sensations that you come across. When I perform a scan on city water, the vibration feels different—less lively, dark. Continue scanning the tap water until you have found this diluted energy.

Next, visualize a protective shield or a symbol of protection around the water in your bowl; you can also physically trace it on the bowl. Now that the water is protected from any dark energy reentering the bowl of water, visualize a large energetic hammer. Visualize this hammer hitting the surface of the water in your bowl. See the power of this hammer striking the negative energy, effectively knocking all toxins and chemicals out of the water.

Another method to remove the dark energy from chemically treated water is to envision sparkling gold energy around the energetic residue that was left behind during the city's treatment. Envision this purifying energy clasping the residue tighter and tighter, like a gold fist manifested out of strong metals, and see the leftover energetic particles explode into nothingness. You can use this technique on microplastics, gasoline, and pretty much any substance that you want to remove from a water source.

Before you continue, perform an energetic sweeping to remove any leftover energy that may still be contained in the surrounding area. You can use an energetic broom or the flooding technique described earlier in this chapter.

Once you have finished cleansing the space, offer gentle energy to the water to soothe and rejuvenate her diluted life force. If you are not attuned to Reiki, use your own personal energies by slowly sending energy from your breath into the bowl. This technique is a powerful way to enhance your visualization as well as any other rituals and energy work that you perform. Reiki practitioners can also use their breath to send symbols to the object of our healing.

When you are finished, state words of love and devotion. Anything that comes to mind will work. Then, take your bowl to your sink and pour the water down the drain. The water's vibrations of healing, purity, and love will mix with the wastewater that it will join. This will spread throughout the city pipelines and your healing will continue, slowly spreading to thousands of homes as this water is repeatedly reused.

Healing for Marine Life and Freshwater Animals

As an energy practitioner who is quite fond of animals, I thoroughly enjoy sending healing energy to them, especially in this time of water pollution. Many freshwater and saltwater creatures have become ill or traumatized in their natural environment due to the plastics, toxins, and chemicals in rivers, streams, ponds, lakes, and oceans. Offering high-vibrational energy to these animals and organisms will offer stress relief and deep relaxation in addition to healing.

You can do this from your home or in person, but offering healing energy to freshwater and saltwater creatures should always be done at a distance. Do not physically touch wild animals while offering healing, both for your safety and theirs. We do not want to cause undue stress when we are attempting to facilitate a stress-free environment for them.

Some Freshwater and Saltwater Creatures

On the following pages, I have listed several species and their spiritual energies as well as where they can be found. I hope this information will assist you as you connect to these creatures and send them healing energies. Afterward, I have included a healing ritual that can be customized to match the animal that you are sending healing to.

At the end of this section, there is a ritual for healing beached whales and a ritual for sanctuary dolphins as well.

Otters

Otters are symbols of adaptability, transformation, creativity, psychic ability, and playfulness. They show us how to maintain balance in life during stressful times. These joyful creatures are found in both saltwater and freshwater.

Manatees
Manatees are symbols of exploration, gentleness, nonviolence, trust, and vulnerability. The manatee reminds us to slow down and reflect on life. These "sea cows" are found in both freshwater and saltwater habitats.

Fish
There are a variety of different species of fish. Fish are associated with bravery, regeneration, fertility, health, abundance, and higher awareness, amongst other things. Fish remind us to search for hidden truths. They can be found in both freshwater and saltwater.

Frogs
Frogs are symbols of rebirth, cleansing, transformation, purity, and good luck. They are associated with removing negativity from one's life and can help guide us through transitions. Frogs can be found in several environments.

Beavers
Beavers are symbols of persistence and hard work. The beaver teaches us the importance of being disciplined in order to achieve our dreams. While normally seen in freshwater, they do sometimes build dams in coastal areas.

Turtles
Turtles are symbols of endurance, wisdom, and strength. They are grounded and mature, and they can show others how to practice self-reflection and patience. They can be found in both saltwater and freshwater environments.

Whales
Whales are seen as symbols of spiritual awareness, unconditional love, and communication. The whale teaches us to speak our inner truth and embrace our emotions. They are the oceanic masters of music! These underwater performers are found in saltwater.

Dolphins

Dolphins are seen as symbols of rebirth, guidance, and gentleness. Some see them as symbols of protection and good luck. With their playful tendencies, dolphins remind us not to take life too seriously. These lively and intelligent creatures are predominantly found in saltwater, though river dolphins can be found in freshwater.

Seals

Seals are seen as symbols of innocence, curiosity, opportunity, and intelligence. They remind us to nurture the creativity within us. This is a species that genuinely cares for one other. With the exception of one type of seal, these spunky creatures are all found in saltwater.

Sharks

Sharks are symbols of invincibility, survival, and independence. They teach us how to make decisions in uncertain situations. These fast-moving and powerful creatures are found in saltwater, though some species of sharks do tolerate brackish water, which is a mixture of fresh- and saltwater.

Sea Lions

Sea lions are symbols of community, perseverance, strength of spirit, and creativity. They can help us remember our connection to the inner rhythms of the sea. Sea lions live in saltwater environments.

Jellyfish

Jellyfish represent regeneration, immortality, and intuition. This mystical creature reminds us to change, adapt, and flow with the ever-changing tide. For the most part, jellyfish live in saltwater, but there is one species of freshwater jellyfish that has been found worldwide.

Penguins

Penguins are symbols of loyalty, devotion, and unity. These birds encourage us to find meaning in life. Most of the world's penguins can be found in their natural habitat in the Southern Hemisphere, where they spend a large amount of time in saltwater.

Customizable Animal Healing Ritual

This is a practice to extend gifts of healing to our water-based friends, one that is completely customizable to suit your own energy-healing practice. This ritual works for both in-person and distance healing sessions.

When you are getting ready to send healing to your chosen creature in their natural habitat, I always advise a couple of essentials. Of course, you can decide what the situation requires at the present moment—just be prepared to facilitate a variety of healings, as you never know what you may need. I personally keep a kit of healing supplies in the trunk of my vehicle in case I need them.

Recommended Ritual Tools
- A singing bowl
- Crystals that align with the spiritual characteristics of the animal
- Sacred water, to offer blessings with
- Incense, to ritually cleanse any negative energy
- A blanket to sit on
- Paper and a pen or pencil
- Matches and a candle
- If performing distance healing: a picture of the animal, or an animal-shaped object such as a sculpture

Once you have decided which animal you would like to send healing to, gather your ritual tools and arrange them on your energy- or water-based altar. If you are performing a distance healing, do not forget to include whichever animal picture or item you have chosen.

Take a couple of minutes to focus on the energy that is associated with the animal. For instance, if you are sending healing to frogs, you could focus on their rebirthing and cleansing properties. In your mind's eye, really *see* the animal that you chose to focus on.

Make sure that you are really focused on your animal, then release your natural-born energies to the cosmos. State your intention of where exactly you want the energy to go. The universe will naturally direct the energy to your healing subject. Visualize your healing manifestations, then send those out as well.

If you are a Reiki practitioner, activate and state the Distance Healing Symbol that allows you to access the bridge across time and space. Send your gifts of Reiki and the symbols that you are using. Make sure to close that bridge when you have finished your distance session.

At the close of your healing ritual, release any spiritual and expectational attachments you may have. Let your healing manifestations be taken by the universe, and let them heal the intended animal in the way that it is needed. Cut your spiritual attachment by visualizing invisible scissors. A Reiki practitioner may use the "Raku" symbol to complete the process.

Ritual for Beached Whales

Whales have been honored and worshiped for centuries by people from all walks of life. They are associated with music, wisdom, protection, life, death, and compassion.

Around the world, whales are viewed in a variety of ways. In Vietnam, whales are seen as protectors of the sea, seafarers, and their ships. Native Hawaiians see the whale as "the god of the ocean" and believe that whales are connected to the divine.[56] The Māori people of New Zealand have a creation story about whales; they believe that the whale is a descendant of the god of the ocean. For many Indigenous Pacific Islanders, whales bring happiness and good fortune.

Seeing a swimming whale is often a sign of good luck, but when whales are beached, they can be seen as a bad omen, potentially indicating illness among the community. When whales become beached, they risk death caused by dehydration, collapsing under their own weight, or drowning when the high tide covers their blowholes. These gentle giants deserve our help, and they greatly need our assistance when trapped on land.

We can offer healing energy to beached whales in hopes that we can make a difference. While you may be in close proximity to the ocean in an area where whales are known to wash up onto the shore, most people do not have access to that kind of closeness. Personally, I have only seen beached whales on television,

---

56. Stanton, "Whale Meaning & Symbolism & the Whale Spirit Animal."

usually on a news station, or on social media. To make this practice as accessible as possible, this healing ritual will be done at a distance.

Ritual Tools
- One large container, crystal or silver
- Blessed rainwater
- Three crystals (fluorite, Lemurian seed quartz, and lapis lazuli)
- A picture or drawing of a whale (optional)

Find a space where you will not be disturbed, maybe a place that reminds you of the water in some way. Your water altar is a great option, or you could sit alongside a body of water near your home.

Place the container on your altar, the ground, a tree stump, or anywhere that you see fit for your healing ritual. If you have a picture of a whale, place it somewhere you can easily see it.

Pour the rainwater into the container. Rainwater provides physical and energetic rejuvenation.

Next, hold your fluorite crystal in both hands. Feel the magic of this balancing crystal as it clears away mental fog and confusion, rebalances scattered energies, soothes anxiety, and repairs any issues with the whale's energy field. Feel these strong yet gentle healing properties in your palms. Say, "I cleanse and soothe the whale with this crystal," then place it in the container of rainwater.

Now, pick up your Lemurian seed quartz crystal and hold it between your hands. This beautiful crystal embodies the soft and loving energies of the cosmos, allowing the whale to find harmony and release any painful feelings of being separated from its natural habitat. Feel these energies within you, as you are the purest energy. Say, "This whale is now at harmony. There is no more fear, only the softest of love." Then place the crystal into the container.

The final crystal, lapis lazuli, is an ancient spiritual stone that has been used by healers all over the world. Take your crystal and place it between your palms. Take a minute to understand the energy that this crystal is offering to beached whales. This stone will balance the whales' mental, spiritual, emotional, and physical levels. It will bring knowledge, cleanse and release negative thoughts, and inspire clarity and understanding. Try to feel the power that this crystal offers as you hold it in your hands. Say, "This whale has been balanced and given the gift of clarity and understanding so that she or he may be able to handle the situation with positivity and inner wisdom." Place this crystal into the container of rainwater.

Place your hands over the bowl of healing crystal and rainwater elixir and imbue it with the power of your natural energy. Feel the energy of the universe flowing down through your body and bursting out of your palms, giving the container an additional boost of healing.

In your mind's eye, see the energies within this magical healing vessel. See the harmony, peace, soothing, understanding, soft love, and your personal frequency becoming wisps of mist, slowly lifting out of the container. This energy travels across the planet, where it finds a beached whale and infuses and settles itself along the length of the whale.

While the whale is experiencing deep inner healing, envision it once more. Visualize the whale being returned to the sea. Watch as the whale rolls onto its back, being playful once more, showing its underbelly before it dives into the dark abyss of the ocean. Hear the musical song that emerges from the deep, allowing you to experience the vibrational sounds of the whale's call as it begins singing once more. The whale is back where it needs to be, free again.

When you are ready, gather your tools and cleanse them. You can pour your rainwater outside on the ground or pour into a body of water; do not pour it down the sink. After you have finished cleaning up, meditating with the energy of the whale is a great way to start building a relationship with them.

Ritual for Dolphins in Captivity

Dolphins are majestic, intelligent, and social creatures. They have captivated us for as long as we have been aware of their existence. Unfortunately, many dolphins are confined to tanks. While I do not agree with dolphins being used for entertainment or being held for a long period of time in a sanctuary, I do know that there are benefits, such as scientists learning more about conservation needs, health and wellness, and how to protect dolphins from their natural environment if it has been polluted or is being destroyed. However, dolphins in captivity live in small spaces, losing their open freedom, and are fed dead fish instead of being able to catch their own food. They may also suffer from stress and anxiety if they are forced to perform tricks for the entertainment of humans, depending on where and why they are being held.

We can send vibrational healing energies to dolphins in captivity. (I have focused on dolphins here, but this ritual can also be used for whales, sharks, and other aquatic life in captivity.) While we may not be able to physically release the dolphins, we can help these precious, intelligent ocean dwellers find peace and joy in times of struggle and uncertainty. Our intention is to create a better and more trusting relationship between dolphins and people while offering healing.

Since the majority of people do not have access to a dolphin sanctuary, this practice will be performed with distance healing. If you are not attuned to Reiki, you may use your natural vibrational frequency. If you are attuned to Reiki, in order to send Reiki energy from a distance, you must be attuned as a Level 1 and 2 practitioner.

Ritual Tools
- One larimar crystal
- An image of a dolphin (sculpture, artwork, picture, etc.)

First, place your dolphin image on a flat surface, then place your larimar stone beside it. Larimar is considered to be the stone of the dolphin because it carries the energies of water and represents healing, tranquility, and love. Interestingly, some believe that meditating with this crystal allows the practitioner to communicate with dolphins, who in turn respond through their vibrational frequency.

When you are ready, pick up the larimar and cup it in the palms of your hands. Imbue this stone of the sea, of water, of dolphins, with energy. If you are not attuned to Reiki, do not worry, for we are all natural healers, and each of us can send healing energy. Visualize a bright, radiant blue light within you, building and growing stronger and brighter. In your mind's eye, see the dolphins you are sending this energy to.

For Reiki practitioners, invoke or visualize the Distance Healing Symbol, "Hon Sha Ze Sho Nen," and state it out loud three times.[57] In your mind's eye, see the dolphins you are sending energy to.

---

57. This symbol is seen as a connection or unity symbol. This symbol transcends time and space; it means "Across past, present, and future" or "The past, present, and future are one." Some practitioners like to use the Power Symbol, "Cho Ku Rei," to activate the Distance Healing Symbol first; opinions vary from practitioner to practitioner. I personally feel that using the Distance Healing Symbol is enough on its own.

Once the crystal is filled with love, healing, and tranquility, place it on top of the picture of the dolphin. Visualize these energies being sent through the interconnected web of vibration that connects us all. Once you feel that the energy has reached a dolphin in captivity, send your Reiki or natural energy through the top of the dolphin's head. See a healing blue mist expanding through the body of the dolphin, gently healing the organs, the vessels, the nerves, and all bodily systems. This energy slowly and gently rotates as it descends to the tip of the dolphin's tail. Direct your energy once more—see the energy relieving worry, stress, and anxiety. See the dolphin full of spirit, playful again.

Continue your healing work for as long as you see fit. When you feel ready, slowly withdraw your energy. Visualize a protective barrier of some type (such as a bubble, clamshell, or shield) around the dolphin so that it may retain the energy you have given it for a longer period of time. I also envision seaweed winding around the dolphin and its energies to neutralize negative vibrations and dispel bad luck.

If you are a Reiki practitioner, you can close the session by visualizing the power symbol over the dolphin, sealing in the healing energy. The power of the universe has found its way to this lovely creature of the sea.

You can leave the image and crystal on your altar space so you can send additional healing to the dolphin each day, or you can keep the items for reuse if needed—just be sure to cleanse them with smoke before using them again to remove any negative buildup.

—

If you want to learn more about how to send healing energy to dolphins and other marine life, visit www.globalwaterhealing.org or www.magnificentu.com /free-guided-equinox-meditation-for-water-dolphins-whales-and-peace.

Healing for Natural Disasters

Natural disasters, while unfortunate and heartbreaking, do happen. While they are normally events that we cannot physically control, we can still offer healing in times of misfortune. However, providing vibrational healing during a natural disaster can be overwhelming at times. Sending healing, loving energies to a place or organism that has been damaged can create low and heavy negative vibrations. Before you offer healing for a natural disaster, you must learn how to avoid picking up those unwanted vibrations while attempting to raise them.

Protecting Your Energy

Know your limits, set boundaries, and watch your energy as you perform healing during a catastrophic event. There are many methods of protection that you can use to ensure your energy field stays free of unwanted negative frequencies. This is especially important if you are offering healing in a physical location, where you are more likely to absorb energetic toxins that can affect your spiritual and mental well-being and manifest as physical symptoms, including emotional heaviness, low mood, frustration, physical or mental tiredness, and migraine.

The most powerful way to protect your energy is with visualization, so I will share a few of my favorite techniques. However, this list is not exhaustive. Feel free to experiment with these techniques and find one that provides adequate protection.

Take note that while these techniques do offer protection, they take energy to maintain, so be mindful of your physical and spiritual needs. Make sure these needs have been met if you are going to take advantage of them for long periods of time.

Energetic Protection Field

This simple visualization allows you to protect your biofield or aura, the energy field around your physical body, when going into a situation that may be energetically hostile.

Sit in silent meditation to gain clarity, taking deep breaths until your mind is clear and focused. When you are ready, imagine that you are standing inside a cobalt blue bubble, shield, or shell, as blue is one of the colors associated with protection, healing, and peace. This bubble, shield, or shell encompasses you, flowing with your movements.

Next, visualize yourself shrouded in the energy field of pink rose quartz, which only allows love and healing to enter and emerge. This shield reaches into the sky above you and the earth below you.

See the energy of the universe pulsating through your shield. It has the unbreakable bond of tungsten. Rest assured that your shield will protect your energy from anything external that may be harsh and intrusive during your endeavors.

When you are finished with your work, simply end the visualization by allowing the shield to dissolve. You can do this by seeing the shield disappear into nothingness in your mind's eye. Any negative energy that the shield has protected you from will dissolve with it.

Cloak of Energetic Protection

In the same way that a shield protects your energy, this cloak protects your energy field from people, places, things, and circumstances beyond your control. You may need to protect yourself quickly at times, and the cloak of protection is a wonderful option.

To begin, simply visualize a cloak that covers you entirely from head to toe, protecting you from outside sources. Choose colors of protection and healing. Black or gray can be used for the entire cloak, as these protective colors place a barrier between your energy and outside energies. Gold or silver thread can "stitch" magical symbols onto the material. I enjoy using a cloak of universal white light, envisioning the universe wrapping me in a cocoon of protective energy. You can change the appearance of the cloak to fit your needs in the present moment.

Dry Bathing (Kenyoku)

Kenyoku, known as "dry bathing," is a purification practice that originated in Japan. This energy sweeping can be used for many occasions; it is a wonderful and easily accessible way to purify your energy for just about any purpose. I normally practice dry bathing before a ritual or Reiki session to cleanse myself. Attunement to Reiki is not required to use this energy practice.

This practice allows you to disconnect from energy that is not your own at the same time that it restores your energy. It removes excess energy by cleansing and unblocking your energy channels, which allows new energy to flow through you to facilitate healing. In addition, dry bathing will heal tears or holes in your aura to prevent energy leakage.

To perform your energy sweeping, first set your intention of what you would like to achieve. For example, the intention is to sweep away and cleanse toxic, congested energy from your energy field before and after offering healing during a disaster.

Find a private space if you feel inclined. For a couple of moments, take a few deep breaths to center yourself. With each exhale, see the stress and toxins leaving you.

Next, place your right hand on your left shoulder. Sweep it across your stomach and to the opposite hip. Repeat this process on the opposite side of your body: place your left hand on your right shoulder, sweeping it across your stomach and to the opposite hip.

Extend your left arm and place your right hand on your left shoulder. Stroke the full length of your arm and then shake your right hand into the air to dispel any negative energy that you have released. Repeat this process on the opposite side of your body: extend your right arm and place your left arm on your right shoulder. Sweep down the full length of your arm, then shake your left hand in the air to dispel any negative energy that you have released.

Lake Protection Shield

Water can range from being healing and loving to unyielding and dangerous. When I need extra assistance protecting myself, I use a lake reflection shield, as the surface of a lake resembles a mirror. I enjoy using this visualization when I want to deepen my spiritual connection with water and need a shield for energetic protection during my water practices.

Lakes are dark, deep, quiet, reflective spaces that hold a lot of magical power. To start, envision a favorite lake of yours, or any lake that comes to mind. Then, visualize yourself on the edge of the lake, connecting to its waters. In your mind's eye, see yourself swimming deep into the lake, then submerge yourself beneath the lake's surface. Now the reflective surface of the lake is above you while you are nestled deep within its watery womb. The lake's reflective, mirrorlike surface shields and protects you, its child, from unwanted energy.

Shower of Light

If you are feeling anxious or mentally cluttered while offering healing, another quick way to cleanse your energy is by showering in the light of the universe. Envision yourself under the radiant energy of the cosmos, with its bright, glowing light showering down on you and your energy. The shower of light gently yet powerfully evaporates anything negative or hostile.

Mirror

Visualize a wall of mirrors surrounding you. The glass, facing out, will reflect all undesired, negative energy—energy will bounce off of your shield of mirrors and go elsewhere. This shield can be maintained while performing healing, or it can be used only when the circumstances require it.

On the following pages, you will find healing options for a variety of water-based natural disasters. I have included an array of multiple climates and environments in the hopes that at least one of them will be useful for you.

Healing During a Drought

A drought is a long period of dry weather. A lack of rain, snow, and groundwater for weeks, months, and sometimes years can wreak havoc on a region and ultimately damage the environment. Marshes and wetlands can dry up, and rivers can slowly diminish and eventually stop flowing. Freshwater organisms, birds, and other animals are affected by the lack of water; as the drought continues, they have to travel farther in search of water. Over time, extinction of wildlife species could occur. There is also a much higher possibility of wildfires occurring. Humans are also at risk during droughts, which can affect nutrition, hygiene, and mental health.

As energy workers, our goal is always to love and care for the earth and its inhabitants. Send vibrations to drought-stricken areas in the hopes that we as a collective can offer soothing properties and encourage rain flow to diminish suffering.

Ritual Tools
- None

To soothe the dehydrated earth during a drought, you only need access to your personal vibration or Reiki, as well as a dry place on the ground that does not have any plants or grass.

When you are ready, face toward the direction of the drought that you are sending healing to. Place your hands on the earth with your palms facedown. Close your eyes and feel the sensation of the vibrational energy of the universe flowing through you.

Visualize soothing, calming blue and green colors gently imbuing the soil beneath your hands. See the colors spreading. Watch as they imbue one grain of soil to another, continuously illuminating the earth with their luminescent energy. The soothing colors travel through the landscape, toward the drought, at the speed of vibration and light, leaving an energetic pathway.

Once the energy has reached its destination, visualize this radiant energy creating a containment of some type around the region experiencing drought. Imagine this energy moving up toward the sky, coming together, and connecting with the energy that has risen on all four sides, like a three-dimensional cube. This technique blocks the sun's rays from overheating the dry land and contains the healing energy you sent to the soil, which will infuse the drought-stricken area with its soothing energy.

After you have completed your energy work, you can encourage rain by saying aloud, "Rain, rain, come this way. Bring your gray clouds here, with heavy, soothing drops plummeting toward the ground. I ask that you hydrate this land that burns afire." Chant this repeatedly to build up the energy of a rainstorm, and visualize it—see it manifest into existence over this area.

If you feel called to do so, you can also perform the following ceremony.

Make It Rain Ceremony

Rainmaking ceremonies are still performed in many countries, especially in regions where rain is scarce. I have created this ceremony to request rain that will nourish the parched lands around the world.

Ritual Tools
- One silver or crystal bowl
- Matches
- Blue chime candle
- Rainwater
- Sea salt

Place your chosen bowl in the center of your altar and pour rainwater into the bowl. Visualize the water in your bowl connecting to the clouds in the sky, dripping down to the earth. Then, take your sea salt and create a circle around the bowl on the flat surface of your altar.

Using a match, light your candle. While doing so, state, "Mother Earth, let your rain pour down on me." Chant this a few times to build up energy, imagining and feeling the sensation of water coming down from the heavens and touching your skin; smell its cleansing energy as it hits the soft earth. You can chant this for as long as you would like.

When you have finished, you can blow out your candle, or you can let it burn. It is usually best to allow a candle to burn down completely for the magic to be most effective.

Healing During a Flood

Flooding creates devastation and chaotic circumstances while generating feelings of helplessness and despair. Water is very diverse: it can be flowing and elegant, but in a flood, it easily disrupts gas and electrical power lines and pollutes clean drinking water. The effects on the environment are immediate. Roadways, houses, and other buildings become damaged by mud and landslides caused by excess water; vehicles are destroyed beyond repair. Many lives are lost, especially during flash flooding. Flood waters can range from being a few inches deep to being taller than your home.

Here, I have provided a ritual to assist with severe flooding and help those who are in the vicinity to the storm. If you are not close to the storm but still have a desire to assist, you may perform this ritual from your home via distance healing.

Ritual Tools
- A glass jar with lid
- Three pieces of rope
- Floodwater (optional)

One way to assist a place during severe flooding is to perform an energetic binding to keep the flood from causing harm. Before beginning, you will need to find an area where you can perform this ritual safely. Do not perform this ritual if it is not safe to do so. If you are unable to find a safe location for ritual work, you can facilitate this energetic binding at your altar, using the water in your home.

If you have found a safe space for ritual work, stand at the edge of the water with your hands placed over the surface, palms facing down. Begin to send your energy into the violent waters while visualizing your energy binding the floodwaters into place and locking them, keeping them from moving forward or retreating.

Pick up the three pieces of rope and hold them tightly, then dip them into the floodwater, making sure to drench them effectively. Be very careful during this step.

Once the ropes are wet, braid the three pieces together. Place the braided rope into a jar and seal the lid.

Hold the jar with both hands and say, "Harsh and vicious, turbulent waters, you are now bound from hurting yourself and others." Feel free to add extra language here—make sure you have made your binding intentions clear.

Finally, send healing energy to this jar and the water inside. This will allow the flood outside to feel its calming effects and reduce in severity. During the flood, continue to periodically send healing and visualization to this jar to maintain its effects. After the flood has ended, you can release the water back to the earth. If there is no foreseeable end to the flood, you can place the jar into your freezer as long as it is freezer-safe; this will assist in binding the excessive floodwaters.

Healing During a Hurricane

Hurricanes are destructive forces that whirl onto land and bring raging winds, rip currents, storm surges, heavy rainfall, flash flooding, and tornadoes. Buildings, homes, and bridges are destroyed by strong, damaging winds upward of one hundred miles per hour. These winds toss debris into the air, which can be deadly. Beach and marsh erosion, dune destruction, and overwash are just a few of the environmental issues that occur on the coast during a hurricane.

While these devastatingly natural disasters are an event that we unfortunately cannot prevent, we can energetically contain them, release their chaotic energies, and offer protection and healing to the people and animals affected.

When you become aware that a hurricane is fast approaching, the first thing that may come to mind is to ensure that others within the storm's path are safe. This can be achieved through visualization. Envision a solid white, oval-shaped shield of glimmering energetic protection cocooned around subjects that you wish to protect from the storm's energy; this will prevent that energy from interacting with theirs.

Ritual Tools

- None

Removing chaotic energy from a hurricane will lessen the effects of the storm. To reduce the severity of this type of storm through vibration, you will need to send healing energy directly to the hurricane. Only perform this ritual if it is safe to do so.

If possible, find a place outside where it is relatively windy. This ritual can be performed without severe wind, though it may take longer for your energy to arrive at its destination. Once you are ready, stand or sit outside, facing the direction of the intended hurricane.

Place both hands in front of you with your palms facing out. Experience the vibrational healing power of the universe flowing through your body.

In your mind's eye, envision gleaming yellow and white energy emanating from your palms into the open air. Watch as this energy twists and turns, dancing effortlessly in the wind. It leaves a suspended pathway as it travels through the sky in search of its destination.

See the energy as it surrounds the storm, getting closer with every whirling rotation. Your energy is slowly being drawn into the clouds of the storm until it is part of the hurricane itself.

In your mind's eye, see the vibration of the universe compressing the energetic properties. Then, visually release the unwanted negative energy streaming through the top of the hurricane. Your gift of healing is slowing the energy of the hurricane, appeasing its chaotic energy and lessening its wind speed.

Healing During a Tsunami

Tsunamis are giant waves caused by earthquakes or volcanic activity beneath the sea. They can also be caused by large explosions above or below the water. As the sea floor shifts, it creates a massive displacement of water. Tsunami waves begin in deep water, and as they travel closer to shore, they become taller as the water becomes shallower.

The impacts of a tsunami are catastrophic. They crumble seawalls and bridges. Trains and ships crash into buildings, houses overturn, and fires start as a result of damaged oil storage tanks. Sewage and wastewater systems are damaged. Trees and plants are uprooted. Land animals and humans are drowned, and marine animals who get caught in this wave may become sick and die after being introduced to chemicals on land. Not only do these violent waters kill thousands of people per year, tsunamis also create immense damage and pollution that take years to correct.

Using energy, we can manipulate these large waves and redirect them in the hopes that we can protect all life. To change the course of a tsunami, all you need is your energy and your ability to manifest.

Ritual Tools
- None

When you are ready, position yourself so that you are facing directly toward the storm. First, visualize these cold, angry waves in your mind's eye. See the pressure and power of thousands of pounds of water, crashing and building up speed as they head for the shore. The energy moves with purpose and deadly intent.

As this tsunami continues to travel forward, send Reiki or your personal energy toward it. Visualize the energy wrapping itself around the waves like a rope coiling around a wrist, pulling tighter in the center.

Grab your energetic rope and pull it. This will redirect the waves of the storm from its original path and back toward the sea. Continue to send energy to the storm as it heads away from land, as this will lessen the intensity of the waves and return them to a calm state of being, preventing others from being hurt at another location.

Healing During an Ice Storm

Ice storms carry powerful and dangerous energy. Ice is harsh, merciless, and cold, with a highly unforgiving nature—and it is stunningly beautiful when its crystalline structures reflect the light. In an ice storm, high winds cover the land with a glaze of ice. Heavy, thick ice on trees can cause them to break in half, and slick, treacherous roadways become even more dangerous when a tree blocks the road, especially if the tree brought down electrical wires with it.

You can soothe an ice storm using Reiki or your natural energy. In your mind's eye, see the universal healing energy flowing from your hands and softly wrapping itself around the jagged edges of the ice. See your energy slowly compressing the shards of ice until the damaging negative energy dissolves and the ice shatters.

Another way to heal an ice storm is to envision a spinning ball of energy, discussed in the following ritual.

Ritual Tools
- None

To begin, place your hands in front of your chest about six inches apart, with your palms facing each other. Move your hands closer to each other, then back away. Start to visualize the shape of a ball in between your hands. You should be able to notice pulling or tingling sensations in your palms while doing this. If you do not, that is okay—learning to work with energy takes time. Even if you cannot feel anything, the energy is still there and being manipulated with your hands.

Once you can visualize the ball in between your hands, visualize healing the ice storm. Imbue this ball with soothing properties and colors such as light blue, soft green, pink, and violet.

Offer healing intentions to this vibrational ball of energy. You can state a mantra or chant of some type, such as, "I calm your storm. I soothe your daggered ice. I release your shards of cold and deadly glass. Leave this space in peace tonight." Continue to chant to build up your energy; you may experience pulsing sensations.

When you feel ready, send your ball of energy to the ice storm. See it making its way closer to the ice storm. When it reaches the edge of the storm, watch as the ball's colors slowly diminish as they are absorbed into the body of the storm. This ball of energy will expand throughout the storm, lessening its intensity.

Healing Water's Past

Water has been polluted, misused, and disrespected for so long. It has witnessed and carried an immeasurable amount of hate, fear, and anxiety. There have been countless natural disasters that have caused catastrophic damage and killed innocent people and animals. While we cannot change the past, we can send universal healing energy to the past to release trauma and heavy emotions. In addition, we can send our forgiveness and love directly to the water through an energetic gateway, which will hopefully minimize the effects that this event had and heal the water that we are familiar with. Because it has no boundaries, energy can access and heal across time and space.

Ritual Tools
- None

To send healing to the past, you will need to choose a certain event that took place, one that is associated with water; you can send this energy as far back in time as you wish. Then, let go of all expectations. Trust that the energy will bring the best outcome possible.

Prepare a sacred space. This ritual can be performed anywhere in your home or outside. Cleanse the space of any residual energy as well as negative energy; you do not want to unintentionally send negative energy to the past, as it will cause further harm.

Before you begin, you may want to set up protective boundaries to shield yourself; I recommend the cloak technique described earlier in the chapter.

When you are ready, ground yourself. State your intention for the distance healing that you will be performing. For example: "My intention is to release pain and fear from the Industrial time period, due to excessive pollution, for its highest good."

Once you have stated your intention, meditate for a few moments. Take some deep breaths and connect to the energy of the universe, feeling its loving energy enveloping you.

Now, you must create a bridge to the past. In your mind's eye, see your own energetic body separating from your physical one. Watch as it moves backward at the speed of light. See the many colors of the universe—bright white, intense violet, galaxy blue, and the deepest black, filled with glittering stars—soaring past you. Think about the time and place that you want to send healing to, then stop at that time period.

While you are still inside the energetic, interconnected divine, envision a small gold circle, rotating and sparkling in front of you, and slowly open this portal to the physical world. Place your hands in front of you, palms facing outward, and send your energy to this moment in history. Hold your position until you feel the energy shifting in your palms or your intuition tells you it has fulfilled its purpose, which symbolizes that this place has received its fill of energy.

To close this gateway, place your hands above and below the gold circle. Slowly compress the circle until it has completely sealed itself, and then simply perform these steps in reverse to close the portal and return to your body. Visualize yourself flowing backward through time and space. See your spirit self return to your physical body.

If you are a Reiki Master, the process is similar. Visualize or draw the Distance Healing Symbol, "Hon Sha Ze Sho Nen," to create a gateway across time and space, connecting you and the past. This symbol will always facilitate healing if the receiver accepts the energy being offered.

See a white beam of Reiki energy traveling across this bridge to the past event that you have chosen. Allow the white and gold haze of the energy to settle around that moment, imbuing it with your intention. Do not forget to let go of all expectations.

When you are ready, draw the Distance Healing Symbol again and imagine that the bridge is dissolving, cutting off access to the past.

After you have finished, you may reflect on your experience and jot down any reminders that you wish to leave yourself. Record your feelings about sending energy to the past—how did you feel when opening an energetic portal?

Healing for Any Body of Water

Sand is an abundant and magical tool. Wherever you find sand, there is usually water. Because of this, we can use sand to send distance healing to any body of water, no matter where you are located.

Sand Spell Jar

Different types of sand have different properties when used in energy work: Sand from the beach itself is great for working with purification or grounding. Sand from the seafloor is useful for banishing negative emotions, as well as transformation and rebirth. Sand from the desert can assist in releasing the past or drying up negative emotions tied to water pollution. Lake sand is known for offering serenity; river sand represents transformation; swamp sand can bind. White sand is for wisdom; red sand promotes courage; pink sand promotes emotional healing; black sand works well for protection against spiritual and physical attacks. When using sand, sometimes there may be ashes or remains of bones and shells mixed in, especially if you take sand straight from the beach for it. These ashes typically allow one to let go of pain and suffering.

The kind of sand used in your spell jar largely depends on what kind of healing you want to send to the water. While this simple spell only requires a jar and some sand, you may want to include seashells, crystals, or other materials that align with your healing intentions.

Ritual Tools
- Jar with lid, any size
- Sand
- Seashells, crystals, or other materials (optional)

First, decide which body of water you would like to send healing to. What is your intent? Use that to determine which type of sand to use in this spell. (If you do not live near the type of sand that you would like to use, you can order sand online. I use Etsy.) When you are ready, place the chosen sand inside your jar, then seal it.

Hold the jar in your palms and imbue it with your energy. Then, imbue the jar with energy that aligns with the type of sand you have chosen.

In your mind's eye, see this energy traveling from the sand in your jar to the sand at your chosen location. The sand at your chosen location has received your gift of energy, and with each caress of the water against the sandy shore, it releases the energies you have sent.

You can return the sand to its natural home or keep this sand jar in your ritual space, as it can be reused. Make sure to reenergize the sand jar periodically.

Shield of Protection Water Ritual

I created this energetic shield protection ritual to protect the water in the same way a practitioner protects themselves from negative energy. In this ritual, you can cast a vibrational shield of protection around a body of water using only energy—either your natural energy or Reiki.

Ritual Tools
- Two crystals, black obsidian and selenite (optional)

Choose a body of water that you would like to protect from future negative energy or events. You can travel to this location or perform this ritual from a distance, perhaps at your home. Find a comfortable place to sit.

Close your eyes. Visualize the universe's loving, protective energy flowing through you, then open your eyes.

You must cleanse any negative energy remaining in the body of water before casting your shield. To do this, hold a black obsidian crystal in one hand. This crystal is a natural shield from negative energy. In your other hand, hold a piece of selenite. Selenite is used for cleansing, as it provides bright and positive vibrations that elevate surrounding energy.

Hold the crystals against your chest so that they may be filled with the power of love. Visualize your natural life force energy flowing into the crystals as you hold them near your heart. Say, "I channel the energy of my personal vibration into these crystals to assist me in activating the protective and cleansing properties."

Set the crystals in front of you, placing your hands on top of them. Say, "I send the power of my loving universal soul into these crystals to empower and assist me in casting an all-powerful vibrational shield of protection. I cast this shield around you, water, to protect you from future harm and negative energy."

If you are attuned to Reiki, draw the Power Symbol, "Cho Ku Rei," three times in the air while stating the symbol's name out loud. This will activate the symbol and bring the entire power of the universe into your ritual, which will clear the water by absorbing and removing energetic blockages.

Now, visualize the radiant multicolored energy of the universe swirling down to your chosen body of water. See this energy slowly enclosing the water in its protective embrace. The pulsating and loving heat of the universe locks in its waves of impenetrable energy by settling around the edges of the water, creating a glittering dome of protection.

To make the shield even stronger, state, "Sacred water, giver of life, I have cleansed you from all negative blockages with the power of the universe. You are now safe and protected from the outside world by a shield, intertwined with the most powerful healing energy in the universe."

The water's vibrational shield is now activated. If for some reason you would like to remove the shield in the future, you can simply visualize this ritual in reverse.

Journal Prompts

1. Jot down your thoughts on the practices here. Which rituals in this chapter did you perform? Did you feel that you were successful in healing the water?

2. Did you perform healing during a natural disaster using one of the rituals in this chapter? If so, document the ritual, as well as the outcome and any insights you experienced.

3. What rituals were you not drawn to? Why?

Chapter 8
WATER RITUALS, CEREMONIES, AND BLESSINGS

If there is magic on this planet, it is contained in water.
—Loren Eiseley

This chapter is a collection of water blessings, ceremonies, and rituals. The rituals in this chapter are longer than those shared previously, and they may not be as easy to perform in the spur of the moment.

New Beginnings Blessing of the Water

The Blessing of the Rivers ceremony held in Australia, discussed in chapter 2, inspired me to create my own version. This ritual calls upon the universe to bless the water and to ask for healing and new beginnings for sacred waterways around the world.

Ritual Tools
- Healing herbs (lavender, cedar, juniper, lilac, and/or palo santo)
- A vessel of water (spring water or rainwater recommended)
- Matches
- A fireproof dish of some kind (abalone shell or silver bowl recommended)

Choose a local body of water you would like to offer a new beginning.

Once you are at your chosen location, light your healing herbs. Infuse the area that you will be working in with the smoke. This will cleanse the area of negative impurities. Make sure to contain the hot ashes on a fireproof dish to prevent an unwanted fire. You can let the herbs continue to burn or snuff them out for another day. I prefer to let them burn throughout the entire ceremony to ensure that purification is successful.

Then, take your water vessel and embrace it with both hands. Say aloud, "Healing energy, I call upon your true power, your ability to transform the sick and hurt with your love and light, to bring new beginnings to our abundant waters. Healing energy, bring your presence deep into the water so that it may be whole and renewed once more."

Visualize your container of water glowing brighter and brighter with each pulse of powerful yet gentle energy as it transforms and revitalizes the water. Really feel the energy flowing through you and into the vessel using the power of your voice and intention.

When you are ready, take the vessel of sacred water and pour it into your chosen body of water. Then, state an intention that offers inspiration for the water's new beginning, such as "Water, you are renewed" or "Water, your new beginning has begun."

Give thanks to the universe for allowing you to call upon and utilize its assistance. I also recommend offering your love to the water after each ceremony, blessing, or ritual.

Finally, sit with the water and meditate. Journal about the experience if you would like to refer to your water blessing at a later time.

New Moon Reawakening Ritual

This ritual was inspired in part by one of the deities I have worked with for some time in my pagan practice, The Morrigan. I have called upon her, asking her to allow me to embody her strength and courage during times of battle and weakness in my own life so I can continue to fight for myself and for the water. She must have granted me that, because I am still standing and attempting to create change for what is right.

The Morrigan is the ancient Irish Queen of Sovereignty, Keeper of Death, and a war goddess. Her name translates into either "the Great Queen," which shows her connection to sovereignty, or "the Phantom Queen."[58] As a sover-

---

58. "The Morrígan."

eignty goddess, The Morrigan is protector of the land. As the Keeper of Death, she is the transporter of life and death and gathers the souls of the slain in the aftermath of battle. As a war goddess, she terrorizes armies, who instantly die from fear at the sound of her terrible voice. The Morrigan is quite a complex goddess and carries many roles, as she is a triple goddess with multiple identities: The Morrigan, Babd, Nemain, and Macha.

For our ritual, we will call on The Morrigan as the goddess of sovereignty. (Working with her is not a closed practice—she is open to all who reach out to her, including nonpagans.) She teaches us to protect our power, our land, and our water and to fight for what is right and honorable. While she is not associated with any wells or springs, The Morrigan is associated with freshwater rivers.

This ritual should be performed on a new moon. Working under this moon phase allows us to release deep trauma and pain from the rivers of the past and present all over the earth so that rivers may be renewed and reclaim their sovereignty once more.

Perform this ritual at night if you can; if you would rather perform it during the day due to safety reasons, you may do so.

Ritual Tools

- Cleansing herbs (rosemary, juniper, or cedar)
- Ritual cloth, black or red
- One chime candle, black or red
- A large crystal bowl
- Sacred water (water made holy)
- One black obsidian crystal or another dark crystal that absorbs negative energy
- A statue, painting, or drawing of The Morrigan or an animal that is symbolic of her (raven, crow, horse, eel, or cow)
- An offering (red wine, water, whiskey, meat, honey, apples, or milk)
- Matches
- A fireproof dish of some kind (abalone shell or silver bowl recommended)

Choose a river that is sacred to you. This can be any river, anywhere, because The Morrigan's reach extends all over the world. You could visit the river you chose (if it is local) or a nearby river. If you live somewhere that currently has more frozen rivers than flowing, it is totally okay to choose a frozen river.

Then, decide where you would like to perform your ritual. If you are using frozen river water, I recommend taking it home to allow the water to melt. You can then perform this ritual indoors at your altar.

Once at your chosen location, take a bundle of your cleansing herb(s) and light it. Sweep the ritual area with the smoke to remove unwanted negative energy. Make sure to prevent unwanted fire by placing a fireproof dish underneath your herb bundle to catch the ash.

Spread out your ritual cloth and lay the remaining tools on the cloth, with your large bowl in the center.

Then, set an intention for the ritual. Be clear on your purpose when working with The Morrigan (or any other deity). For example, your intention may be: "To remove the deep trauma and pain that no longer serves the water so that water can reclaim its own sovereignty and rule once more."

Pour your sacred water into the glass bowl. Then place the black obsidian crystal into the bowl; it will continue to remove any negative energy that the water may absorb.

Next, sit on the ritual cloth. Light your black candle, state the intention you decided upon, and invoke The Morrigan. To do so, first sit in silence for a couple of minutes, feeling The Morrigan's energy and visualizing her presence. Then say, "Goddess of Sovereignty, I call upon you to assist me in healing our sacred waters. Rivers, as ancient and powerful as you, have been in battle and war for thousands of years. I call upon you to assist me in releasing the pain and trauma from your freshwaters. You are the giver of life and of death, I ask you to give life to our water and assist it in reclaiming its sovereignty."

Sit quietly and see if you can sense The Morrigan's answer. If she has blessed your ceremony, you may feel as if you have been given intense power, or she may send corvids (ravens or crows) your way. If neither of those things occur, use your intuition. If you feel that The Morrigan has blessed your ceremony and agreed to assist you, take the black obsidian out of the bowl, then lift the bowl and pour its contents into the river that you have chosen. When you are ready, say, "With the power of The Morrigan and the new moon, I wash away the deep trauma and pain from the freshwaters of the world. You have been torn into pieces and renewed so that you, water, can reclaim your sovereignty once again."

Wait for the candle to fully burn down out of respect for The Morrigan's blessing and to enhance the magic. (If you cannot wait that long, you may blow out the candle, but relight it as soon as possible and allow it to burn down completely.) Sit in collaboration with The Morrigan and give thanks to the Great Queen and the water. You may wish to journal about your experience so that you can reflect on it later.

Water Connection Ceremony

This ritual is an immersive water ceremony. Water ceremonies have been done for thousands of years by people all over the world.

Your first task is to choose a location for this ceremony. It could be a local river, lake, or other water resource near your home, or it can be a place that is farther than you feel connected to. Since this is an immersion, it cannot be performed from a distance; however, you could repurpose this immersion as a ritual bath in your bathroom.

I like to choose a location by considering how I want to personally connect with our sacred water and what my intentions are for my own ceremonies. There is an option to immerse yourself in this water as part of the ceremony, so if you would like to do so, make sure to choose a safe water source.

Next, determine which offerings you would like to incorporate in your ceremony. If you would like to offer physical items to the water, choose offerings that are natural—unnatural objects might harm the ecosystem. To avoid adding unnecessary chemicals to the water, some safe offerings would be natural flowers, leaves, stones, sand, and shells.

You will also need to prepare prayers, poetry, blessings, mantras, or songs for this ceremony. As I have stated previously, prayer is a highly individual practice based on your religious or spiritual beliefs. I have included what I would use for myself, but you can—and should—modify these prayers to suit your needs.

I enjoy writing heartfelt poetry that relates to the water and myself in some way, then reading it out loud to the water sources that I visit. I have found that these words often do not come from the mind—they come from deep within the soul. Meditating near the water and listening to its natural flow really inspires me and fills me with peace and creativity. If you have not tried meditating near the water and then writing poetry, I recommend that you do.

If you would like to include blessings in your water ceremony, you may customize the length of your blessings to your preference, making them as short or long as you need. Blessings are a beautiful addition that can be offered alongside prayer or on their own.

My favorite mantra is the Om symbol, which is pronounced "AUM." This is the ancient universal sound that connects us all. I use this as my mantra because it has significant meaning for me. If you would like to include a mantra in your water ceremony, choose one that is deeply meaningful to you.

If you create music or if there is a song that is special to you, you can share that with the water as well.

Ritual Tools
- Your chosen prayers, poetry, blessings, mantras, or songs
- Your chosen offerings
- Purification herbs (rosemary, juniper, cedar, or palo santo), dried or as incense
- Matches
- A fireproof dish (optional)
- Candles (optional)
- A ritual cloth (optional)

For your ceremony, place your offerings near the body of water that you have chosen. When setting out your offerings, put them on the natural earth, whether that is on grass, sand, or a tree trunk. I prefer to set my offerings right along the water's edge. You can also bring some type of cloth to lay on the ground and place your offerings on top of it.

Light any incense or candles you may be using in your ceremony, then set them alongside your offerings. If you are using dried herbs to energetically cleanse the area before your ritual, light them and waft the smoke around, catching the hot ashes in a fireproof dish to prevent an unwanted fire.

Sit by the water's edge and take a few moments to connect to your natural surroundings. Take a deep breath. Calmly notice if the water is calm or turbulent. Is it a hot day, or is there a bit of a chill? Are there any birds flying in the air near your ceremony? Is the sun shining, or is it a cloudy day? Ground yourself, meditate, and connect to the environment.

When you are ready, speak aloud your prayers, poetry, mantras, or blessings, or play your song. The following connection prayer can be used, reworded, or rewritten entirely: "Water, life giving mother of the earth, nourisher of life, I am connected to all life through you. Water, your elixir flows through the veins of the earth and through the veins of humanity. Water, nothing is born without your consent. Water, I give myself to you, in my entirety, for your connection is the perfect gift. Thank you, water, for the life you have given me, and for your connection."

Now, stand on the shore and release your offerings into the water while blessing it. If it is safe for you to do so, you could immerse yourself in the water while making your offering instead: Hold your offerings against you while you slowly step into the water. When you are in your desired area, release your offerings.

Once you have released your offerings, it is time to purify yourself by pouring water over your head. Purifying yourself will allow the connection between you and the water to manifest and grow stronger. You can do this on the shore, using your water source or water you brought to the ceremony, or you can do this while immersed in your chosen water source, if it is safe to do so. (You may also skip this step for now and purify yourself later, using water from home.) In any case, hold your hands in a bowl shape and pour water over your head. As you do so, the water will cleanse and renew your soul, mind, emotions, and body. Pour water over your head three times in total.

When you have completed your cleansing, return to the shoreline and sit quietly with the water in silent meditation. Let thoughts of love and gratitude fill your mind as you contemplate. As you wrap up your ceremony, you may again offer prayers, poetry, blessings, mantras, or songs to the water.

Afterward, you may write the details of your ceremony down. Journal about the feelings, sensations, or impressions that you had during the ritual. I tend to forget things, so writing them down is helpful when I need to recall something from the ceremony; otherwise, I could lose meaningful information.

Self-Love Healing Ritual

Aphrodite, the Greek goddess of the sea, love, beauty, and sexuality, was born in the depths of the ocean, coming into existence within the frothy sea-foam. Amongst many other things, Aphrodite reminds us to embody self-love. This ritual serves to remind the water of the beauty and power of self-love so that the water may remember its worth and honor on its path to healing.

Ritual Tools
- A large crystal or silver bowl
- A nontoxic marker or a pencil
- Pink Himalayan salt
- Strawberries or apples
- Seawater, if you have access to it, or sacred water (water made holy)
- Honey
- Three pink seashells
- Pink rose petals
- One rose quartz crystal
- One moonstone crystal
- One pearl
- A blanket to sit on (optional)

Choose a location where you can perform this loving ceremony in private, if possible. If you are located near the sea or a lake, a location with sand is preferable. Performing this ceremony on the full moon would work in place of a setting with sand, as the moon is directly associated with the sea and divine feminine energies.

Place your ritual tools near the edge of the water or on your altar, if you are doing this ritual at home. Then, sit and meditate for a couple of minutes, letting the energy from the moon and from Aphrodite, the goddess of love, fill you. When you are ready, ask Aphrodite to bless the ceremony that you will be facilitating in her name. Always make sure that you are respectful, never demanding.

Next, pour your sacred water or seawater into your bowl. Add the pink Himalayan salt, the fruit, honey, and pink rose petals to the bowl. These items are associated with self-love and will offer water loving and healing properties.

Hold your rose quartz, moonstone, and pearl in your hands, bringing them to your heart. Say aloud, "Goddess of love and of the sea, I ask you to imbue these stones with the love of your heart so that I may offer the gift of self-love to the water, your true home, so she may feel worthy and honored once more." Then, place the crystals and the pearl into your sacred bowl of water.

Next, pick up one of your pink seashells. Using a nontoxic marker or a pencil, write *self-love* on the shell, then bury it in the sand. Shells that are buried will be left behind so that your requests, blessings, and intentions can continue after your work is finished. If you do not have sand available, place the shell in the bowl of sacred water instead.

Pick up a second shell. Imbue it with your natural-born universal energy. Bury it in the sand or add it to the bowl of sacred water.

On the third shell, draw the outline of a dolphin, as these magical creatures are connected to Aphrodite, the sea, and rebirth. You could also draw the outline of a dove, as these birds are sacred to this goddess and are associated with love. Or, if you are attuned to Reiki, you can draw the Power Symbol, "Cho Ku Rei," so that the power of the universe will amplify your gift of self-love.

After you have buried your last shell or put it into your sacred bowl, pick up the bowl and pour it into your chosen body of water. Say aloud, "Water, I remind you of your sacred self so that you may love yourself once more. Self-love is courage to love yourself during times of change and difficulty. Self-love will give you strength and keep you strong when modern wars are raging around you."

When you have finished your ceremony, sit and meditate with the energies of Aphrodite, self-love, and the water. You may want to write your impressions down in a journal to reflect on later.

Seashell Blessing

Seashells are gifts of nature that have been in existence for hundreds of millions of years. They have been used for thousands of years in magic and ritual, used to connect to water and various water deities around the world. Seashells represent the beauty that remains after death, reflecting the cycle of life that once lived. As such, shells are symbols of life, death, rebirth, spiritual connection, protection, and transformation.

For this ritual, you will need to collect a few seashells. You can use several of the same kind of shell, or you can select different shells. You may want to choose shells that align with the blessings you would like to offer the water. If you are unsure where to begin, conch, cowrie, scallop, clam, nautilus, auger, or abalone shells would all work well.

I am deeply drawn to the ancient nautilus shell, which was in existence long before the dinosaurs. It is a beautiful living fossil that has graced our Earth for the last 480 million years. A nautilus shell is the remains of a life full of learning and constant transformation. This amazing shell grows with the creature that lives inside—always evolving and moving forward. I identify with this, as I have been on a spiritual and physical evolution for my entire life. I am not the person that I was even a few years ago. I use the nautilus shell as a symbol of growth, renewal, and spiritual evolution in my own practice because I connect to its purpose. It may be a good option for you as well.

Ritual Tools
- Your chosen seashells
- A nontoxic marker or a pencil

You can perform this blessing anywhere you can place your seashells into water. When you are ready, grab your seashells and place them over your heart. Visualize your intentions.

Then, when you are ready, set down all but one seashell and pick up your writing utensil. Make sure that your writing utensil is nontoxic and safe for the environment.

Write a blessing on the seashell. When I perform this blessing, I write *evolve* on my first shell, and on my second shell I write *renewal*. You can use these words or choose your own. Write a blessing on as many of the shells as you feel called to.

After you have finished writing, pick up your shells and place them into a body of water of your choosing, watching your blessings as they sink or float away. Thank the water for accepting your gifts of healing. You can sit with the water in contemplation or write about this simple blessing in your journal.

Heart-Opening Cacao Water Ceremony

Cacao is a plant capable of becoming a bitter, pure, and organic dark chocolate. For the ancient Maya civilization, cacao was considered a gift from the gods. This ancient plant medicine was consumed during ceremony for medicinal, ceremonial, and spiritual purposes, and to release past trauma. Cacao ceremonies have carried into modern day—they are still actively facilitated.

Sacred cacao is now used all over the world to nourish our physical and energetic bodies and to return them to natural states of optimal health. Cacao opens emotional centers and allows blockages to be released. I have combined cacao, sound bowl healing, and energy healing into this water ceremony in the hopes that we can open the heart of our waters once more, filling its depths with peace, love, and joy.

Before the ceremony, decide which green or pink crystals you would like to use. I recommend moldavite and other crystals associated with the heart chakra. Also decide which singing bowl you would like to use in the ceremony. Singing bowls are created for a variety of different uses, though any singing bowl will produce healing vibrations. If you want to use a bowl that is specifically made to open the heart chakra, use a singing bowl that has the frequency of F.

Ritual Tools
- Healing herbs (rosemary, palo santo, lemongrass, cinnamon, or lavender)
- Ceremonial-grade cacao
- Ceremonial cup or chalice
- Green and pink crystals
- A singing bowl and mallet
- A glass bowl
- Blessed water
- Matches
- A blanket
- A fireproof dish

The night before your ceremony, create blessed water by leaving a container of water under the moonlight with a piece of silver immersed in it—any silver coin or ring will do. If you are attuned to Reiki, you can draw the Power Symbol, "Cho Ku Rei," over your blessed water. Doing this will place all the universe's power into your sacred water, creating a powerful elixir.

The day of your ceremony, you will need to prepare your cacao. To make your sacred drink, you will need four tablespoons of ceremonial cacao and five to eight ounces of hot water. Melt the cacao over your stove on low heat. Stir consistently, making sure that it does not boil. If you are traveling to a different location, be sure to put your hot cacao into a container that will keep it warm for your ceremony.

Choose a location where you will not be disturbed during this ceremony. Once you have reached your destination, spread out your blanket and place your ritual tools on top of it, with your glass bowl in the center.

First, light your bundle of herbs and thoroughly cleanse the area where you will perform your ceremony with the smoke. This will remove unwanted negative energy from your sacred space. Make sure to catch the ash in a fireproof dish.

Pour your blessed water into the glass bowl. Then, hold one crystal in the palm of your hand. Feel the energies of the heart. Place your other hand on the bowl of water and envision the heart-opening energies of this crystal flowing from one hand to the other, then imbuing the water. When you are ready, place the crystal beside the bowl. Repeat this process for each crystal you are using.

Sit in front of your glass bowl and pick up your singing bowl and mallet. A mallet made of leather or wood is usually included with a singing bowl. Holding the mallet in the same manner that you would hold a pen, apply even pressure against the outer rim of the bowl and move the mallet in a clockwise circle. Take your time, allowing the sound to build up gradually and smoothly. If the sound is uneven, you may need to apply more pressure with your mallet. The singing bowl's vibrations will be felt by the water's physical and energetic properties and allow the water's heart to open.

While using your singing bowl, you can chant a mantra to amplify the healing effects going into the water. I use the universal Om in my practice; however, the mantra Yam relates to the heart and would work well here.

When you are satisfied by the harmonic frequency that your singing bowl has produced, pour your cacao into your ceremonial cup or chalice. Then, draw a symbol that represents the heart on your ceremonial cup or chalice. You could draw a heart shape or another symbol that relates to the heart in some way, such as an apple, swan, seashell, or Celtic love knot. Then, place your hands around the ceremonial cup and imbue it with your natural energy or Reiki, allowing the energy to flow from you into the cup.

Sit mindfully with your sacred gift, feeling your heart center opening and expanding. Meditate on what you want the water to receive from this ceremony. Allow the spirit of cacao to assist you in setting an intention for this ceremony—let it be a personal one. Breathe deeply for a few minutes.

After you have felt your energy shift or when you are ready, pour the contents of your ceremonial cup into the glass bowl, allowing the cacao's ancient medicine to mix with the sacred water that has been imbued with crystal energy, sound healing, and universal vibrations.

Stand, pick up your bowl, and pour its contents into your chosen body of water. If you are at home, working from your altar, you may pour the contents outside on the ground—the water will filter through the ground back to its natural sources.

You may feel called to chant, sing, give blessings, or say prayers. I say something along the lines of "With the magic of holy water, Reiki, and cacao's ancient medicine, I give thanks to the heart of water. I open the heart of water. I heal the heart of the water so that it does not fear those who want to care for it, so that the water may be open to the waterbearers of the world coming together in its name, for the water is sacred and divine."

Once you have finished your ceremony, sit for a few moments and meditate. In your journal, you may want to jot down aspects of your ceremony and how you felt in the moment.

Worldwide Water Crystal Healing Ceremony

To assist in revitalizing our world's water supply, we can offer healing that will affect all water in positive ways using crystals, energy work, and intention.

To perform this ritual, you will need to choose a crystal that has healing benefits. Any crystal associated with healing and purification will work. Selenite is one of my favorites; however, selenite is easily damaged in water, so when I will be immersing a crystal in water, I prefer to use amethyst or clear quartz, which is a master healer. Clear quartz can be used for almost any purpose: it amplifies intentions, draws away negative energy, and balances spiritual and physical aspects.

Once you have decided which crystal you would like to use, make sure that it has been cleansed of negative energy before using it in this ceremony. You can do this by leaving it under the moon's light, flooding the crystal with your personal energy, or cleansing it with the smoke of healing herbs such as cedar or juniper.

Ritual Tools
- Your chosen crystal

Decide which local river you would like to perform this ritual at. Working with a river allows the energy of the ritual to be shared with other life-giving waters.

Sit at the edge of your chosen river. Pick up your crystal and imbue it with your natural energy or the energy of Reiki. State your intentions for your water blessing. Say aloud, "With the power of these combined energies, I ask for the water to be blessed with pure health and unconditional love." You can repeat this blessing as a mantra or add additional prayers.

Find a shallow area of the river, then safely place the crystal in the water. Visualize the river sharing its rejuvenating, purified power with the rest of the world's water. It will radiate positivity everywhere it flows. Sit with this visualization for as long as you need.

Afterward, you can sit and connect to the water and its consciousness. Reflect and journal about your experience.

Healing Mother Water's Womb Ritual

Water is a powerful resource of fertility. It has life-giving abilities. While it has experienced countless cycles of death and rebirth, it continues to birth new life. This ritual will heal the metaphorical womb of the water, reawakening its fertility and allowing the water to reclaim its holy, life-giving abilities. To do so, we must clear the water's past, remove abuse and trauma, and open energetic and physical pathways. We will also offer water's life blood to the earth once more. Life cannot be created without water—we must remember that.

Ritual Tools
- A large silver bowl
- One black obsidian crystal, or another dark crystal that draws out negative energy
- Rainwater or seawater
- A blanket
- Rose petals
- Cedar for cleansing
- Dried herbs (lemongrass, elderflower, calendula, chamomile, rosemary, Angelica root, raspberry leaf, and hibiscus flower)
- Matches
- A fireproof dish

First, decide where you would like to perform this ritual. Choose a local body of water that is sacred to you. If possible, find a place where you can perform this ritual in private.

Spread out your blanket close to the water, then place your ritual tools on top of it.

Pick up your cedar and light it. Use the smoke to cleanse your immediate environment, including your crystal if it was not cleansed beforehand. Prevent an unwanted fire by catching the hot ashes in a flame-resistant container of some kind.

Sit in front of your items. Pour rainwater or seawater into your glass bowl. Then, take your black obsidian crystal and hold it in both hands. State your intention for what you want to heal from the womb of the water; you can cleanse past trauma, abuse, grief, infertility, or energetic and physical blocks. Hold the crystal against your stomach and imagine the sea goddess imbuing the crystal with her essence. (Feel free to imagine a different deity that is in alignment with your own religious beliefs and practices.) Say aloud, "With the divine mother energy of the sea and my intentions, the waters are rejuvenated once again."

Place the crystal into the middle of your bowl. The crystal will cleanse the water and draw out any negative energy.

Next, take your rose petals and healing herbs and place them in the bowl, trying to arrange them around the crystal if possible. All of the herbs listed in the Ritual Tools section have been used medicinally and spiritually to heal conditions that affect the womb, pregnancy, childbirth, infertility, and the menstrual cycle.

Place one hand over this womb-healing elixir of love. Place your other hand on your stomach. Close your eyes and ask the sea goddess or your chosen deity to bless your ritual. Meditate and observe the silence of ancient wisdom. Allow any feelings or emotions to flow through you. Then, imagine a bright orange sunset or a brilliant ball of orange light emitting from your stomach area. See this orange color radiating through your body. Watch as it flows down the arm you are holding above your healing elixir. Release the vibrant energy from the palm of that hand.

Say, "Mother Water, your womb has been cleansed, nourished, and reawakened. You are free to create life abundantly again without fear. You are free to be the earth's nurturing mother once more. Your feminine powers have been reconnected to your children and to yourself."

After you have spoken your blessings and prayers, remove the crystal from the bowl. Then, pick up the bowl and pour this healing elixir into your water source. Envision your offering infusing itself with the water, intertwining with streams and rivers that eventually connect to the sea.

Afterward, sit with the water and connect with your earthly mother. Reflect on your experience and write down any information that you would like to refer to later.

Releasing Spiritual Attachments

A spiritual attachment is unwanted negative energy that can be created by dis-ease, trauma, and imbalances in the spiritual, mental, physical, or emotional levels of our being. This energy can build up, having undesirable effects on a person's health. In the same way that humans absorb energy, water can absorb and react to the physical and spiritual stimuli it is exposed to. In this ritual, we will release any attachments that the water is holding on to.

Ritual Tools
- One black obsidian crystal, or another dark crystal that draws out nega-tive energy

Choose a nearby water source that could use a spiritual or energetic cleansing. This could be a river in your city that carries heavy toxins, or a river in the countryside that collects agricultural runoff from local farms. Maybe you know of a nearby lake that has had industrial waste released into its waters. Use your judgment to determine if a space has a spiritual attachment.

Once you are at your location, sit beside your body of water. I recommend casting a magical circle of protection for yourself since you will be dealing with negative energy. Refer to chapter 7 for information on how to do this.

Visualize the negative energy that you want to remove. Imagine its shape, size, and color. For example, I see a large, dark-gray entity clinging to the edge of the water's glinting surface. Then, in your mind's eye, take a knife, scissors, or other sharp object and cut away the energy so that it is not attached to the water; see it being severed from the water's energy field. With your hands in a bowl shape, visualize yourself scooping out the negative energy and holding it in between your hands. See it being completely removed from your body of water. You can then send a beam of natural energy from your hands to the spiritual attachment to zap it away. If you are a Reiki practitioner, you can send a beam of Reiki with your eyes. These methods will evaporate the unwanted entity as long as you thoroughly saturate it.

Once you have finished removing the spiritual attachment, hold your crystal in your palms. Fill it with your natural energy or Reiki. Then, place this high-vibrational healing crystal into the water to prevent the negative energy from reattaching to its source.

After you have finished, state any blessings or prayers that you wish to share with the water. Stay for a while, connecting to the energy of the water. You may want to write about the experience in your journal so that you can reflect on it later.

Love Offering Water Ceremony

This water ceremony is based on the traits of water goddesses found in cultures around the world, those who offer love and fertility. In this water ceremony, we will ask these sensual goddesses to use their divine love to fertilize the water of the world so that it may be pure again.

There are two variations for this ceremony. The first option is for those who would like to work with the water goddesses. The second version of this ritual does not involve working with any deities.

Ritual Tools (Option One)
- A nontoxic offering (oranges, lemons, or pumpkins)
- Honey
- Ground cinnamon
- Sunflowers

For this ritual, you will need to visit a river of your choice.

Once you have arrived at your destination, hold your personal offering to the water and infuse it with your love and intentions of healing. Then, spend time with the water, meditating and connecting to the water's healing energy.

When you are ready, dig a small hole near the water's edge and place your offering(s) into the hole.

For the sensual water goddesses, place sunflowers and your offering into the hole, sprinkle cinnamon over everything, and add a drizzle of honey. State your personal blessings, prayers, love, and gratitude for the health and love of the water. Ask the water goddesses to give their unwavering love to the water so that it may heal. Then, bury your offering.

Release your blessings, prayers, and healing intentions to your buried offering and then to the water. Say, "I release my offerings, all my love, and highest blessings."

Visualize the powerful healing intentions that you just released, and in your mind's eye imagine this energy dropping down into the water, flowing with the water's current, joining with other rivers, and eventually making its way to the ocean.

Ritual Tools (Option Two)
- A nontoxic offering that symbolizes love (red or pink rose petals, a rose quartz crystal, apples, white-flowered jasmine, dried lavender, or seashells)
- Lavender essential oil
- Honey
- Shredded apples

Decide where you would like to perform this ceremony. You may choose any location, though it is best to perform this at a place where there is flowing water.

Once you have arrived at your destination, hold your personal offering to the water and infuse it with your love and intentions of healing. Then, spend time with the water, meditating and connecting to the water's healing energy. When you are ready, dig a small hole near the water's edge and place your offering(s) into the hole.

Sprinkle a few drops of lavender oil, a drizzle of honey, and a handful of shredded apples over your offering. State your personal blessings, prayers, love, and gratitude for the health and love of the water. Then, bury this love offering.

Release your blessings, prayers, and healing intentions to your buried offering and then on to the water. Say, "I release my offerings, all my love, and highest blessings."

Talk freely to the water before you. Tell the water that your deepest desire is for it to be whole again. Inform the water that your love offering is given so that it may be refilled with love and healing once more.

Visualize the powerful loving intentions that you just released and in your mind's eye, imagine this energy dropping down into the water, flowing with the water's current, joining with other rivers, and eventually making its way to the ocean.

Aura-Cleansing Water Ritual

An aura is the energy field that surrounds the body of all energetic organisms, including plants, animals, rocks, and water. Water shifts and changes energetically when it is affected by the vibrations of other sources and stimuli. Sometimes the vibrations that water has absorbed affect it negatively, and it carries this heavy weight for long periods of time. This high-vibrational ritual will rebalance the water's aura, clearing the stagnant and polluted energies that it has picked up.

Ritual Tools
- A large bowl
- A bundle of rosemary herbs
- Six crystals (amethyst, black tourmaline, clear quartz, rose quartz, celestite, and agate)
- Sacred water (water made holy)
- Dried lavender and rosemary
- Lemongrass essential oil
- Himalayan salt
- Matches
- A fireproof dish

Before you proceed, choose a nearby body of water for your ritual. Pick a place where water naturally flows, such as a river or stream. Finding a space where you will not be disturbed is recommended.

Once you are at your location, light a bundle of rosemary and cleanse the space of negative, unwanted energy with the smoke. Catch any ash in a fireproof dish to prevent an accidental fire. After you have cleansed the space, casting a circle of energetic protection would be wise, as you will be working with darker energies during this cleansing.

Now, place your bowl on the earth. Pour your sacred water into the bowl and then add the Himalayan salt, crystals, lavender, and rosemary, as well as a few drops of lemongrass essential oil. Amethyst and agate both have strong cleansing powers, black tourmaline absorbs toxic energy, celestite produces positivity and reduces negativity, rose quartz offers deep healing and love, and clear quartz rejuvenates the aura. This special blend will assist in removing unwanted negative energy and will spiritually bathe the aura of the water.

Now hold your hand over the bowl. With your finger, draw a cleansing symbol, such as a lotus flower, above the surface of the water. If you are attuned to Reiki, draw "Sei He Ki," or the Harmony Symbol. While this symbol symbolizes harmony, its intent is purification.

Keeping your palm facedown over the water, feel the energy of the symbol flowing through you and into the sacred bowl. Visualize white or gold energy flowing from your palm into the water. Take your time and see if you can sense the energy of the water's aura changing. You may feel tingles, warmth, or a cold sensation.

When you feel ready, say, "Water, your torn and strained aura has been rejuvenated." Remove the crystals from the bowl. Then, take your sacred gift of water and pour it into the body of water you have chosen. Visualize the water from the bowl flowing throughout the river, stream, or ocean, intertwining its purified aura with the body of water to cleanse and rejuvenate.

Afterward, meditate with the water, sending it loving energies and blessings. You may want to journal your thoughts or reflections on this ritual.

Water Blessing Ritual

For this ritual, I have pulled elements from a variety of natural and earth-based practices as well as my own. This ritual focuses on blessing and healing both a physical body of water and its internal spirit, as they are intimately connected. In this way, we will heal the water's physical and energetic bodies.

Ritual Tools
- A bundle of purifying herbs (rosemary, juniper, cedar, and/or palo santo)
- Stones

- A sacred vessel
- Matches
- A fireproof dish
- A nontoxic marker
- A blanket (optional)

Choose a nearby body of water that will be the location for your ritual. If you can, choose a place that is meaningful to you. Also choose a vessel of some kind that you can carry water in. Pick a vessel that is special to you.

Once at your chosen location, gather a handful of stones from the earth that surrounds the body of water. Physically clean the stones off, then place the stones and your vessel in an easy-to-reach location in front of you, either on a tree stump, a blanket, or a large, flat rock.

Pick up your water vessel and carefully use it to collect water from your chosen body of water. Place the vessel back on your flat surface and either stand or sit in front of the vessel and stones.

Next, light your bundle of herbs to spiritually cleanse and remove any negative energy before the next step in the ceremony. Be sure to smoke cleanse the stones that you collected as well. Collect any ash in a fireproof dish to avoid an unwanted fire.

Pick up one of the stones and a nontoxic marker. On one side of the stone, draw a universal symbol that has strong healing effects, such as the spiral sun symbol or a snake. On the opposite side, draw the arrow symbol, which is a sign of protection in various cultures. Draw these same symbols on your vessel, one on each side, to represent both the healing and protective aspects of this ceremony.

If you are attuned to Reiki, draw the "Sei He Ki" symbol on each side of your vessel and on all of the stones that you collected using your finger. This symbol is a double-edged sword that represents healing, harmony, and balance as well as being useful as a protection symbol.

Once you have finished drawing the symbols, place your hands around the vessel of water and infuse it with your universal life-force energy. State any intentions or thoughts that come to mind. When you are ready, move on to each stone, infusing them with your energy one at a time. Feel the energy of the stones strengthen as you infuse them.

Gather the infused stones and stand beside your body of water. Sing or chant a water blessing that has sacred meaning for you. You can create your own or play a song if you wish. If you sing your own song, remember that songwriting is a process, and it does not have to be perfect; if you speak and feel with your heart, the right words will find you. If you choose a song, it is important to find or create one that complements the ritual; try to represent your feelings and emotions in the lyrics. If you are unsure which song to sing, I recommend the Algonquin Water Song, a water blessing created by a Native woman named Irene Wawatie Jerome.[59] It is beautiful and wildly soul-pulling, straight from the heart and true.

Drumming and chanting may be used to raise the energy of your ritual. Chanting usually consists of one to four lines repeated many times over. This will manifest a trance state, which will allow you to focus on this practice more effectively.

As you start to sing or chant a water blessing song, listen to the water and walk alongside it, dropping a stone in an area that speaks to you. Continue to sing or chant while slowly dropping the stones into the water. These stones, imbued with energetic vibrations and symbols, will effectively kickstart the cleansing, healing, and protection process for the water. They will first heal the water and then send out protective energies to maintain the water's newly balanced state.

After you have finished releasing all of the stones, grab your vessel and pour the water back into the body of water.

Afterward, take some time with the water. Connect with the body of water you chose. Breathe deeply and sit in contemplation. If the water spoke to you, what did it have to say, or what did it need? Journal about this experience so you do not forget anything that might be important.

Water Manifestation Ritual

Manifestation rituals are normally used to create the life that you want through a process of bringing your thoughts, visions, and dreams into the physical world. When you combine your vision with action, you bring your manifestation into

---

59. To learn more about the Water Song, visit www.singthewatersong.com.

reality. As healers of the water, we can manifest these hopes and desires into existence.

Imagine that worldwide water pollution starts being taken seriously on a larger scale. All over the world, businesses have started to work together to find better solutions for disposing of waste, toxins, oils, hazardous chemicals, and plastic, as they now refuse to dump in bodies of water and overflowing landfills that cannot safely contain trash. Leaders of countries all over the world have signed water peace treaties that acknowledge that water is a living entity and have made it illegal to pollute any form of water. You are noticing less plastic and trash in the town where you live. Animals are no longer dying from eating plastic; fish, turtles, and other aquatic life are thriving. Everything is being united because of a commitment to change. What would this feel like? Can you imagine how joyous this would be? If you can feel it in your heart, then you can manifest it. It may take a while and be a lot of work, but great and worthy things take time.

Now, you will not have to visualize this for your ritual—this is just an example of the power that manifesting can achieve. In this ritual, you will set your own personal intentions for manifesting change in the water. When manifesting, avoid using words that are past tense. For instance, do not say "The water might be healed." Use words that are in the present tense, and say them with confidence, like you mean it. For example: "The water *is* healed."

Once you know what you will be manifesting, you can choose your candle. The color of your candle should correspond to your manifestation. Purple candles work well for wisdom, peace, and spirituality. Green can be used to promote healing and new beginnings. Blue candles are for forgiveness and balance, red is for courage and strength, orange is for prosperity, and yellow is for positivity. Black candles are for protection and releasing negative energy. White candles are a great default candle because they are associated with serenity, peace, and healing.

I recommend performing this manifestation on a new moon, if possible, as this is a wonderful time that symbolizes rejuvenated intention.

Ritual Tools
- One chime candle in a corresponding color
- A nontoxic marker

- Healing herbs (lavender, rosemary, juniper, cedar, and/or desert sage)
- Matches
- A piece of paper and/or bay leaves
- A fireproof dish

If possible, perform this ritual outside, under the moon's energy. You may stand in your backyard, near your favorite body of water, on the beach, or in the woods. Wherever you choose to perform this ritual, make sure that you have cleansed the space with healing herbs.

Light your candle, then share your intentions with the universe. Writing your manifestations down is a good way to do this. Express your desires on a piece of paper, then read them aloud to the universe with authority as if they have already manifested. As you state your intentions, remember to visualize your manifestations. What do they look and feel like? Make sure you know exactly what you want so that the universe can make it happen. Always be mindful of your thoughts while manifesting—if you are visualizing plastic-free waters but your thoughts are elsewhere or disbelieving, it will not work. Once you have finished reading, safely burn the paper using the flame of your candle, catching the ashes in a fireproof dish.

You could also write your intentions on bay leaves and burn them in the same way. Bay leaves work well because they are associated with manifestation magic, but they require extra caution, as they are incredibly flammable. As with any manifestation, you need to express your desires, then let go of your attachment to the outcome.

If you are a practitioner of Reiki or any other energy-healing modality, you can infuse your visualization and intentions to give them an extra boost of power. If you are attuned to Usui Reiki, visualizing or stating that you are adding the Power Symbol, "Cho Ku Rei," to your manifestation calls the entire power of the universe into making your intentions a reality. Not being attuned to Reiki is not a disadvantage, as this is not necessary for your ritual to be successful.

When you are done sharing your intentions, you must release them to the universe and to the bottom of the ocean. Feel your wants and desires for the water coming to life as a result of your work.

When you are finished, journal about your experience or rewrite your intentions so that you can track the progress of your manifestation.

Clearing Water's Consciousness with Energy

We know that water has an intelligent consciousness, and that its molecular structure can be impacted by the environment. Thus, thoughts and spoken words can transform the water. Using energy medicine and powerful symbols, we can cleanse and release negative energies that the water has been exposed to, returning the water to a harmonious, rejuvenated form.

Prior to beginning this ritual, you will need to purify water. Water can be purified by placing silver into it or by letting it charge under the light of the moon. If you are in a pinch and do not have access to silver or moonlight, you may use water from a stream, spring, or well, as these water sources are associated with cleansing properties.

Ritual Tools
- A large crystal bowl
- Sacred water

This ritual can be performed indoors at home or outdoors at any local water source.

Pour your sacred water into a large crystal bowl. Using your finger, draw a symbol above the surface of the water. This symbol can be anything so long as you associate it with power. If you are attuned to Reiki, draw "Cho Ku Rei," the Power Symbol, over your bowl of water. While doing so, repeatedly chant the Power Symbol out loud. Chanting this symbol will cultivate energy and call in the entire power of the universe so that water's consciousness can receive intense healing. The coil on the Power Symbol will draw out negative energy from the water and prevent unwanted energy from reentering the water.

When you are ready, say, "I remove all unwanted negative energy from this water." Visualize the energy of the universe manifesting your intention.

Next, draw a symbol you associate with harmony over the surface of the water. If you are attuned to Reiki, draw "Sei He Kei," the Harmony Symbol. While doing so, repeatedly chant the Harmony Symbol out loud. Doing this will clear sadness, grief, anger, and worry. It will remove negative thought patterns and promote a more balanced state.

When you are ready, say, "I release all past trauma and fill this water with love and harmony." Visualize the energy of the universe manifesting your intention.

Finally, draw a symbol you associate with cleansing above the bowl of water. If you are attuned to Reiki, draw "Hon Sha Ze Sho Nen," the Distance Healing Symbol, over the water. Again, chant this symbol repeatedly, as it will heal issues that have resulted in past, present, and future imbalances in the water.

When you are ready, state "Water, you are pure and filled with vibrant energy again. You have been cleansed from unwanted negative physical and spiritual energies." Visualize the energy of the universe manifesting your intention.

Now, visualize universal energy being pushed down into the bowl of water. If you are attuned to Reiki, visualize the symbols being pushed into the water instead. This visualization locks in the gifts of cleansing that you have offered the bowl of water.

If you traveled to a local body of water to perform this ritual, pour the contents of the bowl into the water. This healed water will mix with the rest of the water, allowing it to purify the water's consciousness once more. If you are at home, working from your altar, you may pour your water on the ground outside.

When you have finished, sit and meditate. Give blessings of love, gratitude, and devotion. If you wish, you may journal about your experience.

Heal the Future with Energy

Many organizations around the world are striving to build a better future for the earth and all life-forms. To assist in this process, we can send healing energy to the future. Because it has no boundaries, energy can access and heal time and space.

In chapter 7, I shared the Healing Water's Past ritual. Sending energy to the future is different than sending it to the past, but only because we already know what we need to heal in the past, as we have already lived it. The future is uncertain because we have not yet experienced it. To perform this ritual, you will need to let go of all expectations and let the wonderful vibrations of the universe share their ancient knowledge; this will bring the best outcome possible.

Ritual Tools
- None

This ritual can be performed anywhere, either indoors or outside. Wherever you decide to perform this ritual, prepare a sacred space. Cleanse the space of any residual energy as well as negative energy; you do not want to unintentionally send negative energy to the future. Set up protective boundaries if you feel it is necessary to shield yourself.

When you are ready, ground yourself. State your intention for the distance healing that you will be performing. For example: "To heal the water in our future, for its highest good."

Once you have stated your intention, meditate for a few moments. Take some deep breaths and connect to the energy of the universe, feeling its loving energy enveloping you.

In the same fashion that you healed the past in chapter 7, you can use your own personal vibration to open a door that will grant you access to the future. Close your eyes and, in your mind's eye, see your pulsating, vibrant energy. Watch as it moves into the vast universe, traveling through time and space.

When you feel you have reached your designated future, stop. Hold your hand out and trace a circle in front of you. Feel the vibration of this door slowly weakening to the energetic pressure of the universe, creating an open portal. Send your personal vibrations, healing intentions, and love into the future.

When you receive the sensation that the future has been given enough energy healing, you may stop. Then close the vibrational doorway, and travel back to the present. You may close this doorway by repeating the steps in reverse; instead of opening the portal, you will close it. Trace the doorway in the opposite direction and see it fade away. See your astral self slowly returning to your body, and open your eyes when you are ready.

If you are attuned to Reiki, you can visualize or draw the Distance Healing Symbol, "Hon Sha Ze Sho Nen," to create a bridge across time and space, connecting you to the future; this symbol will always facilitate healing if the receiver accepts the energy being offered. See a white beam of Reiki energy traveling across this bridge to the future of water. Allow the white and gold haze of energy to settle, imbuing it with your intentions of its highest good.

Continue to send energy across time until you have received the sensation that the future has been given a thorough dose of healing energy. Then, draw the Distance Healing Symbol again and imagine that the bridge is dissolving, cutting off access to the future. Do not forget to let go of all expectations after your healing is complete.

When you are ready, open your eyes and reflect on your experience. Jot down any reminders that you wish to leave yourself.

Ice Ritual for Binding and Banishing

In ritual work, ice can banish, create curses, and break bonds. It can be used to break unwanted bonds that a toxic person has with the water or to bind a corporation that may be causing harm to the water. It will restrict their actions, thoughts, and energy and keep them from interfering with another place, person, object, or environment. I have successfully used ice rituals myself—they have been holding strong for a couple of years.

Some practitioners believe that ice rituals can be reversed when binding is no longer needed; others are positive that these rituals are permanent and cannot be undone. I have not yet had the opportunity to unbind one of my bindings, as they are still as necessary as they were on the day that I created them. However, I believe in order to reverse and unbind, you would simply perform the ritual backward, though reversing rituals or spells can be complicated depending on what ingredients are used.

In this ritual, I will share how to use ice to bind individuals or corporations that are damaging the water.

Ritual Tools
- Thorns
- Pepper
- Thyme
- Bay leaves
- Rue
- A tempered glass jar with lid, or another freezer-safe container
- Matches
- String
- A photo of the individual or business that you are planning on binding, or artwork that represents them
- One black candle
- A nontoxic marker
- Swamp water or water collected during a storm
- A fireproof dish
- A sewing needle (optional)

Place your freezer-safe jar in a place that is easily accessible, such as on a table. Then, take the image of the corporation or person you are binding and roll it into a tube shape, tying the tube closed with string. You can push a sewing needle through the tube to cut off all ties with the person or place that has been doing the damage. Next, say, "I banish you and bind you from causing future harm and despair to the water. It is so." Place the tube inside the jar.

Light a black candle. While your candle is burning, grab a bay leaf and a non-toxic marker. Write the name of the person or corporation that you are binding on the leaf. Then, on a second leaf, write down what you wish to bind and banish about this person or place. You could write down toxic habits that a person continuously performs toward the environment, for example, or the names of major oil and plastic companies as well as the destructive habits they possess. Use as many bay leaves as you would like to list the toxicity that you are binding and banishing.

When you are finished, hold the bay leaves over the flame one at a time. While burning the leaf, say, "I release your destructive habits, [name]." Once the leaf catches fire, place it in a fireproof dish. This protects your hands, prevents unwanted fire, and holds the burnt ash of the leaves, which will be used later on.

After you have burned the bay leaves, place the thorns, pepper, thyme, and rue into your jar. Pour in your swamp or storm water as well. Finally, add the ash of the bay leaves to your jar.

Put the lid on your jar. Say, "With the power of water, the fire in my heart, and the passion in my soul, I banish you, and I bind you from all future harmful activity to the water that nourishes Mother Earth."

Place your jar in the freezer. If you live in an area that stays around freezing temperature for long periods of time, you could choose to place the jar somewhere safe in your garage or on your porch. Make sure that the contents of this jar stay frozen as long as you would like to maintain the binding.

Snow Rituals

If you live in a colder climate that gets snow, you may feel drawn to use this magical form of water in your practice. I personally love snow; I feel alive during the snowy season, more so than any other time of year.

As it is quite versatile, snow can be used in magic, rituals, and blessings to offer inner healing, rejuvenation, purification, peace, and harmony. It can also release negativity. Finally, snow can be used to rebalance the energies of the water. Here are two simple rituals for working with snow.

Melt Away Trouble with a Foe
This is a quick technique that you can use when you are in a pinch and need assistance. It will remove negative energy or stop someone from causing immediate harm to the environment.

Ritual Tools
- Fresh snow
- A glass, crystal, or silver container

Fill your container with fresh snow. Then, bring the container inside your home, where it is warmer. Place the container on a table and sit directly in front of it. While the snow slowly melts, visualize your foe or the issue at hand. See harmful activities melting away with the snow in the bowl.

When you have finished your visualization, dispose of the contents of the container. Choose a disposal site far enough away that the negative energy contained in the melted snow will not affect your home. I recommend taking it to a heavily wooded area.

Bury Negative Energy
For this simple rite, make sure to use fresh, clean snow that has not been polluted by the city or animal activity.

Ritual Tools
- Bay leaves
- A nontoxic marker

Choose an area outdoors where you will have access to fresh, clean snow. Once you are there, grab a bay leaf and a nontoxic marker. On the leaf, write something that you want to change in regard to our waters. This could be anything from reducing oil pollution to recovering from the plastic crisis to simply removing unwanted negative energy that has built up in ice, water, and snow. Close your eyes and really attempt to imagine the scenario after you have written it down.

Write on as many bay leaves as you would like. When you are ready, bury your bay leaves underneath the snow. As it gets warmer and the snow melts, the water will take your healing energies and disperse them.

Other Uses for Snow

Here are some everyday ways to work with snow that do not require a full ritual.

Place Protective Barriers

To place a protective barrier around sacred places of water, build one with snow; you can place icicles around the barrier for added protection. This is a handy way to protect a birdbath or a small pond. This energetic circle of protection, crafted from snow, will prevent anyone with harmful intentions from crossing the barrier.

Draw Charged Symbols

Draw symbols on the surface of the snow with an icicle. These symbols will become offerings to the water. They can be symbols of healing, protection, or any other type of symbol that you are in need of at the time. When the snow melts, that charged water will make its way into the groundwater, effectively delivering your offering.

Remove Negative Energy from Altar Tools

Snow is as purifying as a clear quartz crystal, and it reenergizes your altar tools, removing stagnant energy that may have built up over time. Rub altar tools with a handful of snow, bury them in the snow overnight, or melt fresh snow and use that water to cleanse them.

Energize Your Rituals and Ceremonies

A great way to energize the rituals in this book is to add a cup of snow to them. You can add snow to any practices that pertain to cleansing the aura, clearing consciousness, removing negative energy, or offering peace and harmony.

However, do not use snow from a blizzard, as that snow has a supercharged chaotic energy that is not a good option for releasing negativity from the water.

Similarly, you can gather fresh, pure snow that is located in a silent place. Use it in rituals to soothe tense situations.

Journal Prompts

1. How did you feel while reading through this chapter? Were there any practices that stood out?
2. Do these practices positively affect your own? Why or why not?
3. One of the rituals involves working with The Morrigan. Do you feel comfortable performing a healing ritual based on a war and sovereignty goddess? Why or why not?
4. If you performed a seashell blessing, what type of seashell did you use, and why were you drawn to that specific shell? Describe its energy. If you did not perform the seashell blessing, are there any shells you feel drawn to?
5. What are your impressions about working with ice and snow?
6. Reflect on this chapter in an informal format. Jot down anything that felt important or raised your awareness in some way. If you wrote in your journal after performing any of the rituals, reflect on your notes now. If you did not write in your journal as you made your way through this chapter, what do you remember about the rituals you performed? In the future, jot down your thoughts after the ritual so they do not become forgotten.

Chapter 9
THE PATH OF THE WATER PRIESTESS/PRIEST/PRIESTEX

I have seen the sea when it is stormy and wild;
when it is quiet and serene;
when it is dark and moody.
And in all these moods, I see myself.
—Martin Buxbaum

By definition, the word *priestess*, which is the feminine translation of the word *priest*, comes from the Greek root *presbyteros*, or "an elder."[60] A priestess is a woman who has been authenticated to facilitate the sacred rites and rituals of her religious practice. In my opinion, religion should never keep someone from becoming a Water Priestess/Priest/Priestex. Water is a part of the earth, intimately intertwined with us, and originally, being a Water Priestess was a path of non-Christian origin. This path was first associated with women, who were documented throughout history as dedicants to the water. Women would lovingly care for the springs, wells, and other water sources that were local to them. Today, the majority of Water Priestesses are still women, though more and more men and nonbinary folks are becoming involved with and tending to water. For the duration of this chapter, I will be using the term Water Priestess, although the information in this chapter applies to all who work with the water, regardless of their gender identity.

---

60. *Vocabulary.com Dictionary*, s.v. "Priestess," accessed April 5, 2024, https://www.vocabulary .com/dictionary/priestess.

The Water Priestess is an individual who is dedicated to spending their life serving water in its various forms, including all water spirits and living organisms found in the water. There are many ways that one can identify themselves when tending to our ancient waters. Calling yourself a Water Priestess is a personal choice, for there are many people who walk this path but refer to themselves using other titles. Some prefer to be called a water healer, a waterbearer, a sea priestess, a water witch, a medicine woman, or a water advocate. The title you choose should be based on your practices, your experience, and what you feel most comfortable with. Your location may influence your path, as some Water Priestesses only work with freshwater due to living inland, while others only work with seawater. However, remember that distance healing will allow you to practice with all kinds of water, no matter where you are. Ultimately, your title does not fully define you as a Water Priestess—your dedication, actions, and the way you carry yourself in the name of water do.

A Water Priestess acts as a containment of water in which they offer ritual washing and healing water rituals to themselves, their family, their coven, and the community that they serve. Water Priestesses offer ritual acts of devotion to the water and its spirits, merfolk, and many gods and goddesses. With that said, honoring deities or believing in any religion is not necessary for one to become a Water Priestess. Even being a member of a coven is not required; many of us who walk this path do it alone. I have been a solitary Celtic pagan for a long time, and while I enjoy the idea of a coven, there is something magical and fulfilling about tuning in to nature all by myself. In all my years as a solo practitioner, I have never felt truly alone—how could I when I am amongst the water?

For the last three years, I have been studying Water Priestess training with Annwyn Avalon, an initiated Avalonian and Water Priestess. While you can and should seek out Water Priestess training from those who have been initiated, you can take that role on yourself in some way if formal training is not accessible to you. Self-study using books such as this one, and seek out hands-on personal learning experiences. The water will witness your efforts and honor you in return.

While you cannot initiate yourself as a Water Priestess, as someone of that path who has the authority and skill would have to perform that sacred bestowing upon you, you can perform a self-dedication rite. A self-dedication ritual will allow you to set this path in motion by making an oath to the water and to yourself. Of course, there is a sense of validation that comes with an official title that others recognize, but in reality, only you can call yourself a true Water Priestess. You are the one going out and putting in that work, building on your foundation, adding bricks with each new experience.

Whether or not you've undergone formal training, honoring the water and devoting yourself to it is the path to becoming a Water Priestess. I am still training, as formal training takes time, but in my heart and in my soul, I am a true Water Priestess. I have offered myself, my energy, and my love to the water countless times. I have stood on the water's shores and facilitated healing rituals for myself and others, performed sacred ceremonies, and recited the intimate poetry that I write only for the water. I have also done plenty of energy work for the water. I am passionate about water *and* energy, so I facilitate the energy within and around myself to heal the water—and to heal others using the water. Like with Reiki, I am the one who facilitates healing, but I am not the healer. I allow the energy of water to flow through my body and my soul, and I give it to the recipient, who takes this glorious energy and then uses it to manifest healing within themselves. I also teach others how to use energy for the purpose of healing the water.

If you are new to this path, mindfully connecting to the water's spirit and essence is a good way to begin each day. Simply sitting in meditation with the water is another great way to start building your practice. Additionally, performing the blessings, rituals, and ceremonies found in the pages of this book will raise the vibration of your energy and strengthen your connection to the water.

No matter how long you have been working with the water, you will never stop learning your craft. You will always deepen your practice as a Water Priestess, initiated or not. You will continue to cultivate a relationship with the water—there are always new lessons to be learned, new connections to be had. Each Water Priestess walks their own path, which transforms as they grow and evolve.

Self-Dedication Water Ritual

The best way to start your watery journey is by performing a self-dedication ritual. This type of ritual is usually done by a solitary practitioner of some type—a person who practices on their own. Anyone from any spiritual path can facilitate one. Keep in mind that these rituals are very powerful.

Ritual Tools
- A bathtub
- A silver bowl
- Spring water (or another type of water—excluding tap or swamp water—that has been made holy with a piece of silver and the moonlight)
- Flower petals of any kind
- Matches
- A purifying herb bundle (sweetgrass, palo santo, chamomile, or lemongrass)

On the full moon, take your herb bundle and light it with a match, then purify your ritual space with smoke to cleanse the area of negative energy. Extinguish the herb bundle, then take a purifying bath (also called ritual bathing), thoroughly cleansing your body and your energy. Be creative and use candles, flowers, herbs, essential oils, and any spiritual items that you feel will be useful in your cleansing process. After bathing, dress in colors that are associated with water: blue, sea green, turquoise, black, or white.

When you are ready, relight the herb bundle and cleanse the bowl that you will be using with smoke. You may state, "I cleanse this bowl with this [herb]. You are now sacred." Then, pour spring water into your sacred vessel and add your chosen flower petals.

Shield yourself (see chapter 7) before proceeding to protect yourself while you are fully immersed in your dedication ritual. Take time to slip into an altered meditative state. Really try to become relaxed and at peace here—block out your surroundings. Once you have reached this state, place your palms above your sacred water and imbue the water with your personal energy.

Then, dip one finger into the water. With that same finger, trace a sacred symbol connected to water on your body. (I favor the Celtic triskele or an upside-down triangle, which is the alchemical symbol for water.) Draw the symbol that you have chosen on your forehead, lips, chest, stomach, arms, hands, legs, and the tops of your feet. While doing so, you may state a dedication prayer. Here is an example:

> *May my mind be blessed so that I may choose to do what is right for*
> *the water. May my lips be blessed so that I may speak only in respect*

for the water. May my heart be blessed so that I may carry devotion and love in my heart for the water. May my abdomen be blessed so that I may honor life's creation. May my arms and hands be blessed so I can use them to heal the water. May my legs and feet be blessed so that I can walk amongst the waves of the sea and the flowing rivers. Water, divine mother, guide me on my journey. I dedicate myself to you today—my blood, my soul, and my body are yours. I vow to honor you in all of your forms. So shall it be.

After you are finished with your prayer, lift the bowl of sacred water and pour it over yourself. This completes the ritual by connecting you to water for life.

Hearing the Call

If you are anything like me, you may have felt the call of the water for a very long time. I did not feel balanced in my life, as if a certain something was missing. But I knew that when I spent time with the water, it drew me in. The water mesmerized me. I couldn't help but sit and watch in wonder as it flowed. I wanted so desperately to dive in and become one with the water. For a period, I did not know what that call really meant or what the water wanted from me.

I began to visit a nearby river and listened to the water rushing by, sitting in meditative contemplation in the hopes that it would direct me on my journey. I conversed with the water, sharing all my fears, my desires, and my deepest secrets. I confessed all my regrets. The water became my best friend in a way that no one else could.

I visited lakes, hoping that the calm and reflective surface of the water, shimmering in the sunlight, would communicate with me more effectively. I did not receive the answer that I thought I was searching for. The water wanted me to change my entire life so I would be willing to heal. I believe the water knew that I was not content with aspects of my personal and professional life; in order to be worthy of the water, to be an advocate, healer, and priestess, I had to become my true self. I could not represent the water correctly if I could not even be true to myself. I had to shed the person that I said I was.

This was not the answer that I expected. I did, however, understand it. While I had grown into spirituality, wisdom, knowledge, and peace, I had not told others who I really was beneath the surface. I kept my spirituality quiet, not wanting to be noticed or judged by others who did not understand. I had to free myself of this way of thinking because to be a waterbearer, to advocate for its sacred worth, I had to cherish and respect my own. When the water wants you to change, it can be messy. Shedding myself was not easy, but the water was right: I did know who I wanted to be.

The water's call made me the best version of myself. However, I had a part to play. I was the water's dedicated servant. Once I was able to serve, I had to find out exactly what was in store for me. Of course, the water does not always provide a direct answer. Symbolism can be strong, but it can also be confusing.

Over time, I started paying more attention to my environment and local waterways. What I saw was heartbreaking. I found seagulls near a lake, swallowing plastic bits as though they were food. Waterways were filled with so much plastic and filth that they looked more like a landfill than a river. In one river near my home, while communing with the spirits of the water, I found an innocent turtle wrapped in plastic, trapped. This precious creature of the water was being strangled around its neck. Seeing that little baby's life in danger because humans created products that the water and environment have rejected filled my soul with passion. I became so angry. We are surrounded by the ancient power, beauty, and magic of water, and we just destroy it without a thought.

Each time I went out after these incidents, my mind was definitely more open. I saw this environmental destruction everywhere—I still do, by the way. We are part of the cycle of life, but many of us are not contributing to that cycle in a positive way. We are not more important than water or animals. Everything needs water to survive. Water is number one, not us, and it can survive and thrive without us.

As a vessel of sacred water myself, I decided to dedicate myself to water pollution, water conservation, and healing water through energy medicine. I am the voice for water when the rest are silent.

Called to Serve

Being called to serve is more than hearing the call of the water—it is taking action to serve the water without hesitation, without stopping, even in times of challenge. I am not perfect in my service to the water, and you don't have to be either. As long as you fight for our waters with your full heart and do not give up, the water will accept you and take you places that you have never been before.

We all have our own path of enlightenment when water is involved. When the water has decided you are ready, it will call you. (Since you are reading these words, you may have already been called!) It is the siren's call that you cannot ignore. When you show the water your respect and loyalty, it will offer healing, purification, and tranquility. It will also break you down and give you challenges and obstacles to overcome. It is both a devastating and magical experience, feeling that spiritual connection and fighting for the water's life at the same time.

Water is always on a path of evolution, never keeping the same shape, always changing rhythm and movement. It watches, waits, and seeks out the ones with pure hearts and souls, those willing to give and sacrifice. As the tide ebbs and flows, the water draws you in and then demands transformation from you. It possesses an ancient wisdom and if you listen, you just might receive everything you have ever needed, which may be very different from what you thought it would be.

Facing Challenges

At this point in history, water has been battling a raging war against pollution for generations. The water relies on us—the waterbearers, advocates, and priestesses of the world—to be the human voice that it does not have so that we may teach and show those who have not heard the water's call that there is a better way. Unfortunately, many of our human brothers and sisters do not listen. People often take water for granted when it is easily accessible to them. This, I am afraid, is a common problem you will run into during your commitment to our sacred waters.

We are called to serve because the consequences are dire if we do not. The water is on a path of destruction that it did not create, and if we do not find ways to inspire leaders and everyday people to take steps to reduce the waste that is released into waterways, then there will be life-altering effects. Many countries are already beginning to face consequences.

Serving the water is exhausting at times; it is not pretty or glamorous. When removing pollution or trash from sacred waterways, you are outside in the elements, wearing heavy protective clothing, drenched in sweat, and picking up filth. Though it is a challenging task, it is a rewarding one. Removing waste from waterways is one of the most important things you can do to serve the water. You may choose to do this on your own or join one of the many water organizations that are available.

Worldwide water pollution has become quite a problem, and even though we want change to happen now, it will take a long time to recover from the damage that plastic, oil, and chemicals have caused. When we speak for the water, we must show patience and love for the water even in times of hate. You may repeat your contributions of ritual work, volunteering, and advocacy over and over again for a period of many years.

Just like the cycle of the seasons that pass us by, each season will bring a new wave of people who have not been informed of the call of water or how sacred our waters are. You will be responsible for communicating with these people in the hopes that they will see water as a living entity that nourishes us all. We must pass on our knowledge to those who are willing to listen. For each person who takes the words of wisdom that the water has blessed us with, it will be shared with dozens more. That is the power of the water's call: when we least expect it, we will be called to serve, and it is for a much grander design, a design that is whole and pure again, connected and free.

What You Can Do

Healing the water requires physical work and spiritual and energetic work. While performing water rituals does spark the universe to create change, magic and energy will only go so far—they cannot go outside and pick up plastic. Water cannot be healed through magic and energy alone. That is why water has called us to serve, because as physical and energetic bodies, we can do physical *and* energetic work. That is our power.

If you serve the water only through energy, vibration, and magic, that may be wonderful and fulfilling for you. It is not a requirement that you clean pollution out of your water sources. If you feel called to serve, keep in mind that everyone's path will be unique. While I am called to perform advocacy, conservation, and energy healing, the gifts that you contribute do not have to be identical. The water is wise, and if it chooses you, your gifts are worthy, no matter what they are.

I understand some people who serve the water cannot physically go outside and participate in cleanups. That is okay! If you want to be an advocate but cannot perform the physical labor that it sometimes requires, water conservation is a great way to raise awareness about water. Teach others how to conserve and manage water so that the earth will not face a freshwater shortage. Writing or blogging about water is another option. In this way, you can raise awareness on the sacredness of water and share how to give back. There are many options for you to explore when it comes to being in service to the water. No matter what path you take, your patience and persistence will win in the end.

Being in service to the water may be difficult at times, but as you prepare to serve, remember this: you are a vessel of water, and you are serving not only Mother Earth, but your own life and the lives of the next generation. I believe that with enough sacred contributions and time, we can once again have a society that is positively centered around water. Unfortunately, as optimistic as I am, I do not believe that it will happen in my lifetime. However, I am positive that it will happen at some point in the future—the fight for water will win.

Performing any of the rituals, ceremonies, and blessings that you have found in this book will build up healing energy over time. Each time you perform a ritual, you are connecting to the energy of the universe, which creates vibrational healing thanks to your personal energy, spoken words, love, and magic. These magical, energetic elixirs will get stronger over time. If you continue to give your healing energy to the water, it will eventually manifest from visualization into reality.

With each day, week, month, and year that passes, a new wave of people will hear the water's call and join the rest of us, adding their love, energy, and healing to our waters. This will create high-vibrational frequencies, and that energy will only continue to build as each person sends their unique positive frequency into the universe via their practice.

Journal Prompts

1. When you performed your Self-Dedication Water Ritual, what sensations or emotions did you feel during and after? How did you feel about dedicating yourself to a lifetime of devotion to the water? Jot these feelings down for later reflection.

2. When did you hear the water's call? What did it feel like to be chosen by the water, and how did you respond?

3. If you have decided how you will serve the water, what will that look like?
4. How do you plan on addressing the challenges you will face as a devotee to our sacred water?

CONCLUSION

Now that you have prepared yourself for the long but life-changing journey of healing the water, I hope that you will reflect back on why you chose this path during moments that may test your commitment to being of service. When I have a bad day, when I do not feel as if I can fight much longer, I take a minute to go deep within my soul, breathe, and remember the passion and fire that I felt the first time I saw that little turtle trapped in plastic.

Work with the water as often as you can. Remember that performing one ritual or healing ceremony per day, or even one per week, will bring positive results much faster and more frequently, slowly diminishing the negatives. Your work will affect even the smallest drops of water. The more that you put out into the universe that the water is healed, the more it will be—your affirming decision makes it so. The love, gratitude, and energy that you have given to the water will bring the water back to life.

If you are interested in more actively fighting pollution, there is an appendix in which I have listed several organizations that are affiliated with water. Get involved with one or more of these organizations. Their work has a major impact on the water, the earth, and the living conditions of all living organisms. The number of people that volunteer for organizations worldwide is astounding, and it tells me that we are on the right path. Efforts to reduce water pollution are not in vain. Humanity can learn, grow, and evolve over time and fight for our waters as one. We are capable of carrying the fate of our water until it is able to flow freely on its own again. It may not be today or tomorrow, but it will happen someday. That I know for certain.

It is my hope that I have brought awareness to our sacred waters and the part that we play in protecting them. I am but one woman in a world of billions, but if I can reach you and others who want to heal the water, imagine the physical and vibrational effects that will occur over time! The transformation of our water will be exceptionally beautiful to all who have the opportunity of witnessing such a miraculous event.

Journal Prompts
1. What is the water asking of you? Meditate on this one.
2. What is your truth? What are you seeking for yourself?
3. Do you feel prepared to be of service to the water? Why or why not?

Appendix
WATER ORGANIZATIONS
AROUND THE WORLD

While the previous chapters have shown that water pollution is a serious issue, I want to give credit to several amazing organizations that are working to heal the water. Thousands of people are devoting an immeasurable amount of time to protect and restore the world's water back to its original state. Each organization showcases caring citizens in their respective countries committing their lives to the cause of water. They are standing on the shores of polluted waters, sunburnt, holding up heavy signs in protest, filled with love for our waters with a fire in their eyes, glowing from deep within. They have yelled, chanted, cried, and repeated themselves in support of our precious water sources. They have spent countless hours dragging plastic and other pollutants out of the water by the thousands—and at times, millions—of pounds. Covered in grime, feces, oil, and mud, these water advocates have put their blood, sweat, and tears into healing the water. Their time and tears are willingly sacrificed because the result is well worth it. They continue to spread the word through their never-ending diligence. Their efforts are not in vain. These organizations are the lifeblood of water.

National and Global Organizations

I have attempted to be as thorough as possible when sharing these organizations. It is my hope that one or more are affiliated in your region of the world and that you can access them easily.

Alliance for the Great Lakes

Alliance for the Great Lakes is a nonprofit working in the massive Great Lakes region to protect the fresh, clean, and natural waters of these magnificent lakes. They are protecting the Great Lakes by removing pollution, wastewater, stormwater, and invasive species from the waters. Each year they remove thousands of pounds of pollution from the Great Lakes, and about 85 percent of that is plastic.

There are multiple ways that you can get involved. The Alliance for the Great Lakes is always looking for volunteers to assist in coastal beach and water cleanups. You can volunteer as a team leader to set up and organize the cleanup events, which is what I currently do. If you are not physically able to do that kind of work, you can make a donation so that the organization can continue to make these projects possible. You can become a brand ambassador and speak at events to spread the word about the threats to the Great Lakes. They also offer free curriculum and lesson plans on their website, which can teach children from kindergarten to twelfth grade about the Great Lakes.

Visit www.greatlakes.org to learn more.

For Love of Water (FLOW)

Another organization that has dedicated themselves to preserving the nation's Great Lakes and fighting against environmental threats is For Love of Water. FLOW maintains that the Great Lakes are for everyone to defend because they belong to all of us, and they are a public trust. This essentially means that the Great Lakes are held and handled for the benefit of the public, and no one can claim ownership. FLOW is devoted to protecting groundwater as well, calling it the sixth Great Lake.

FLOW uses the principles of the trust to educate, advance, and provide solutions to energy, water, and climate issues that affect the region and the planet. They are currently involved with multiple projects, including Clean Water for All, which works to close the water infrastructure funding gap in the state of Michigan so that wastewater, stormwater, and drinking water can be effectively managed. FLOW is also one of several organizations working to get the Line 5 pipeline shutdown. Line 5 is an old oil pipeline running underneath some of the Great Lakes, and it poses a serious threat to the freshwater basin. (See chapter

3 to learn more about Line 5.) In addition to these projects, FLOW has a campaign called Get Off the Bottle that encourages people to use less bottled water.

Visit www.forloveofwater.org to learn more.

Oil & Water Don't Mix

In 2012, an article brought attention to the outdated Line 5 oil pipeline. It caused an outcry from local citizens, who put together a rally that attracted the media and hundreds of people. As a result, Oil & Water Don't Mix was created by people dedicated to protecting the Great Lakes from major oil spills.

The mission of Oil & Water Don't Mix is to keep oil out of the Great Lakes. They are passionate about removing Line 5 and keeping oil pipelines out of the water for good. They speak out about water quality, oil pollution, the harmful effects of tourism, and Indigenous rights, as Enbridge's pipeline violates tribal treaty rights. There are several petitions that you can sign on their site, as well as templates for contacting your local representatives.

Visit www.oilandwaterdontmix.org to learn more.

US Water Alliance

This member-based, nonprofit water alliance—a coalition of leading organizations—envisions a future where all water is valuable. Members have numerous benefits and can help shape what US Water Alliance focuses on. This organization is transforming the way that the United States values and holistically manages our most precious substance. Members work to educate Americans about the true value of water through strategic approaches.

Visit www.uswateralliance.org to learn more.

Planet Water Foundation

Active in twenty-eight different countries, and supporting over four million people, this nonprofit organization focuses on providing safe drinking water. They primarily work in impoverished communities in Asia and Latin America, creating safe water solutions for children and local communities by installing water filtration systems that remove harmful and potentially deadly bacteria, viruses, and pathogens. This organization also offers educational programs that promote handwashing and water hygiene, both within local schools and to the community. Planet Water Foundation also works to provide safe drinking water after natural disasters and other emergencies.

Visit www.planet-water.org to learn more.

World Water Council

Created in 1996, this international water council has member organizations from over fifty countries. World Water Council focuses on a variety of issues, though the main goal of this organization is to work internationally to convince major decision-makers that water is a political priority. World Water Council promotes and fights for water security on a global scale and advocates for water to be clean and accessible to all.

Visit www.worldwatercouncil.org to learn more.

Charity: Water

Over seven hundred million people do not have access to safe drinking water. Since 2006, Charity: Water has been on a mission to change that. They have provided clean water to twenty-nine countries and counting, partnering with local organizations to bring safe drinking water to even the most remote areas. Over one hundred thirty thousand water projects have been funded by Charity: Water, and over seventeen million people have benefited from their work. They have a 100 percent model, meaning that 100 percent of public donations fund clean water projects worldwide.

Visit www.charitywater.org to learn more.

WaterAid

Over forty years ago, this nonprofit water organization was created to bring clean water to millions of people living without it. They work with communities to introduce sustainable water, and they also work to end the sanitation and hygiene crises by providing decent toilets and other hardware as well as good hygiene education. WaterAid currently has programs in twenty-two countries. They are dedicated to creating change on a global scale, stating that they will work until there is no need for their organization any longer.

Visit www.wateraid.org to learn more.

Water.org

This global organization is looking to bring clean water and sanitation to the world. They are also working toward making water and sanitation as safe, cost-effective, and accessible as possible. So far, they have changed the lives of 63 million people in eleven different countries. There are several ways you can get involved with their cause.

Visit www.water.org to learn more.

Thirst Project

This global water organization—which claims to be the world's largest youth water organization—is predominantly made up of high school and college students. The organization focuses on bringing clean drinking water to impoverished communities and developing countries by building or funding wells. They have built or funded wells in thirteen different countries and are currently working to make sure 100 percent of people who live in the Kingdom of eSwatini have access to safe drinking water.

Visit www.thirstproject.org to learn more.

Global Water Challenge

The Global Water Challenge collective partners with over fifty companies, agencies, and organizations to ensure WASH (water, sanitation, hygiene) access for all. Since 2005, they have helped more than three million civilians across North and South America, Asia, and Africa. Currently, there are eight programs listed on their website that you can explore and get involved with.

Visit www.globalwaterchallenge.org to learn more.

BIBLIOGRAPHY

"A Brief History of Chalice Well." Chalice Well Trust. Accessed January 22, 2024. https://www.chalicewell.org.uk/our-history/a-brief-history-of-chalice -well.

"A Brief History of Pollution." National Ocean Service. Accessed February 6, 2024. https://oceanservice.noaa.gov/education/tutorial_pollution/02history .html.

"Addressing Water Quality Challenges Using a Watershed Approach." United States Environmental Protection Agency. Updated December 4, 2023. https://www.epa.gov/nps/addressing-water-quality-challenges -using-watershed-approach.

Admin. "Rainmaking Hot Springs of the Ba Tonga." *The Patriot*, October 16, 2014. https://www.thepatriot.co.zw/old_posts/rainmaking-hot-springs-of -the-ba-tonga.

"AFN National Chief Perry Bellegarde on World Water Day 2018: 'We Must Redouble Our Efforts to End All Drinking Water Advisories by 2021.'" Assembly of First Nations, March 22, 2018. https://afn.ca/all-news/news /afn-national-chief-perry-bellegarde-on-world-water-day-2018-we-must -redouble-our-efforts-to-end-all-drinking-water-advisories-by-2021.

Africanews with AFP. "Plastic Pollution Clogs Hydropower Dam in DR Congo." *Africa News*. Updated March 21, 2022. https://www.africanews .com/2022/03/21/plastic-pollution-clogs-hydropower-dam-in-dr-congo.

Albom, Rhonda. "Lourdes, France – A Town of Healing Water and Miracles." *Albom Adventures* (blog). Updated January 13, 2024. https://www.albom adventures.com/lourdes.

Asadu, Chinedu. "Nigeria's Osun River: Sacred, Revered and Increasingly Toxic." *The Associated Press*, August 18, 2022. https://apnews.com/article /sacred-rivers-religion-osun-nigeria-2cb638faba9adffd33ce7170d4ce62f7.

The Associated Press. "Bolivia's Lake Titicaca Yields Trove of Relics." Phys Org, October 9, 2013. https://phys.org/news/2013-10-bolivia-lake-titicaca-yields -trove.html.

———. "Federal Judge Gives Enbridge 3 Years to Close Line 5 on Bad River Tribal Land." PBS Wisconsin, June 21, 2023. https://pbswisconsin.org /news-item/federal-judge-gives-enbridge-3-years-to-close-line-5-on-bad -river-tribal-land.

Baker, Kayla. "What Is a Sound Bath?" All Tree Roots, May 4, 2023. https:// alltreeroots.com/article/what-is-a-sound-bath.

Barchfield, Jenny. "Study: Rio de Janeiro Waterways Full of Human Waste, Dangerous Viruses." *Detroit Free Press*, August 1, 2016. https://www.freep .com/story/news/world/2016/08/01/rio-de-janeiro-water-olympics/8790 7882.

Barrett, Olivia. "The Secrets of Guatemala's Atlantis: The Maya Ruins of Samabaj." *The Collector*, February 5, 2022. https://www.thecollector.com /maja-ruins-samabaj-guatemala-atlantis.

"The Baths at the Sanctuary of Our Lady of Lourdes." Lourdes Office de Tourisme. Accessed April 2, 2024. https://en.lourdes-infotourisme.com /explore/have-a-spiritual-experience/explore-the-sanctuary/the-unmissables /the-baths-at-the-sanctuary-of-our-lady-of-lourdes.

"Bath World Heritage." City of Bath World Heritage Site. Accessed January 25, 2024. https://www.bathworldheritage.org.uk/bath-world-heritage.

Baurley, Thomas. "Holy Wells." *Naiads* (blog). Accessed January 19, 2024. https://naiads.org/holy-wells.

Beavis, Laura. "Tasmania's Polluted King and Queen Rivers Draw of PhD Student Research." *ABC News Australia*, September 23, 2016. https://www.abc.net.au/news/2016-09-24/fix-the-rivers-challenge-for-tas-phd-students/7874112.

Beckerman, Jane. "Holy Wells and Healing Springs of North Wales: Ffynnon Elian, Llanelian … the 'Cursing' Well?" *Holy and Healing Wells* (blog), December 19, 2016. https://insearchofholywellsandhealingsprings.wordpress.com/2016/12/19/holy-wells-and-healing-springs-of-north-wales-st-elians-well.

Bell, Dorothy, and Bill Bell. "Chichén Itzá – The Sacred Cenote." *On the Road in Mexico* (blog). Accessed February 23, 2024. https://www.ontheroadin.com/Mexico%20Archeology/Chichen%20Itza%20The%20Sacred%20Cenote.htm.

Biles, Mike. "The Chalice Well." *A Bit About Britain* (blog). Updated August 23, 2023. https://bitaboutbritain.com/the-chalice-well.

Boissoneault, Lorraine. "The Cuyahoga River Caught Fire at Least a Dozen Times, but No One Cared Until 1969." *Smithsonian Magazine*, June 19, 2019. https://www.smithsonianmag.com/history/cuyahoga-river-caught-fire-least-dozen-times-no-one-cared-until-1969-180972444.

Brady, Heather. "Native Community Fights to Defend Their Sacred River from Dam." *National Geographic*, July 27, 2018. https://www.nationalgeographic.com/culture/article/sacred-san-pedro-river-dam-mapuche-chile.

"Bridget." Behind the Name. Updated January 21, 2022. https://www.behindthename.com/name/bridget.

Broholm, Tessa. "The Effects of Plastic Pollution on Seabirds." Ocean Blue Project. Accessed January 19, 2024. https://oceanblueproject.org/the-effects-of-plastic-p-on-seabirds.

Brys, Marek. "Spotted Lake, British Columbia." WorldAtlas, August 9, 2021. https://www.worldatlas.com/lakes/spotted-lake-british-columbia.html.

Buckley, Nick, Elena Durnbaugh, and Trace Christenson. "The 2010 Enbridge Oil Spill Reshaped the Kalamazoo River and Provided a Cautionary Tale." *Battle Creek Enquirer*, July 24, 2020. https://www.battlecreekenquirer.com /story/news/2020/07/24/2010-enbridge-oil-spill-kalamazoo-river-line-5 -cleanup/5472623002.

Buntaine, Mark T., Bing Zhang, and Patrick Hunnicutt. "Citizen Monitoring of Waterways Decreases Pollution in China by Supporting Government Action and Oversight." *PNAS* 118, no. 29 (July 2021). https://doi.org /10.1073/pnas.2015175118.

"Bush Community Gathers for Blessing of the Rivers Ceremony." Catholic Religious Australia, March 11, 2019. https://www.catholicreligious.org.au /news/2019/3/11/blessing-of-the-rivers-ceremony-a-real-community-event.

Cafasso, Jacquelyn. "How Many Cells Are in the Human Body? Fast Facts." *Healthline*. Updated July 18, 2018. https://www.healthline.com/health /number-of-cells-in-body.

Carrington, Damian. "Microplastics Found in Human Blood for First Time." *The Guardian*, March 24, 2022. https://www.theguardian.com/environment /2022/mar/24/microplastics-found-in-human-blood-for-first-time.

"Cenotes in the Maya World." Archaeology's Interactive Dig. Accessed February 23, 2024. https://interactive.archaeology.org/cenotes/cenotes.html.

"Chambered Nautilus." Monterey Bay Aquarium. Accessed February 19, 2024. https://www.montereybayaquarium.org/animals/animals-a-to-z/chambered -nautilus.

Chapman, Michael. "6 Facts You Didn't Know About Icelandic Water." Guide to Iceland. Accessed January 19, 2024. https://guidetoiceland.is/history -culture/6-facts-you-didn-t-know-about-icelandic-water.

Chariot Energy. "How Long Does It Take for Plastic to Decompose?" Chariot Energy, February 13, 2024. https://chariotenergy.com/blog/how-long-until -plastic-decomposes.

Chauhan, Priya. "Cost of Color: Textile Dyeing Industry Is Slowly Killing Rivers in Asian Countries." Planet Custodian, September 9, 2021. https://www.planetcustodian.com/dyeing-industry-polluting-asian-rivers/15641.

Cheng, Johnny. "Mitchell Falls." World of Waterfalls, June 9, 2006. https://www.world-of-waterfalls.com/waterfalls/australia-mitchell-falls.

Clark, John. "Bladud of Bath: The Archaeology of a Legend." *Folklore* 105 (1994): 39–50. https://www.jstor.org/stable/1260628.

Clifford, Eva. "One of the Last Surviving Pagan Communities in Russia." Feature Shoot, February 27, 2017. https://www.featureshoot.com/2017/02/one-of-the-last-surviving-pagan-communities-in-russia.

"Climate Change: The Challenge." Monterey Bay Aquarium. Accessed January 19, 2024. https://www.montereybayaquarium.org/act-for-the-ocean/climate-change/the-challenge.

"The Clootie Well, Munlochy." Black Isle, June 23, 2006. Archived at the Wayback Machine. https://web.archive.org/web/20060623211132/http://www.blackisle.org/clootiewell.htm.

"Coal." World Wide Fund for Nature. Accessed January 22, 2024. https://wwf.panda.org/discover/knowledge_hub/teacher_resources/webfieldtrips/climate_change/coal.

Coeln, Alexandra. "Discover the Cradle of Incas Civilisation with a Visit to Lake Titicaca." Uncover South America, October 20, 2023. https://www.uncoversouthamerica.travel/blog/discover-the-cradle-of-perus-civilisation-with-a-visit-to-lake-titicaca.

Collier, Roger. "Swallowing the Pharmaceutical Waters." *Canadian Medical Association Journal* 184, no. 2 (Feb. 2012): 163–64. https://doi.org/10.1503/cmaj.109-4086.

Conaway, Cameron. "The Ganges River Is Dying Under the Weight of Modern India." *Newsweek Magazine*, September 23, 2015. https://www.newsweek.com/2015/10/02/ganges-river-dying-under-weight-modern-india-375347.html.

Cook, Bill. "Facing the Facts." Michigan State University Extension: Forestry. September 5, 2019. https://www.canr.msu.edu/news/facing-the-facts.

Corbin, Amy. "Zuni Salt Lake." Sacred Land Film Project, November 1, 2003. https://sacredland.org/zuni-salt-lake-united-states.

Coutsoukis, Photius. "Russia Environment – Water Quality." Photius. Updated February 12, 2008. https://photius.com/countries/russia /geography/water_quality.html.

Crow, Alexander. "Why Do Celts Hang Rags on Trees?" Culture Trip, February 23, 2017. https://theculturetrip.com/europe/united-kingdom/scotland /articles/clootie-wells-the-celtic-tradition-of-hanging-rags-on-trees.

Crowley, Aleister. *Magick in Theory and Practice.* 6th ed. New York: Castle Books, 1992.

Crystal, Ellie. "Inca Creation Myths." Accessed February 23, 2024. https:// www.crystalinks.com/incacreation.html.

Cymres, Winter. "Brigid: Survival of a Goddess." Druidry, February 11, 2020. https://druidry.org/resources/brigid-survival-of-a-goddess.

Danan, Tammy. "Rebuilding and Reclaiming: Wunambal Elders Preserve Indigenous Culture." Urth Magazine, July 14, 2023. https://magazine.urth .co/articles/wunambal-elders-fighting-to-preserve-indigenous-culture.

Davies, Nia. "Pride and Prejudice: The Janeites Bathing in Sulis." *Nia Faraway* (blog), December 2023. https://niafaraway.com/pride-and-prejudice-the -janeites-bathing-in-sulis.

Davis, Faith. "How Ancient Cultures Used Crystals & What We Can Learn from Them." Cosmic Cuts, February 1, 2021. https://cosmiccuts.com/blogs /healing-stones-blog/ancient-cultures-and-crystals.

"Deepwater Horizon – BP Gulf of Mexico Oil Spill." United States Environmental Protection Agency. Updated August 14, 2023. https://www.epa.gov /enforcement/deepwater-horizon-bp-gulf-mexico-oil-spill.

Dempsey, Jim. "Tobar Bride: St Brigid's Holy Well." *Megalithic Ireland* (blog). Accessed January 19, 2024. http://www.megalithicireland.com /St%20Brigid's%20Well,%20Kildare.html.

Denchak, Melissa. "Fossil Fuels: The Dirty Facts." NRDC, June 1, 2022. https://www.nrdc.org/stories/fossil-fuels-dirty-facts#sec-whatis.

DiLonardo, Mary Jo. "The Mystery of Canada's Magical Spotted Lake." *Treehugger*. Updated June 17, 2020. https://www.treehugger.com/mystery -canada-spotted-lake-4869731.

"Don't Let Nature Go to Waste." WWF-Australia. Accessed April 5, 2024. https://wwf.org.au/get-involved/plastic-pollution/dont-let-nature-go-to -waste.

Doyle, James. "Into the Centipede's Jaws: Sumptuous Offerings from the Sacred Cenote at Chichén Itzá." The Met, May 21, 2018. https://www .metmuseum.org/blogs/now-at-the-met/2018/golden-kingdoms-sacred -cenote-chichen-itza.

Easterby, Jony. "King River Queen River." Jony Easterby. Accessed January 19, 2024. https://www.jonyeasterby.co.uk/portfolio/king-river-queen-river.

"Easter: What Is the Origin of the Tradition of Getting Wet on Glory Saturday." Infobae, April 16, 2022. https://www.infobae.com/en/2022/04/16 /easter-what-is-the-origin-of-the-tradition-of-getting-wet-on-glory-Saturday.

Egbejule, Eromo. "Photos: The Pollution of Nigeria's Sacred Osun River." *Al Jazeera*, September 2, 2022. https://www.aljazeera.com/gallery/2022/9/2 /photos-the-pollution-of-nigerias-sacred-osun-river.

Eller, Donnelle. "Pollution and Habitat Loss Make Mississippi River Among Nation's Most Endangered." *Des Moines Register*, April 19, 2022. https:// www.desmoinesregister.com/story/money/agriculture/2022/04/19 /mississippi-river-map-endangered-american-rivers-list/7332940001.

"Enbridge Line 5 Pipeline in the Great Lakes." FLOW (For Love of Water). Accessed February 7, 2024. https://forloveofwater.org/line5.

Evans, R. J. "The Spotted Lake of Osoyoos." Kuriositas, December 3, 2017. https://www.kuriositas.com/2014/06/the-spotted-lake-of-osoyoos.html.

Evers, Jeannie, ed. "Great Pacific Garbage Patch." *National Geographic*. Updated February 1, 2024. https://education.nationalgeographic.org /resource/great-pacific-garbage-patch.

"Exploring the Mysteries and Scientific Wonders Behind Canada's Spotted Lake." Explored Planet. Accessed February 1, 2024. https://www.explored planet.com/en-route/exploring-the-mysteries-and-scientific-wonders-behind -canadas-spotted-lake.

"Exxon Valdez: Oil Spill | Prince William Sound, Alaska | March 1989." Damage Assessment, Remediation, and Restoration Program. Updated August 17, 2020. https://darrp.noaa.gov/oil-spills/exxon-valdez.

Faerywolf, Storm. "Into the Realm of Enchantment: Pop Culture and Magical Consciousness." *Llewellyn* (blog), January 9, 2017. https://www.llewellyn .com/blog/2017/01/into-the-realm-of-enchantment-pop-culture-and -magical-consciousness.

Farid, Farid. "The Mighty Nile, Threatened by Waste, Warming, Mega-Dam." Phys.org, March 20, 2020. https://phys.org/news/2020-03-mighty-nile -threatened-mega-dam.html.

Fava, Marta. "Ocean Plastic Pollution an Overview: Data and Statistics." UNESCO, May 9, 2022. https://oceanliteracy.unesco.org/plastic-pollution -ocean.

"Final Programmatic Damage Assessment and Restoration Plan and Final Programmatic Environmental Impact Statement." Gulf Spill Restoration. Accessed April 4, 2024. https://gulfspillrestoration.noaa.gov/media /document/chapter-2incident-overview508pdf.

Fontaine, Andie Sophia. "Pagans Are the Largest Non-Christian Faith in Iceland." The Reykjavík Grapevine, May 22, 2020. https://grapevine.is/news /2020/05/22/pagans-are-the-largest-non-christian-faith-in-iceland.

"FOSC Desk Report for the Enbridge Line 6b Oil Spill Marshall, Michigan." Environmental Protection Agency, April 7, 2016. https://www.epa.gov/sites /default/files/2016-04/documents/enbridge-fosc-report-20160407-241pp .pdf.

Fox, Demelza. "All About the Avalonian Tradition." Rockstar Priestess, September 8, 2014. http://www.priestesstraining.com/avalonian-tradition.

Fraley, Scott. "95% of Michigan Rivers Too Polluted to Swim, New Study Finds." *Manistee News Advocate*, April 1, 2022. https://www.manisteenews .com/news/article/95-of-Michigan-rivers-too-polluted-to-swim-new -17048964.php.

"'Ganga Receives 2,900 Millions Ltrs of Sewage Daily.'" *Hindustan Times*, September 9, 2015. Archived at the Wayback Machine. https://web.archive .org/web/20150909164033/http://www.hindustantimes.com/newdelhi /ganga-receives-2-900-million-ltrs-of-sewage-daily/article1-842037.aspx.

"Gayndah-Biggenden Loop." Drive Inland. Accessed April 4, 2024. https:// driveinland.com.au/itinerary/gayndah-biggenden-loop.

Gibson, Carolyn. "Water Pollution in China Is the Country's Worst Environmental Issue." The Borgen Project, March 10, 2018. https://borgenproject .org/water-pollution-in-china.

"God's Acre Healing Springs." SC Picture Project. Accessed January 22, 2024. https://www.scpictureproject.org/barnwell-county/healing-springs.html.

Gonzales, Jenny. "Pharmaceutical Water Pollution Detected Deep in the Brazilian Amazon." *Mongabay*, March 21, 2022. https://news.mongabay .com/2022/03/pharmaceutical-water-pollution-detected-deep-in-the -brazilian-amazon.

Goyal, Anuradha. "India's Profound Kinship with Water." *Hinduism Today* 26 (October/November/December 2021). https://www.hinduismtoday.com /environment/indias-profound-kinship-with-water.

"The Great Lakes." National Wildlife Federation. Accessed January 24, 2024. https://www.nwf.org/Educational-Resources/Wildlife-Guide/Wild-Places/Great-Lakes.

"Great Lakes Plastic Pollution." Alliance for the Great Lakes. Accessed January 19, 2024. https://greatlakes.org/great-lakes-plastic-pollution-fighting-for-plastic-free-water.

Greeley, June-Ann. "Water in Native American Spirituality: Liquid Life—Blood of the Earth and Life of the Community." *Green Humanities* 2 (2017): 157–79. https://digitalcommons.sacredheart.edu/cgi/viewcontent.cgi?referer=&httpsredir=1&article=1124&context=rel_fac.

Greenpeace International. "A Monstrous Mess: Toxic Water Pollution in China." Greenpeace, January 23, 2014. https://www.greenpeace.org/international/story/6846/a-monstrous-mess-toxic-water-pollution-in-china.

Grimond, Georgia. "Brazil's Goddess of the Sea: Everything You Need to Know About Festival of Iemanjá." Culture Trip, April 12, 2022. https://theculturetrip.com/south-america/brazil/articles/brazils-goddess-of-the-sea-everything-you-need-to-know-about-festival-of-iemanja.

"Groups Aim to Make Iemanjá Day More Sustainable." *Folha de S.Paulo*, February 2, 2024. https://www1.folha.uol.com.br/internacional/en/culture/2024/02/groups-aim-to-make-iemanja-day-more-sustainable.shtml.

"A Guide to the Holy Springs of Tirta Empul: Bali's Sacred Water Temple." Wonderful Indonesia. Accessed January 22, 2024. https://www.indonesia.travel/gb/en/destinations/bali-nusa-tenggara/bali/the-holy-springs-of-tirta-empul.

Gully-Lir, Caroline. "Lady of Avalon." The Wheel of Britannia. Accessed April 2, 2024. https://www.skylightpublishing.com/gullylir/avalon-about.htm.

Haggerty, Bridget. "The Holy Wells of Ireland." Irish Culture and Customs, November 25, 2023. https://www.irishcultureandcustoms.com/ALandmks/HolyWells.html.

Haghighi, Anna Smith. "What Effects Does Water Pollution Have on Human Health?" Medical News Today, November 23, 2020. https://www.medicalnewstoday.com/articles/water-pollution-and-human-health.

Håland, Evy Johanne. "The Life-Giving Spring: Water in Greek Religion, Ancient and Modern, a Comparison." *Proteus: A Journal of Ideas* 26, no. 1 (Spring 2009): 45–54. https://www.ship.edu/globalassets/proteus/volume 26-45-haland.pdf.

Hamilton, Denise. "The Secret Sacred Spring in West LA." *Alta Journal*, March 30, 2020. https://www.altaonline.com/dispatches/a6456/kuru vungna-secret-sacred-spring-in-west-l-a.

"Harbin Hot Springs Water." Heart Consciousness Church of Harbin Hot Springs. Accessed February 2, 2024. http://art.net/studios/lile/.h/water .html.

Hayes, Amy. "The Troubles of Pollution: Environmental Impact of Industrialization." *The Collector*, November 11, 2022. https://www.thecollector.com /environmental-impact-industrial-revolution-pollution.

Hays, Jeff. "Water Pollution in Russia." *Facts and Details* (blog). Updated May 2016. https://factsanddetails.com/russia/Nature_Science_Animals/sub9_8c /entry-5064.html.

———. "Yellow River." *Facts and Details* (blog). Updated June 2022. https://factsanddetails.com/china/cat15/sub103/item448.html.

"Healing Powers of Unusual Spotted Lake in Canada." Pando Trip. Accessed January 22, 2024. https://www.pandotrip.com/healing-powers-of-unusual -spotted-lake-in-canada-3208.

Heiser, Christina. "What the Beach Does to Your Brain." *NBC News*. Updated July 15, 2018. https://www.nbcnews.com/better/health/what-beach-does -your-brain-ncna787231.

Higgs, Karen A. "Uruguay Festivals – Sea Goddess Day on February 2." Guru'Guay. Updated January 26, 2023. https://www.guruguay.com /uruguay-festivals-sea-goddess-day.

"History and Traditions of Reiki." International Association of Reiki Professionals. Accessed February 12, 2024. https://iarp.org/history-of-reiki.

History.com Editors. "Exxon Valdez Oil Spill." *History*. Updated March 23, 2021. https://www.history.com/topics/1980s/exxon-valdez-oil-spill.

———. "Water and Air Pollution." *History*. Updated March 30, 2020. https://www.history.com/topics/natural-disasters-and-environment /water-and-air-pollution.

"History of the Springs." Harbin Hot Springs. Accessed January 19, 2024. https://harbin.org/update/history.

"History of the Water Song." Sing the Water Song. Accessed January 22, 2024. https://www.singthewatersong.com/history-of-the-water-song.

Holloway, April. "Maya Water Temple Complex Discovered Where Ritual Offerings Were Made to Placate the Rain God." Ancient Origins. Updated January 28, 2015. https://www.ancient-origins.net/news-history -archaeology/maya-water-temple-complex-discovered-where-ritual -offerings-020181.

Howard, Adele. "A Mercy Prayer Ritual for a Local Blessing of the Rivers Ceremony." Mercy International Association. Accessed January 19, 2024. https://www.mercyworld.org/f/45074/x/3467ad6e9f/mercy_ritual_botr _final_120219.pdf.

"How Bad Is Water Pollution in Australia?" Earth Reminder, August 15, 2022. https://www.earthreminder.com/water-pollution-in-australia.

"How Many Birds Die from Plastic Pollution?" WWF-Australia, October 8, 2018. https://wwf.org.au/blogs/how-many-birds-die-from-plastic-pollution.

HRCap, Inc. "Surfrider Foundation Beach Cleanup." HRCap, August 11, 2022. https://www.hrcap.com/post/hrcap-outreach-surfrider-foundation -beach-cleanup.

Hughes, Austin. "Effects of Water Pollution in Egypt." The Borgen Project, July 24, 2022. https://borgenproject.org/water-pollution-in-egypt.

"Indians – 07 Belief and Ritual of Crater Lake." Crater Lake Institute. Accessed April 4, 2024. https://www.craterlakeinstitute.com/index-of -general-cultural-history-books/index-of-books-and-articles-about-native -americans/1-02/indians-07.

Indosphere Culture. "Agama Tirtha: Holy Water in Indonesian Hindu Ritu- als." Medium, September 19, 2019. https://medium.com/@Kalpavriksha /agama-tirtha-holy-water-in-indonesian-hindu-rituals-cc5b5ab47952.

Irfan, Umair. "The Alarming Trend of Beached Whales Filled with Plastic, Explained." Vox. Updated January 16, 2020. https://www.vox.com/2019 /5/24/18635543/plastic-pollution-bags-whale-stomach-beached.

Ivanova, Nadya. "The Smoke of Change: Indigenous Colombians Pray for Water Conservation." Circle of Blue, April 16, 2009. https://www.circle ofblue.org/2009/world/the-smoke-of-change-indigenous-colombians -pray-for-water-conservation.

Jenkins, Olaf P. "Spotted Lakes of Epsomite in Washington and British Columbia." *American Journal of Science* 275 (Nov. 1918): 638–44. https://zenodo.org/records/1450202.

Jones, Allison. "Lake Legends of Wa She Shu." *Northwoods Tahoe* (November/ December 2018): 3–4. https://issuu.com/communityinkinc/docs/north woodstahoe_novdec_finalproof 2/3.

Jones, Rachel. "Hindu Cremations at Nepal's Pashupatinath Temple." *SevenPonds* (blog), July 30, 2019. https://blog.sevenponds.com/cultural -perspectives/hindu-cremations-at-nepals-pashupatinath-temple.

"Kailash Mansarovar Tour with Everest Base Camp Guru Pornima 03 July 2023." Kailash Tour Package. Accessed April 2, 2024. https:// www.kailashtourpackage.com/kailash-mansarovar.html.

Kamah, Wahyuni. "An Evening of Worship, Spiritual Reflection Along the Ganges River." Jakarta Globe, October 5, 2015. https://jakartaglobe.id /news/evening-worship-spiritual-reflection-along-ganges-river.

"Karnak Temple – Largest Religious Site of the Ancient World." Egypt Tours Plus. Updated May 3, 2023. https://www.egypttoursplus.com/karnak-temple.

King, Jon. "As the Anniversary of Enbridge's Refusal to Shut Down Line 5 Approaches, Groups Press Biden Admin." *Michigan Advance*, May 10, 2023. https://michiganadvance.com/2023/05/10/as-the-anniversary-of-enbridges-refusal-to-shut-down-line-5-approaches-groups-press-biden-admin.

"Kiyomizudera Temple." Japan-Guide. Accessed January 22, 2024. https://www.japan-guide.com/e/e3901.html.

Knebel, Don. "Column: Karnak Temple's Sacred Lake." *Current Publishing*, March 13, 2017. https://youarecurrent.com/2017/03/13/column-karnak-temples-sacred-lake.

Kois, Dan. "Iceland's Water Cure." *The New York Times Magazine*, April 19, 2016. https://www.nytimes.com/2016/04/24/magazine/icelands-water-cure.html.

Kraker, Dan, and Kirsti Marohn. "30 Years Later, Echoes of Largest Inland Oil Spill Remain in Line 3 Fight." *MPR News*, March 3, 2021. https://www.mprnews.org/story/2021/03/03/30-years-ago-grand-rapids-oil-spill.

"Lakehead Pipeline Company; Grand Rapids, Minnesota." IncidentNews. Accessed May 22, 2024. https://incidentnews.noaa.gov/incident/6793.

LaPier, Rosalyn R. "Why Is Water Sacred to Native Americans?" *Open Rivers* 8 (Fall 2017). https://doi.org/10.24926/2471190X.3283.

Lardieri, Alexa. "BP Takes $1.7 Billion Charge on Deepwater Horizon; Costs Now Top $65B." *US News*, January 16, 2018. https://www.usnews.com/news/national-news/articles/2018-01-16/bp-takes-17-billion-charge-on-deepwater-horizon-costs-now-top-65b.

"The Largest Inland Oil Spill in US History Happened in Minnesota." Stop Line 3, March 3, 2017. https://www.stopline3.org/news/2017/3/6/appy-anniversary-the-largest-inland-oil-spill-in-us-history-happened-today-in-minnesota.

Larmon, Jean, and Erin Benson. "Drought and Pilgrimage at the Cara Blanca Pools, Belize." Illinois News Bureau, June 13, 2016. https://news.illinois.edu /view/6367/372910.

Lee, Ilchi. "Energy and Consciousness: Something from Nothing." *Brain World*, May 8, 2019. https://brainworldmagazine.com/energy-and -consciousness-something-from-nothing.

"The Livenza Springs: Magical Act of Nature in 'Technicolour.'" *Italy-Tours-in-Nature* (blog). Accessed January 19, 2024. http://www.italy-tours-in-nature .com/livenza-springs.html.

Livingston, Jill. "'Taking the Waters,' Historic Mineral Springs in Siskiyou County, Far Northern California." Living Gold Press. Accessed January 22, 2024. https://www.livinggoldpress.com/TakingtheWaters.htm.

Lysaght, Gary-Jon. "Indigenous Sacred Site Lake Torrens Faces Exploratory Drilling for Resources." ABC News, September 27, 2020. https://www .abc.net.au/news/2020-09-28/lake-torrens-sacred-site-faces-exploratory -mining/12696750.

Majola, Nokulunga. "'Massive' Oil Spill in Umbilo River." *GroundUp*, October 21, 2020. https://groundup.org.za/article/massive-oil-spill-umbilo-river.

Malzer, Clara. "The Sacred Power of Cacao: How an Ancient Plant-Medicine Can Open Our Hearts." The Conscious Club, November 12, 2019. https://theconsciousclub.com/articles/2019/10/9/the-sacred-power-of -cacao-how-an-ancient-plant-medicine-can-open-our-hearts.

"Mami Wata: Arts for Water Spirits in Africa and Its Diasporas." National Museum of African Art. Accessed January 19, 2024. https://africa.si.edu /exhibits/mamiwata/intro.html.

"Manasarovar Lake." Wonders of Tibet. Accessed January 22, 2024. https:// www.wondersoftibet.com/destinations/western-tibet/manasarovar.

Manco, Jean. "The Mystery of Bladud." *Bath Past* (blog). Updated December 5, 2004. https://www.buildinghistory.org/bath/medieval/bladud.shtml.

Marinacci, Michael. "Harbin Hot Springs and the Heart Consciousness Church." *Califia's Children* (blog), December 28, 2014. https://califias .blogspot.com/2014/12/harbin-hot-springs-and-heart.html.

"Maya Sacred Ceremonial Site at Chichen Itza, Yucatan, Mexico." Yucatan Adventure, February 8, 2007. https://www.yucatanadventure.com.mx /mayanrituals.htm#Here_are_some_of_the_programed_Maya_Ceremonies _and_Spiritual_Rituals_at_Sacred_Ceremonial_Site_of_Chichen_Itza, _Yucatan,_Mexico_for_the_Year_2007.

McBride, Pete. "The Pyres of Varanasi: Breaking the Cycle of Death and Rebirth." *National Geographic*, August 7, 2014. https://www .nationalgeographic.com/photography/article/the-pyres-of-varanasi -breaking-the-cycle-of-death-and-rebirth.

McBurney, James. "The Cult of Sulis-Minerva at Bath: The Religious Ritual of the Patron Goddess at Bath." Master's thesis, Victoria University of Wellington, 2016. https://researcharchive.vuw.ac.nz/handle/10063/6483.

McCleery, Adam. "Ban Ban Springs Historically Important." *The Courier Mail*, May 31, 2017. https://www.couriermail.com.au/news/queensland/central -and-north-burnett/ban-ban-springs-historically-important/news-story/5c 31345374cb9898fa896b88be0f292b.

McClure, Matthew. "What Are the Causes and Effects of Water Pollution in Africa?" Greenpeace, September 1, 2021. https://www.greenpeace.org/africa /en/blogs/49015/what-are-the-causes-and-effects-of-water-pollution-in -africa.

Michael, Fady. "Egypt and Water Pollution." Save the Water, April 1, 2014. https://savethewater.org/egypt-and-water-pollution.

"Michigan Water Quality Issues." Michigan Water Stewardship Program. Accessed January 24, 2024. https://miwaterstewardship.org/michigan -water-issues.

Milligan, Mark. "Aquae Sulis – Roman Bath." Heritage Daily, May 30, 2020. https://www.heritagedaily.com/2020/05/aquae-sulis-roman-bath/129611.

Millmore, Mark. "Karnak Temple Sacred Lake." Discovering Egypt. Accessed January 22, 2024. https://discoveringegypt.com/karnak-temple/karnak-temple-sacred-lake.

Miler, Kate. "A Tale of Celtic Folklore: The Clootie Well in the Scottish Highlands." Scotland Itinerary Planning, January 28, 2022. https://scotlanditineraryplanning.com/the-clootie-well.

Mingren, Wu. "The Ancient Ruins On and Beneath the Sacred Lake Titicaca." Ancient Origins. Updated September 11, 2018. https://www.ancient-origins.net/news-ancient-places-americas/ancient-ruins-and-beneath-sacred-lake-titicaca-004012.

Min, Jia. "Hindu Beliefs." *Religion and Pollution* (blog). Accessed April 2, 2024. https://blogs.ntu.edu.sg/hp3203-1819s2-u15.

Misachi, John. "Which Country Has the Most Fresh Water?" WorldAtlas, September 24, 2018. https://www.worldatlas.com/articles/countries-with-the-most-freshwater-resources.html.

"Mitchell Falls, the Sacred Waterfalls of Australia." MyBestPlace. Accessed February 26, 2024. https://www.mybestplace.com/en/article/mitchell-falls-the-sacred-waterfalls-of-australia.

Monardo, Clare. "An Exploration of the Irish Holy Wells of St. Brigid." University of St. Thomas, November 2, 2016. https://blogs.stthomas.edu/arthistory/2016/11/02/an-exploration-of-the-irish-holy-wells-of-st-brigid.

Moreira, Jose Roberto. "Water Use and Impacts Due Ethanol Production in Brazil." International Water Management Institute. Accessed April 5, 2024. https://www.iwmi.cgiar.org/EWMA/files/papers/Jose_Moreira.pdf.

"The Morrigan." Coru Cathubodua Priesthood. Accessed January 22, 2024. https://www.corupriesthood.com/the-morrigan.

Mossolle, Maitlynn. "Iargo Springs Is a Michigan Hidden Gem That's Worth a Road Trip." 94.9 WMMQ, July 24, 2021. https://wmmq.com/iargo-springs-michigan-road-trip.

"Mrs. Takata Talks about Reiki." The International Center for Reiki Training. Accessed February 12, 2024. https://www.reiki.org/mrs-takata-talks-about -reiki.

Nasike, Claire. "The Polluted Lakes of Kenya." Greenpeace, April 8, 2021. https://www.greenpeace.org/africa/en/blogs/13461/the-polluted-lakes-of -kenya.

Nolan, Katherine. "Rag Trees." *DoChara* (blog), October 9, 2006. Archived at the Wayback Machine. https://web.archive.org/web/20061009200520 /http://www.dochara.com/tips/ragtree.php.

Oberlander, Elana. "A New Theory in Physics Claims to Solve the Mystery of Consciousness." Neuroscience News, August 11, 2022. https://neurosciencenews.com/physics-consciousness-21222.

"Ocean and Coastal Acidification." United States Environmental Protection Agency. Updated December 18, 2023. https://www.epa.gov/ocean -acidification.

Ochs, Rebecca. "Many European Lakes and Rivers Have Water Quality Issues." *European Scientist*, July 5, 2018. https://www.europeanscientist .com/en/environment/many-european-lakes-and-rivers-have-water-quality -issues.

Ohaire, Shannon. "St. Brigid's Well." Atlas Obscura, January 7, 2014. https://www.atlasobscura.com/places/st-brigid-s-well.

"Oil Pollution Act of 1990 (OPA)." United States Coast Guard. Accessed January 22, 2024. https://www.uscg.mil/Mariners/National-Pollution -Funds-Center/about_npfc/opa.

Oirere, Shem. "Chinese Involvement in Sierra Leone Fishing Development Project Criticized by Environmental Groups." SeafoodSource, May 24, 2021. https://www.seafoodsource.com/news/supply-trade/joint-sierra-leone -and-chinese-fisheries-project-strongly-opposed-by-environmental-groups.

P., Olive. "Water Pollution in Russia." StoryMaps, April 21, 2021. https:// storymaps.arcgis.com/stories/9b921568ab934d319ab057119b43888a.

Pang, Kelly. "Lake Manasarovar: A Mystical Sacred Lake in Tibet." China Highlights. Updated November 14, 2023. https://www.chinahighlights .com/nagri/lake-manasarovar.htm.

Parish, R. B. "An Abecedary of Sacred Springs of the World: Some Swedish Sacred Källa." *Holy and Healing Wells* (blog), July 19, 2019. https:// insearchofholywellsandhealingsprings.com/2019/07/19/an-abecedary -of-sacred-springs-of-the-world-some-swedish-sacred-skalla.

———. "An Abecedary of Sacred Springs of the World: Denmark – St. Magnus's Well, Mogenstrup." *Holy and Healing Wells* (blog), April 19, 2017. https://insearchofholywellsandhealingsprings.com/2017/04/19/an -abecedary-of-sacred-springs-of-the-world-denmark-st-magnuss-well -mogenstrup.

———. "An Abecedary of Sacred Springs of the World: The Hot Springs of Yemen and Zimbabwe." *Holy and Healing Wells* (blog), December 19, 2019. https://insearchofholywellsandhealingsprings.com/2019/12/19/an -abecedary-of-sacred-springs-of-the-world-the-hot-springs-of-yemen -and-zimbabwe.

———. "An Abecedary of Sacred Springs of the World: Latvia." *Holy and Healing Wells* (blog), December 19, 2017. https://insearchof holywellsandhealingsprings.com/2017/12/19/an-abecedary-of-sacred -springs-of-the-world-lithuinia.

Parker, Laura. "US Generates More Plastic Trash than Any Other Nation, Report Finds." *National Geographic*, October 30, 2020. https://www .nationalgeographic.com/environment/article/us-plastic-pollution.

Paul, Madhumita. "Sanitation Woes Cost Africa 115 Lives Every Hour." *Down to Earth*, November 26, 2020. https://www.downtoearth.org.in/news/africa /sanitation-woes-cost-africa-115-lives-every-hour-74417.

Perry, Nick. "New Zealand River's Personhood Status Offers Hope to Māori." *AP News*, August 14, 2022. https://apnews.com/article/religion-sacred -rivers-new-zealand-86d34a78f5fc662ccd554dd7f578d217.

Peters, Kirsten. "Origin Stories of the Lake." Crater Lake Institute. Accessed January 22, 2024. https://www.craterlakeinstitute.com/smith-chronological -history-of-crater-lake/sources-and-articles-of-interest/orgin-stories-of-the -lake.

Phillips, Dom. "The Lagoon in Front of Rio's Olympic Park Is So Filthy the Fish Are Dying." *The Washington Post*, July 21, 2016. https://www .washingtonpost.com/world/the_americas/the-lagoon-in-front-of-rios -olympic-park-is-so-filthy-the-fish-are-dying/2016/07/20/fcffbe98-4cfe -11e6-bf27-405106836f96_story.html.

PhotoBlog. "Prayer for Rain Ceremony Takes Place in Guatemala." *NBC News*, May 18, 2012. https://www.nbcnews.com/news/world/prayer-rain -ceremony-takes-place-guatemala-flna780871.

Pike, Jimmy. "Rainbow Serpent Dreamtime Story." Japingka Aboriginal Art Gallery. Updated February 2020. https://japingkaaboriginalart.com/articles /rainbow-serpent.

Pinto, Elcy. "Hindu Perspective on Water." St. Andrew's College. Accessed January 22, 2024. https://standrewscollege.ac.in/wp-content/uploads/2019/11 /Cardinal-Paul-Poupard-2011-Hindu-perspective-on-water.pdf.

Pippo, Tommaso De, Carlo Donadio, Marco Guida, and Carmela Petrosino. "The Case of Sarno River (Southern Italy): Effects of Geomorphology on the Environmental Impacts." *Environmental Science and Pollution Research* 13, no. 3 (May 2006): 184–91. https://doi.org/10.1065/espr2005.08.287.

"Plastic Polluter: Brazil Recycles 'Almost Nothing.'" *France 24*, May 24, 2019. https://www.france24.com/en/20190524-plastic-polluter-brazil-recycles -almost-nothing.

"Plastic Pollution Facts." Plastic Oceans. Accessed January 19, 2024. https:// plasticoceans.org/the-facts.

"Plastic Pollution Is Killing Sea Turtles: Here's How." WWF-Australia, June 30, 2021. https://wwf.org.au/blogs/plastic-pollution-is-killing-sea-turtles-heres -how.

"Polluted Water in the UmBilo River System in Durban's eThekwini Municipality." Ecohubmap. Accessed January 22, 2024. https://www.ecohubmap .com/hot-spot/polluted-water-in-the-umbilo-river-system-in-durban%E2 %80%99s-ethekwini-municipality/ekh0ml93wf6mo.

Prats, J. J. "Kawehewehe: Waikīkī Historic Trail." The Historical Marker Database. Updated February 10, 2023. https://www.hmdb.org/m.asp?m=13225.

Priestley, Samantha. "Is Overtourism Ruining an Ancient English City?" *Fodor's Travel*, November 13, 2023. https://www.fodors.com/world/europe /england/experiences/news/is-overtourism-in-bath-england-ruining-the -ancient-city.

"The Problem with the Line 5 Oil Pipeline." Oil & Water Don't Mix. Accessed January 22, 2024. https://www.oilandwaterdontmix.org/problem.

Rademacher, Ron. "Iargo Springs." Michigan Back Roads. Accessed April 4, 2024. https://www.michiganbackroads.com/daytrips/iargosprings.html.

Ritter, Kayla. "Pollutants and Heavy Metals Taint Moscow's Water Supply." Circle of Blue, April 12, 2018. https://www.circleofblue.org/2018/europe /pollutants-and-heavy-metals-taint-moscows-water-supply.

"River Sarno Emergency." Protezione Civile (Civil Protection Department). Accessed January 19, 2024. https://emergenze.protezionecivile.gov.it/en /environmental/sarno-river-reclamation.

Rodrigues, Alex. "More than 50% of Brazilians Do Not Have Access to Sewage Networks." *Agência Brasil*. Updated December 18, 2021. https:// agenciabrasil.ebc.com.br/en/geral/noticia/2021-12/more-50-brazilians-do -not-have-access-sewage-networks-says-mdr.

Ronalds, Geoff. "Ban Ban Springs – Aboriginal Sacred Ground – Great Bird Photography Area with the Nikon 200-500 mm f/5.6E ED VR AF-S Lens." All Digital Photography, January 15, 2017. https://www.alldigi.com/2017 /01/ban-ban-springs-aboriginal-sacred-ground-great-bird-photography-area.

Root, Tik. "US Is Top Contributor to Plastic Waste, Report Shows." *The Washington Post*, December 1, 2021. https://www.washingtonpost.com/climate-environment/2021/12/01/plastic-waste-ocean-us.

Rumpler, John. "What Is the Clean Water Act?" Environment America, October 19, 2022. https://environmentamerica.org/articles/what-is-the-clean-water-act.

"Running Out of Water." USC US–China Institute, April 22, 2021. https://china.usc.edu/running-out-water.

Rusnell, Charles. "Enbridge Staff Ignored Warnings in Kalamazoo River Spill." *CBC News*, June 22, 2012. https://www.cbc.ca/news/canada/edmonton/enbridge-staff-ignored-warnings-in-kalamazoo-river-spill-1.1129398.

Sagarino, Michele. "Catholics Provide Clean Water in Three African Countries." Cross Catholic Outreach, December 28, 2022. https://crosscatholic.org/blogs/2022/12/catholics-provide-clean-water-in-three-african-countries.

"Sarno Is the Most Polluted River in Europe." EcoHubMap. Accessed February 5, 2024. https://www.ecohubmap.com/hot-spot/sarno-is-the-most-polluted-river-in-europe/5g4uyml7kr5v64.

Schlicht, Jennifer, and Sean McBrearty. "Remembering the Kalamazoo." Clean Water Action, July 26, 2022. https://cleanwater.org/2022/07/26/remembering-kalamazoo.

"Sempaya Hot Springs." Elephant Whispers Safari. Accessed January 22, 2024. https://whisperssafarisuganda.com/sempaya-hot-springs.

Sorrentino, Joseph. "Rain Ritual Keeps Community Close to Its Heritage and In Tune with Nature." *Mexico News Daily*, June 30, 2021. https://mexiconewsdaily.com/mexico-living/rain-ritual-keeps-community-close-to-its-heritage.

"Sound vs Fjord – What's the Difference?" Aurora Expeditions. Updated November 29, 2023. https://www.aurora-expeditions.com/blog/sound-vs-fjord-whats-the-difference.

"Sources and Currents: Who Is Mami Wata?" National Museum of African Art. Accessed January 22, 2024. https://africa.si.edu/exhibits/mamiwata/who.html.

Spanne, Autumn. "What Are the Health Worries Around Pesticides?" Environmental Health Sciences, February 7, 2023. https://www.ehn.org/pesticides-2659319421.html.

Sperling, Vatsala. "Tradition: Diving Deeply into Water and its Near-Magical Role in Human Health and Hindu Ritual." *Hinduism Today* 18 (October/November/December 2019). https://www.bluetoad.com/publication/?i=619137&article_id=3476990&view=articleBrowser.

Spray, Aaron. "Visit the Sacred Cenote That Was Once Home to Chichen Itza's Tributes & Rituals." The Travel, March 12, 2023. https://www.thetravel.com/visit-the-chichen-itza-sacred-cenote-in-mexico.

Stanton, Kristen M. "Whale Meaning & Symbolism & the Whale Spirit Animal." *UniGuide* (blog), July 20, 2023. https://www.uniguide.com/whale-meaning-symbolism-spirit-animal.

Streich, Marianne. "How Hawayo Takata Practiced and Taught Reiki." *Reiki News Magazine* (Spring 2007): https://www.reiki.org/sites/default/files/resource-files/TakataArticle.pdf.

Stringer, Mary. "The Remarkable Tale of King Bladud and His Pigs." *Visit Bath* (blog), September 20, 2018. https://visitbath.co.uk/blog/read/2018/09/the-remarkable-tale-of-king-bladud-and-his-pigs-b81.

"Summary of the Clean Water Act." United States Environmental Protection Agency. Updated June 22, 2023. https://www.epa.gov/laws-regulations/summary-clean-water-act.

Taylor, Ian. "Ffynnon Elian, Llanelian yn Rhos." *Well Hopper* (blog), April 11, 2015. https://wellhopper.wales/2015/04/11/ffynnon-elian-llanelian-yn-rhos.

Thomas, Jeffrey L. "St. Cybi's Well." The Castles of Wales. Accessed January 25, 2024. https://www.castlewales.com/stcybi.html.

"3 Sacred Spring." Roman Baths, November 2, 2007. Archived at the Wayback Machine. https://web.archive.org/web/20071102122621/http://romanbaths .co.uk/index.cfm?fuseAction=SM.nav&UUID=F9F320C4-1A95-4C04 -AC609094E5B5DFD3.

Tikkanen, Amy. "New Seven Wonders of the World." *Encyclopaedia Britannica*, February 14, 2018. https://www.britannica.com/list/new-seven-wonders-of -the-world.

Tokach, Marilyn. "More Animal Symbolism: Whale Symbolism." Pure Spirit. Accessed January 19, 2024. http://www.pure-spirit.com/more-animal -symbolism/509-whale-symbolism.

"The True Story of Deepwater Horizon." Ensynox. Accessed February 7, 2024. https://www.ensynox.com/the-true-story-of-deepwater-horizon.

Unruh, Trent. "The Washoe Tribe and Their History Around Lake Tahoe." Visit Lake Tahoe. Accessed January 22, 2024. https://visitlaketahoe.com /attractions/the-washoe-tribe-and-their-history-around-lake-tahoe.

Varner, Gary. "Cenotés and Other Sacred Waters of the Americas." *Holy and Healing Wells* (blog). Accessed April 2, 2024. https:// insearchofholywellsandhealingsprings.wordpress.com/the-living-spring -journal-contents/cenotes-and-other-sacred-waters-of-the-americas.

Venkatachari, M. "Udaka Shanti Pooja | Importance and Purpose of Udaka Shanthi Puja." *Lifestyle Tips* (blog), May 28, 2017. https://vnktchari .blogspot.com/2017/05/importance-and-purpose-of-udaka-shaanti.html #.ZBjdBBTMJPY.

Villazon, Luis. "Why Do Beached Whales Die So Often?" *Science Focus*. Accessed January 22, 2024. https://www.sciencefocus.com/nature/why -do-beached-whales-die-so-often.

"Wakka Wakka Native Title Continues the Work of Past Generations." Queensland Law Society Proctor, April 13, 2022. https://www.qlsproctor .com.au/2022/04/wakka-wakka-native-title-continues-the-work-of-past -generations.

Warren, Karen. "Roman Spa and Hot Springs of Bath: A Continuous Tradition." *Worldwide Writer* (blog), January 3, 2024. https://www.worldwidewriter.co .uk/roman-spa-and-hot-springs-of-bath.html.

"Water and Hinduism." *All You Need to Know About Hinduism* (blog). Accessed January 19, 2024. http://history-of-hinduism.blogspot.com/2010/06/water -and-hinduism.html.

"Water Blessing." Australian Red Cross. Accessed January 22, 2024. https://www.redcross.org.au/stories/together-as-partners/water-blessing.

"Water in First Nations Ceremonies." Safe Drinking Water Foundation. Accessed January 19, 2024. https://static1.squarespace.com/static /583ca2f2d482e9bbbef7dad9/t/5d69c7d1f0b2850001ed8c7a/1567213 524800/10-12+Lesson+1+Water+in+First+Nations+Ceremonies.pdf.

Water Science School. "Water, the Universal Solvent." US Geological Survey, June 9, 2018. https://www.usgs.gov/special-topics/water-science-school /science/water-universal-solvent.

"Water – The Sacred Element." Udara Bali. Accessed January 22, 2024. https://www.udara-bali.com/water-the-sacred-element.

"We Are All Connected." Quantum-Serendipity. Accessed February 12, 2024. https://quantum-serendipity.com/connections.

"What Causes Water Pollution in Africa?" The Last Well, June 28, 2019. https://thelastwell.org/2019/06/what-causes-water-pollution-in-africa.

"What Is Kalash?" Eshwar Bhakti. Accessed January 19, 2024. https:// pujayagna.com/blogs/pooja-havan-yagya/what-is-kalash-in-puja.

"What Is the National Environmental Policy Act?" United States Environmental Protection Agency. Updated October 5, 2023. https://www.epa.gov/nepa /what-national-environmental-policy-act.

Whelan, Ed. "Divers Find Hundreds of Ritual Offerings in Lake Sacred to the Maya." Ancient Origins. Updated February 11, 2019. https://www .ancient-origins.net/news-history-archaeology/maya-relics-found-lake -0011463.

"Where Is Lake Titicaca?" Lake Titicaca. Accessed January 19, 2024. https:// laketiticaca.com.

"Why Swimming in Roman Baths Can End Badly." Bright Side. Accessed April 2, 2024. https://brightside.me/articles/why-swimming-in-roman -baths-can-end-badly-815315.

Williams, A. R. "Centuries-Old Inca Offering Discovered in Sacred Lake." *National Geographic*, August 4, 2020. https://www.nationalgeographic .com/history/article/centuries-old-inca-offering-discovered-sacred-lake.

Wockner, Gary. "Population, Pollution, Pandemic—The Race to Save Lake Atitlan in Guatemala." Medium, July 7, 2020. https://garywockner .medium.com/population-pollution-pandemic-the-race-to-save-lake -atitlan-in-guatemala-61640b7ac321.

Wong, Kenneth. "12 Universal Laws: How to Use Them." *The Millennial Grind* (blog), October 4, 2023. https://millennial-grind.com/the-12-laws -of-the-universe-explained.

Young, Peter T. "Halekūlani Hotel." Images of Old Hawaiʻi, August 31, 2022. https://imagesofoldhawaii.com/halekulani-hotel.

———. "Waikīkī, Place of Healing." *Hoʻokuleana* (blog), October 31, 2013. https://totakeresponsibility.blogspot.com/2013/10/waikiki-place-of-healing .html.

Zelenková, Barbora. "Iemanja: A Uruguayan Celebration of the Yoruba Goddess of the Sea." *The Ethnologist* (blog), April 25, 2019. https://ethnologist .info/2019/04/25/iemanja-a-uruguayan-celebration-of-the-yoruba-goddess -of-the-sea.

"Zuni Salt Lake." Springerville-Eagar Chamber of Commerce. Accessed January 19, 2024. https://springervilleeagarchamber.com/wp-content/uploads /2022/04/Zuni-Salt-Lake-01-02-21.pdf.

To Write to the Author

If you wish to contact the author or would like more information about this book, please write to the author in care of Llewellyn Worldwide Ltd. and we will forward your request. Both the author and publisher appreciate hearing from you and learning of your enjoyment of this book and how it has helped you. Llewellyn Worldwide Ltd. cannot guarantee that every letter written to the author can be answered, but all will be forwarded. Please write to:

Catharine Robinette
℅ Llewellyn Worldwide
2143 Wooddale Drive
Woodbury, MN 55125-2989

Please enclose a self-addressed stamped envelope for reply,
or $1.00 to cover costs. If outside the U.S.A., enclose
an international postal reply coupon.

Many of Llewellyn's authors have websites with additional information and resources. For more information, please visit our website at http://www.llewellyn .com.